New Orleans, Louisiana,
& Saint-Louis, Senegal

NEW ORLEANS, LOUISIANA & SAINT-LOUIS, SENEGAL

Mirror Cities in the Atlantic World, 1659–2000s

Edited by Emily Clark, Ibrahima Thioub, and Cécile Vidal

LOUISIANA STATE UNIVERSITY PRESS
BATON ROUGE

Published by Louisiana State University Press

Manufactured in the United States of America
First printing

DESIGNER: Michelle A. Neustrom
TYPEFACE: Adobe Garamond Pro
PRINTER AND BINDER: Sheridan Books, Inc.

LIBRARY OF CONGRESS CATALOGING-IN-PUBLICATION DATA

Names: Clark, Emily, 1954– editor. | Thioub, Ibrahima, editor. | Vidal, Cécile, editor.
Title: New Orleans, Louisiana, and Saint-Louis, Senegal : mirror cities in the Atlantic world, 1659–2000s / edited by Emily Clark, Ibrahima Thioub, and Cécile Vidal.
Description: Baton Rouge : Louisiana State University Press, [2019] | Includes bibliographical references and index.
Identifiers: LCCN 2019005200 | ISBN 978-0-8071-7111-0 (cloth : alk. paper) | ISBN 978-0-8071-7170-7 (pdf) | ISBN 978-0-8071-7171-4 (epub)
Subjects: LCSH: New Orleans (La.)—History. | Saint Louis (Senegal)—History. | Blacks—Louisiana—New Orleans—Social conditions. | Blacks—Senegal—Saint Louis—Social conditions. | Slavery—Louisiana—New Orleans (La.)—History. | Slavery—Senegal—Saint Louis—History. | New Orleans (La.)—Race relations—History. | Blacks—France—Colonies. | Port cities—Case studies.
Classification: LCC F379.N557 N485 2019 | DDC 976.3/35—dc23
LC record available at https://lccn.loc.gov/2019005200

The paper in this book meets the guidelines for permanence and durability of the Committee on Production Guidelines for Book Longevity of the Council on Library Resources. ♾

CONTENTS

1 Introduction
CÉCILE VIDAL, EMILY CLARK, AND IBRAHIMA THIOUB

PART I: NEGOTIATING SLAVERY AND FREEDOM

35 The Role of Slavery in the Economic and Social History of Saint-Louis, Senegal
MARTIN A. KLEIN

55 Wives, Soldiers, and Slaves: *The Atlantic World of Marie Baude, la femme Pinet*
JESSICA MARIE JOHNSON

75 The Streets, the Barracks, and the Hospital: *Public Space, Social Control, and Cross-Racial Interactions among Soldiers and Slaves in French New Orleans*
CÉCILE VIDAL

PART II: ELUSIVE CITIZENSHIP

103 The Prison of Saint-Louis: *French Expansion, Social Control, and the Early Development of the Penitentiary Institution in Senegal, circa 1834–1895*
IBRA SENE

125 Citizenship and the Abolition of Slavery after 1848: *Conflicts of National Allegiance among the French in New Orleans*
MARIEKE POLFLIET

146 Asserting Citizenship and Refusing Stigma: *New Orleans Equal-Rights Activists Interpret 1803 and 1848*
REBECCA J. SCOTT

168 French Citizenship and Colonial Rule in Saint-Louis, Senegal
LARISSA KOPYTOFF

PART III: MYTHIC PERSISTENCE

191 Transatlantic Currents of Orientalism: *New Orleans Quadroons and Saint-Louis Signares*
EMILY CLARK AND HILARY JONES

210 Reflections of Senegambia in New Orleans Jazz
BRUCE BOYD RAEBURN

233 Acknowledgments

237 Selected Bibliography

245 Contributors

247 Index

New Orleans, Louisiana,
& Saint-Louis, Senegal

INTRODUCTION

CÉCILE VIDAL, EMILY CLARK, AND IBRAHIMA THIOUB

On March 19, 1731, a wedding ceremony took place in the New Orleans church that brought together the worlds of Senegambia and Louisiana. The Capuchin missionary Hyacinthe united Simon Vanon, a "free negro" "born in Senegal," with Marie Anne, a "Senegalese" "free negress."[1] This marriage was exceptional for several reasons. At the time, the Louisiana capital comprised very few free blacks. Before Simon Vanon and Marie Anne's union, only one marriage between free blacks had been celebrated, and afterwards very few would be until the end of the French Regime.[2] Most notable of all is that the priest followed the traditional form employed for whites when he recorded the ceremony in the parish registers: he specified where the spouses were born and addressed the publication of the banns, a set of three formal announcements of the impending wedding that allowed any legal or religious impediments to the union to be raised.[3] Both Simon and Marie Anne came from "Senegal."[4] According to slave trade historian Philip Curtin, "a slave identified as Senegalese might [. . .] be either (a) an individual shipped from Saint-Louis, whatever his nationality, (b) a Wolof of Cayor or Walo in the immediate vicinity of the town, or (c) a Pular-speaker from Futa Toro in the middle valley of the Senegal."[5] Simon Vanon and Marie Anne probably did arrive in New Orleans from Saint-Louis. However, it is impossible to decipher their precise ethnic backgrounds and to know whether they arrived free or obtained their freedom in the Mississippi Valley. Their union, nevertheless, testifies to the early entangled histories of Saint-Louis and New Orleans and invites a consideration of the two port cities over the course of the Atlantic age that spawned their earliest connection with one another. By mirroring their histories, this collective volume aims at recovering the crucial role played by port cities in the integration of the Atlantic world. It also argues that Africa must be given the same place as the Americas in Atlantic studies and that historians need to reconsider how the interplay of imperialism, colonialism, and slaving that defined the early Atlantic world operated and evolved differently on both sides of the ocean. Finally, it seeks to contribute to a better understanding of the particularities of the French Empire within the Atlantic world.

WHY SAINT-LOUIS AND NEW ORLEANS, SEPARATELY AND TOGETHER?

Saint-Louis and New Orleans were two river towns created ex nihilo by the French, the former in West Africa and the latter in North America, at the time of French early imperial expansion in the Atlantic world. Both became important port cities of their own continents, the Atlantic world as a whole, the African diaspora, and the Atlantic portion of the French Empire. Saint-Louis was founded first, in 1659, with the internationalization of the transatlantic slave trade. Whereas the Portuguese had dominated the commerce of slaves to the Americas for most of the sixteenth century, the Dutch, French, and English breached their monopoly over the course of the seventeenth century. Senegambia was a particularly attractive region because it was close to both Europe and the Americas. These three European powers created zones of influence to supply the colonies they had simultaneously begun to develop in the Caribbean. New Orleans was established much later, in 1718, after the transatlantic slave trade had greatly expanded and plantation slavery was already well entrenched in the French Antilles. The French had started to settle in Louisiana in 1699 to impede the English from getting closer to the Spanish and to block their westward expansion. The first phase of settlement had taken place on the Gulf of Mexico, but the colonizing effort was redirected toward the Mississippi Valley after the monopoly on the Louisiana trade was granted to the Company of the West—later named Company of the Indies—in 1717. The Company's initial project, besides exploiting the mythic gold mines of the Illinois Country and expanding trade with neighboring Spanish colonies, was to develop a plantation society and economy, growing tobacco and indigo with a mixed labor force of African slaves and European indentured servants and convicts.

The sites of Saint-Louis and New Orleans were chosen because they controlled the mouth of a river that gave access to the interiors of West Africa and North America, respectively. The ocean is much nearer in Saint-Louis than in New Orleans. The former was founded fifteen miles from the mouth of the Senegal River, on an inhabited island in the middle of the river that could be easily defended, separated from the ocean by a sandbar named the Langue de Barbarie. Located at a distance of about one hundred miles from the Gulf of Mexico, New Orleans was established on the top of a meander of the Mississippi River, in the vicinity of a Native American portage that gave two points of access to the sea, through the Mississippi River and through Lake Pontchartrain. The location of each city, nevertheless, allowed it to maintain connections with and even to control over time a large continental hinterland: for Saint-Louis, much of the Western Sahara, the upper and middle Niger Valleys, and the north of Senegambia; and for New Orleans, the whole Mississippi Basin. Yet, during the early modern period, the territories acquired and occupied by European or US imperial powers were discontinuous and limited mostly to coastal enclaves in Senegambia, and in Louisiana to a corridor, with the city and a line of plantations, supplemented by an archipelago of posts, forts, and missions. Beyond Saint-Louis, sovereignty belonged to the kingdoms of Waalo, Kajoor, Bawol, Djolof, Siin, and Saalum between the Senegal and Gambia Rivers, to the Peul and Haalpulaar aristocracies in the Fuuta Tooro region in the Senegal Middle Valley, and to the Soninke state of Gajaaga in the Senegal Upper Valley. As for the vast territory claimed by the French in the Mississippi Basin, it remained to a large extent Indian Country throughout the French Regime. The indigenous populations of Greater Louisiana remained high, even though they suffered demographic losses because of the pathogens brought by Europeans. The number of settlers and slaves never exceeded that of the Choctaw, for instance, one of the largest and most powerful nations to which the French were allied.[6] In both places, it was only during the nineteenth century that the appropriation of continuous and extensive territories was achieved, Saint-Louis and New Orleans each serving as a bridgehead in this process.

Saint-Louis and New Orleans were the first urban settlements created in their respective regions by Europeans, but the establishment of both hinged on the cooperation of native populations. Saint-Louis could only be founded with the permission of the surrounding kingdoms, and the Louisiana city depended on the assistance of the nearby *petites nations* (small Native American nations).[7] However, only New Orleans was immediately conceived as a city, while Saint-Louis remained a slave trading post (a "*comptoir*") and a multiethnic African town with a dominant Muslim and Wolof culture that had no urban planning before the early decades of the nineteenth century.[8] Still, both places occupied for a very long period a prominent position in the urban networks that developed over time in Louisiana and Senegambia/Senegal, and fulfilled major political, cultural, and administrative functions. New Orleans functioned as the only true urban center in the Mississippi colony during the French Regime.[9] It became the Louisiana capital in 1722 and retained this political and administrative function until 1849, throughout French, Spanish, and the first forty-five years of American rule. Saint-Louis constituted, after Gorée Island, the most important slave trading post established by the French in Senegambia. It became the capital of the colony of Senegal after Louis Faidherbe's territorial conquest began in 1854 as well as that of Mauritania from 1872. From 1895 to 1902, it was also promoted to the rank of capital of Afrique occidentale française (French West Africa), before Dakar, colonized only in 1857, assumed this function. Saint-Louis, nevertheless, remained the capital of the colony of Senegal and Mauritania. When Senegal became independent in 1960, Dakar, which had become much more demographically and economically important than Saint-Louis, was chosen as capital of the new republic.

As they constituted central places of the French Empire, the history of both cities was heavily impacted by the imperial rivalry between the French and the British. In North America, French Louisiana, which theoretically extended from the Great Lakes to the Gulf of Mexico and from the Alleghenies to the Rocky Mountains, was located between territories claimed by the British and the Spanish. In Senegambia, the French had to face competition from the British slave trading posts located near the mouth of the Gambia River. The British seized and occupied Saint-Louis for a few months in 1693, then for a longer period from 1758 to 1779, and once again from 1809 to 1816. From 1817, Saint-Louis, once again in the hands of the French, had to face the competition of Portendick in Mauritania, under British rule, for the gum trade. At the end of the Seven Years War, New Orleans and the western bank of the Mississippi River were ceded to Spain by the Treaty of Fontainebleau in 1762, while Great Britain obtained the eastern part of the colony, the capital excepted, by the Treaty of Paris one year later. In 1800, the Treaty of San Ildefonso gave Spanish Louisiana back to France, but the French took possession of the colony only three weeks before the Louisiana Purchase in 1803. The failure of the Leclerc expedition to quash the slave rebellion in Saint-Domingue, resulting in the birth of the Republic of Haiti, and the fear that the British would conquer Louisiana after the renewal of war in May 1803, explain Napoleon's choice to sell the colony to the United States during Thomas Jefferson's presidency.[10]

The two cities occupied a singular place within the French Empire for opposite reasons. New Orleans did not remain long under French sovereignty—hardly two generations. However, although Louisiana was effectively no longer part of the French Empire after 1763, it remained part of the French Atlantic dynamic well into the nineteenth century, sharing demographic, cultural, economic, and political features shared by France and its colonies.[11] Francophone migrations from France and the Caribbean were much more important in the first half of the nineteenth century than during the French Regime. After the arrival of some Acadians in the 1760s, New Orleans welcomed thousands of refugees of Saint-Domingue and then a steady flow of migrants from France.[12] French speakers remained a majority in the Louisiana capital until 1850.[13] Because of this large and diversified francophone population, which included many French citizens, politics and events in the French Empire continued to impact New Orleans well into the nineteenth century.

In contrast, Saint-Louis belonged to the French Empire for three centuries with few interruptions. This long-lasting French imprint is enshrined in the present-day designation of the city, which is still officially named Saint-Louis, Ndar being its name in the Senegalese lingua franca, Wolof. The port city helped to maintain continuity between the first and second French Empires.[14] Its past as a slave trading post disputed between the French and the English explains why Saint-Louis benefited from an exceptional political status in the nineteenth and twentieth centuries, which resulted in the colonial capital's right to elect local officials. During the British occupation in the 1760s and 1770s, the *habitants*—the term designated the free city dwellers of mixed and African descent—succeeded in winning representation by a mayor, and the French could not but maintain this function when they regained the slave trading post. Since the Euro-African and African population of Saint-Louis remained economically and politically powerful in the first half of the nineteenth century, the habitants then obtained a *Conseil général* in 1840 to discuss their local affairs, though this office was suppressed in 1848 and only reinstated in 1879. In 1848, they were also granted a seat as a deputy at the National Assembly, which was suppressed in 1852 and subsequently reinstated in 1871. Hence, they had already benefited from a tradition of political representation before the actual conquest and colonial occupation of Senegal by the French that had started by the mid-nineteenth century. In 1872, Saint-Louis and Gorée became the first *Communes,* granted the same rights as French cities. Their urban dwellers were considered French citizens, whereas in the rest of Senegal the indigenous inhabitants had the status of subjects.[15] However, as Mamadou Diouf recalls, "this tradition of local government, like that of citizenship, was never entirely established. It was the object of constant daily attacks by certain governors and colonial judges."[16] Moreover, control of these representative political institutions and positions was the object of fierce struggle between the various components of the urban population.[17]

For most of the eighteenth century, Saint-Louis and New Orleans shared similar demographies. In both places, slaves constituted a substantial part of the urban population. Saint-Louis comprised 1,401 inhabitants in 1758, 3,000 in 1779, and 9,000 in 1819. Its population rose thanks to a constant flow of free and enslaved African migrants. Slaves quickly came to represent about 60 percent of all urban dwellers. Saint-Louis's economy rested not only on the slave trade but also on the gum trade and the commerce in grain that sustained the slave trade. Following a phase of expansion in the first half of the eighteenth century, slave exports declined after 1750 for a variety of reasons, including the growing demand for slave labor in the Senegalese Valley in combination with a series of famines and wars. The gum and grain trades then became more important.[18] Likewise, the Louisiana capital's population rose to around 3,000 inhabitants (48 percent of them slaves) at the end of the Seven Years War in 1766 and around 8,000 (34 percent slaves and 17 percent free people of color) at the time of the Louisiana Purchase in 1803.[19] New Orleans remained a secondary Caribbean port city for a long time, attracting very few migrants. It slowly grew thanks to trade with nearby Spanish colonies during the French period and the export of pelts and furs, tobacco, indigo, and lumber throughout the eighteenth century.[20]

In the nineteenth century, by contrast, New Orleans experienced dramatic demographic and economic growth. After the development of steam navigation on the Mississippi River following the War of 1812, the port started to export the agricultural production of the Midwest and Deep South and to supply those regions with manufactured goods from Europe and the northeastern United States. New Orleans quickly came to rank as the second port in traffic in the country after New York, a position it kept throughout the antebellum period. Its population rose to 27,176 inhabitants in 1820, 102,193 in 1840, and 168,675 in 1860. The greatest growth was in the white population, which rose from 46.5 percent of the city's population in 1820 to 58.2 percent in 1840 and 84.7 percent in 1860. The percentage of enslaved hovered at about 20 percent between 1820 and 1840, dropping to 8.3 percent on the eve of the Civil War in 1860. The most dramatic demographic change occurred among free people of color, who made up a substantial proportion of the city's free population for several decades, constituting 36 percent of the population in 1820 and 23 percent in 1840, but only 8 percent in 1860.[21] New Orleans was then one of the most important US ports of immigration: migrants from France, Germany, and Ireland poured into the city. Hundreds of thousands of slaves from the Upper South also passed through the harbor.[22] The vast extent of this internal slave trade fueled the expansion of slavery in the Deep South. Louisiana itself experienced the embedding of a deadly regime of plantation slavery based on the cultivation of sugarcane and cotton.[23] Although the city declined after the Civil War—after 1880 it fell from the list of the ten largest American cities in which it had appeared since 1810—it remained one of the largest cities in the South, with a population of 339,075 in 1910 and 494,537 in 1940.

Saint-Louis benefited from some demographic and economic growth throughout the nineteenth century, even though this growth was much more modest than in New Orleans.[24] In the first half of the nineteenth century, "the commerce of Saint-Louis made it one of the most important ports of trade in West Africa. While many other Atlantic ports went into decline because of the gradual abolition of the Atlantic slave trade, Saint-Louis was transformed into a bustling urban center by the export trade in gum arabic."[25] The composition of the population was affected by the establishment of a few French resident merchants but also by the arrival of numerous free African migrants. After midcentury, the development of peanut cultivation and exportation superceded the gum trade. The city also attracted freed and fugitive slaves who formed the majority of immigrants between 1848 and 1900. Hence, its population slowly rose to 12,138 inhabitants in 1845, 15,480 in 1869, and 18,824 in 1882.[26] The European component reached around 1,000 individuals in 1900 before declining as colonists grew to prefer living in Dakar. Throughout the first half of the twentieth century, the demographic growth of Saint-Louis accelerated, the population rising to around 23,000 in 1914 and then 40,000 in 1945.[27] Saint-Louis, nonetheless, never acquired the stature of New Orleans in international trade during the antebellum period.[28]

The slave trade not only played a crucial role in the demographic and economic growth of both Saint-Louis and New Orleans, but also directly connected the two cities. The Company of the Indies ran the Senegambia slave trading posts and the Mississippi colony simultaneously from 1719 to 1731.[29] Having acquired the trade monopoly of Louisiana in 1717, the Company of the Indies incorporated the Company of Rouen in 1719 and gained the trade monopoly of the Senegambia slave trading posts. From 1720 to 1725, the Company also obtained the exclusive privilege of engaging in the slave trade. Between 1719 and 1731, it transported roughly 6,000 African slaves to New Orleans, two-thirds of whom were shipped from Saint-Louis or Gorée.[30] As the exclusive buyer and seller for the French, the Company was in a position to more easily and cheaply acquire slaves in Senegambia and to sell them at a profit in New Orleans. As a result, Louisiana did not experience a transition from indentured to slave labor, as did many American colonies founded during the seventeenth century. Instead, slave labor was important from the outset. It very quickly became even more prominent because most of the European indentured servants who had come with the single migratory wave that French Louisiana experienced between 1717 and 1721 died or left the colony. Very few moved to the colony afterwards. Consequently, a black majority emerged as early as 1726 in the colonial settlements of the Lower Mississippi Valley outside New Orleans. After the Natchez Wars of 1729–1731, the Company decided to abandon its trade monopoly, and in 1731

Louisiana again became a royal colony. The Company of the Indies nevertheless retained its monopoly on the slave trade to Louisiana after 1731, though it stopped sending slave ships. By contrast, some sixty years passed before the French state definitively took over trading companies in Saint-Louis in 1791.

The connections between Saint-Louis and New Orleans were not entirely disrupted after 1731, although only scattered evidence for individuals linking the two has been found so far. Pilots and sailors born in Senegambia, for example, worked on ships that landed in New Orleans throughout the French Regime.[31] Such relationships persisted after New Orleans came under Spanish and then American sovereignty. The d'Erneville family, for instance, had members in both New Orleans and Saint-Louis over the course of the eighteenth century. Pierre Henri d'Erneville was a French military officer who made his career in Louisiana throughout the French Regime. One of his domestic slaves, Charlotte, was his illegitimate daughter. Although she purchased freedom for herself in 1773, the son she bore in 1754 was refused freedom by his grandfather and master, even when he reached adulthood. With his wife Pélagie Fleuriau, the daughter of an attorney general, Pierre Henri d'Erneville also fathered at least five other children. One of them, Charles Jean Baptiste, born in New Orleans in 1752, left Louisiana to train as an artillery captain in France. After serving in the Grenoble Regiment, he took part in the military expedition sent to Saint-Louis to reestablish French control in 1780. In the slave trading post he wed Catherine Miller *à la mode du pays,* a customary form of marriage between Europeans and Africans that was recognized by the parties to the union but not by the church or in law. Catherine, born in 1760, was the daughter of a French trader who arrived in Saint-Louis during the British occupation and an unknown African woman. In 1789, Jean Baptiste d'Erneville left Saint-Louis for Gorée to fulfill his new assignment as governor. There he married another woman of color named Hélène Pateloux à la mode du pays. He died in Gorée in 1792. His children with Catherine Miller gave rise to a highly prominent métis family in Saint-Louis.[32]

At roughly the same time, the lives of other individuals took them in the opposite direction, from Saint-Louis to New Orleans. Rebecca Scott and Jean Hébrard have followed the trajectory of Rosalie, "black woman of the Poulard nation," who was probably captured in the valley of the Senegal

River and transported as a slave to Saint-Domingue, where she obtained her freedom before taking part in the migration of Saint-Domingue refugees to Cuba and then to New Orleans at the outset of the nineteenth century.[33] Even after the abolition of the international slave trade at the beginning of the nineteenth century (in 1807 for the United Kingdom, 1808 for the United States, and 1815 for France), some slaves continued to be transported, though illegally, from Saint-Louis to the Americas, particularly to the Antilles and Louisiana.[34]

Saint-Louis and New Orleans also share a similar treatment by historians, who for a long time adopted an exceptionalist perspective, describing each of them as a Creole city.[35] Their work focused on people associated with French culture and Catholicism and on *métissage* and hybridity, and mythologized free women of color known as *signares* in Saint-Louis and quadroons in New Orleans.[36] This shared historiographical preoccupation has had the effect of simplifying social and ethnic dynamics and downplaying colonial exploitation and ethnic or racial tensions. Novels and historical books written by self-taught historians have contributed to popularizing the trope of the charming signares in Saint-Louis.[37] On the one hand, these romanticized visions have fueled the sociopolitical marginalization of Saint-Louis within African and Muslim Senegal and of New Orleans within the English and Protestant United States. On the other hand, they have also served the development of tourism and the preservation of each site's architectural heritage, bringing much-needed revenues to the two impoverished cities. Tourists are attracted by the architecture Saint-Louis and New Orleans preserve from their colonial past. In New Orleans, they visit the French Quarter, in particular, though it is only nominally French, since the great fires of 1788 and 1794 completely consumed the French city. In Saint-Louis the so-called houses of signares, before which visitors marvel as they imagine a romanticized Creole past, most often belonged to Muslim merchants.[38]

Each city also hosts an acclaimed international jazz festival that attracts music lovers from all over the world. Two years after we held, in Saint-Louis, the first of two international conferences on which this collective volume is based,[39] a post on the *National Geographic* website promoted the 2014 session of the Saint-Louis jazz festival. The author started his note by asking: "Riverboats, wrought iron balconies, Creole culture, a famous jazz fest, and flamboyance in the face of hardship. Where else could this describe but . . . Saint-Louis, Senegal?" To leave no ambiguity about the parallels with New Orleans, he ended his paper quoting "Marie-Caroline Camara, who turned a 19th-century timber warehouse into the chic Au Fil du Fleuve guest-house," who observed that, "American visitors say we're like New Orleans."[40] The conference organizers had met Marie-Caroline Camara in 2012 during our stay in Saint-Louis.[41] Paradoxically, we had involuntarily contributed to the perpetuation of this common romanticized Creole vision of the two cities!

CONFRONTING AND INTEGRATING AFRICAN AND AMERICAN HISTORIES

In the present collective volume, we would like to approach Saint-Louis and New Orleans together in a different way, one that avoids the kind of comparison that can lead to oversimplifications such as the cities' conflation as interchangeable Creole sites. Instead, we are confronting the histories of the two port cities on the *longue durée.*[42] Our hypothesis is that their respective historical trajectories, with their points of intersection and divergences, should allow us to better understand their singularities as they were shaped by the dynamics at play in the Atlantic world and beyond. Several historical fields cross urban history with the history of imperialism, colonialism, and/or slaving, but often these fields do not converse with each other, and they have rarely considered American and African port cities together. The history of "colonial cities" and African urban history both focus mainly on the modern period.[43] By considering them in relation to New Orleans over the longue durée, they can be put into conversation with the history of American urban slavery that has started to expand after Ira Berlin's call in the 1980s for a greater attention to time and space in the study of slavery.[44] The same is true for Atlantic history, with its renewed interest since the 1990s in port cities as nodes of connections and networks.[45]

By confronting the histories of Saint-Louis and New Orleans, we are following the path of a pioneering collective volume, *The Black Urban Atlantic in the Age of the Slave Trade,* which recently gathered very interesting essays on port cities located on both sides of the Atlantic. Yet we are also distancing ourselves from the choice made by the editors of that volume, who decided to focus on the "victims of the slave trade" (although it is less obvious in the chapters themselves). The essays in our volume, by contrast, acknowledge that what characterized African slave trading posts was the fact that some Africans controlled the slave trade, while others were victims of it. Moreover, a slave system also developed within these African societies to sustain the transatlantic slave trade that was itself different from the one that bloomed in the Americas. In the same way, we find that using the category "black" and writing about the "black urban Atlantic" and "black communities" in all the port cities located on both sides of the Atlantic, either in Africa or in the Americas, tends to oversimplify and obscure the contrasted social and cultural dynamics and processes of identification in which African and African-descended populations took part.[46]

The choices made by the editors of *The Black Urban Atlantic in the Age of the Slave Trade* conform to a more general problematic tendency of Atlantic studies. Although Atlantic historians are supposed to analyze the relationships among Europe, Africa, and the Americas and their impact on all the societies of these four continents, their main focus is very often on the Western Hemisphere, the territories that were the most transformed by Atlantic dynamics. Atlantic studies have contributed to taking Africans and Africa into better account and to illuminating the crucial role they played in the formation of new societies in the Americas.[47] Still, Africa mostly appears in the historiography on the Atlantic world with reference to the transatlantic slave trade and the African diaspora. The impact of the Atlantic slave trade on power relationships in Africa, particularly among ruling elites, has been widely studied, but the dramatic transformations in the social and, especially, cultural realms have been neglected. Moreover, those studies of African societies are not included, most of the time, in syntheses on the history of the Atlantic world.[48] Consequently, historians of the Atlantic world customarily agree to end Atlantic history with the independence of most American colonies in the late eighteenth and early nineteenth centuries, or with the last abolitions of slavery in Cuba and Brazil in the late nineteenth century. However, these dates are meaningful only for the Western Hemisphere. Neither slaving nor colonization, two dynamics that spawned and animated the Atlantic world, ceased in Africa at these junctures. Indeed, it was quite the contrary.[49]

We aim in this volume to contribute to a better integration of African and American histories and of imperial and Atlantic histories. For that purpose, the volume includes essays dealing with the age of the transatlantic slave trade as well as the period after the forced migration ended. The goal is to better understand three interrelated phenomena that are often not clearly distinguished from one another—imperialism, colonialism, and slaving—to analyze how these three phenomena intersected with each other differently according to time and place. We are especially interested in how various configurations of imperialism, colonialism, and slaving shaped in different ways distant port cities of the Atlantic world, and in exploring what roles port cities played in these phenomena. *Imperialism* is here understood to be the project and process of building an empire through territorial expansion and the imposition of sovereignty over vast territories, whereas the term *colonialism* refers to the project and processes of conquest, settlement, and exploitation of remote territories to the benefit of the colonizing power. When imperialism and colonialism do not combine, the imperial project can work with only a very small group of representatives of the central power, leaving much autonomy to the local populations provided that the political, geopolitical, military, fiscal, and/or economic goals are reached. Colonialism, in contrast, aims to impose a greater control on every aspect—political, economic, and sociocultural—of the life of the colonized, although this desire for control varied over space and time. Moreover, to legitimize the colonial order, the colonizers need to produce and reproduce a symbolic separation and distance between the colonizers and the colonized. Through discourses and practices, they position themselves as radically different on the basis of race or ethnicity.[50]

Throughout the eighteenth century, both Saint-Louis and New Orleans were caught in the French imperialist project, but it was only in New Orleans that imperialism and colonialism combined. Saint-Louis was integrated into the French Empire despite the fact that it was, to a large extent, a multiethnic African city that could not serve as the bridgehead for a project of conquest and colonization of the interior before the middle of the nineteenth century. The port city constituted a zone of contact between several sovereignties. For nearly two centuries, the payment of tribute (*coutumes*) by the French recognized the sovereignty of surrounding kingdoms that controlled the slave trade. By the early eighteenth century, the monarch of Kajoor and Bawol was unable to impede the French from establishing an exclusive commercial zone in coastal Senegambia between Saint-Louis and Gorée, but he could impose a boycott on the food supply as a way to extract the payment of higher customs. Likewise, although the French established a fort named Saint-Joseph two hundred miles upriver in Galam (Gajaaga) and ran a specialized fleet of river boats to facilitate trade in the interior, they "paid customs to Fuuta Tooro and to Gajaaga for the right to open markets and trade, and to provide protection for the river fleets."[51] Even within Saint-Louis, the European population was reduced to a few dozen or hundreds of men and turnover was high. No European women migrated to the slave trading post, while many of the men succumbed to deadly diseases upon arrival, and those who survived this "seasoning" stayed for only a short time before returning to Europe. In the absence of a stable, sizable European population, the Afro-European and African merchants of the city quickly came to control the various trades to the overall benefit of the Atlantic French Empire that connected Louisiana and Senegambia.

In contrast, Louisiana was almost immediately founded as a colony with the project of settling and exploiting the entire Mississippi Valley from the strategic vantage point of New Orleans. The port city was conceived as a trading entrepôt on the river whose functions were to defend access to the interior of the continent, structure the colonizing process, and exercise dominion over a vast hinterland. Although New Orleans was initially dependent on food supplied by Native Americans, this dependence quickly decreased and then completely disappeared. Moreover, the population of the Louisiana capital only comprised a few Indians, and most of them were enslaved. Only the competition of older and better-located colonies and the lack of resources invested in this project explain why the colonial population was still of modest size when the Spanish took possession of the colony in the 1760s. Consequently, the most important Native American nations were able to maintain sovereignty over their territories for a long time.[52] Yet by the end of the French Regime two generations of European inhabitants had succeeded in giving root to a settler society in the Lower Mississippi Valley. This was centered in New Orleans, where 27.3 percent of Lower Louisiana's colonial population was concentrated in a long-lasting effect of the Natchez

Wars. Outside the main colonial settlements, the French had also built an imperial infrastructure consisting of missions, forts, and stores that brought the French presence to the heart of Indian country. These forts, stores, and missions were crucial, both to assert French sovereignty against English or Spanish encroachments and to develop the fur trade on which the French-Native alliance was based. Most Native Americans were considered alternatively or simultaneously as allies or subjects of the French king.[53] Although most Indian nations in the Lower Mississippi Valley took part in the Gallic alliance, the French had more conflicted and warlike relationships with the Chickasaw and the Natchez.[54]

By the end of the Seven Years War, French Louisiana had not only formed a settler society but also a slave society. Nearly from the outset, the French in the Mississippi Valley wanted to follow the Saint-Domingue model by developing a plantation economy supported by the apparatus of a slave society. Thanks to the early shipments of captives from Senegambia, slaves quickly formed the majority of the colonial population and allowed Louisiana to establish the commitment to enslaved labor that is the foundation of a slave society, that is, a society in which slavery was "pivotal to the entire institutional structure and value complex."[55] This was the case everywhere in the Lower Mississippi Valley, not only in the plantation area surrounding New Orleans, but also in the port city itself.

Like New Orleans, seventeenth- and eighteenth-century Saint-Louis was a slave society.[56] In fact, slavery existed in Senegambia for centuries before Europeans began their initial forays along the West African coast in the fifteenth century, but the African institution was transformed and expanded by the rise of the transatlantic slave trade. This was true within as well as outside Saint-Louis. The transatlantic slave trade was at the heart of the system of trades that connected Europe, Africa, and the Americas throughout the early modern period, which deeply transformed societies on both sides of the Atlantic. This does not mean, however, that a single system of "Atlantic slavery" existed in the Atlantic world. After the Seven Years War, the "Atlantic system" (the system connecting Europe, Africa, and the Americas that rested mainly on the transatlantic slave trade and the colonial trade of merchandise produced with slave labor in the Western Hemisphere) entered a phase of intensification, acceleration, and transformation. The balance between the French and British Empires was shaken by the territorial cessions of the Treaty of Paris, including Louisiana and Senegambia. All European colonial empires discussed and implemented reforms that sought to consolidate metropolitan control on their colonial territories, while the debate on the necessity to soften laws restricting commerce within each empire to the benefit of the metropole, known as the *Exclusif*, intensified. Although Saint-Louis did not benefit from the movement except in the 1780s and 1790s, the transatlantic slave trade rose very quickly at this historical juncture. At the same time, abolitionist ideas and movements began to develop. Both British and French abolitionists started to see the colonization of Africa as an alternative to the transatlantic slave trade and American slavery.[57]

The abolition of the international slave trade by France in 1815 coincided with the return of the French to Saint-Louis two years later. Though the transatlantic slave trade had preserved Senegambia from colonialism, if not imperialism, its official suppression propelled both the expansion of local slavery and the formation of the "*colonie du Sénégal*" ("colony of Senegal"). In the first half of the nineteenth century, a period of transition, the project of turning Senegal into a genuine colony, transformed Saint-Louis. It led to the implementation of a new colonial government based in the city, the first policy of urban planning, the arrival of the first female migrants from Europe, the establishment of missionaries, and the replacement of the merchant directors and employees of trade monopolies by resident French merchants who competed with the habitants and African merchants for the control of the river trade. Outside Saint-Louis, the colonizing project also materialized with a series of territorial explorations, the construction of a string of forts on the Senegal River, and experiments in plantation agriculture with free laborers and indentured servants. The agricultural schemes failed. They provoked wars, and Euro-African and African merchants in Saint-Louis fought to continue the gum trade as they had done for more than a century.[58] The gum trade rested on a rise of the slave labor force both in and outside Saint-Louis.

The midcentury witnessed two major upheavals with the French abolition of slavery in 1848 and the beginning of continental appropriation through conquest and negotiations in 1854 to impose colonial rule, with the goal of developing the cultivation and export of peanuts under the control of French trading companies.[59] Even though the 1848 law potentially concerned the resident slaveholders of French citizenship in New Orleans, it had, most of all, an immediate and profound impact on Saint-Louis. Globally, the abolition of slavery and the imposition of colonial rule intersected in multiple ways. In Europe, the liberation of slaves was used as an argument to justify colonialism along with the civilizing mission. In Saint-Louis, emancipation financially weakened or even ruined most of the habitants, despite the indemnities they received, and the whole process helped the French trading companies to assert their economic domination. Outside Saint-Louis, the issue of slaving played a crucial role in the imposition of "free trade," replacing the system of customs payments to African states on the river. This facilitated the process of territorial appropriation and the construction of a different status for the territories and populations of conquered Senegal. Until the outset of the twentieth century, outside of Saint-Louis, slavery was tolerated and the principle of free soil, according to which a slave was freed as he or she put foot on French soil, suspended. Unless they came from Saint-Louis or the other former slave trading posts, runaway slaves were sent back to those masters who were not in conflict with the colonial regime. Nevertheless, Saint-Louis attracted many fugitives and some *villages de liberté* were formed in its surrounding area.[60]

As in Senegal, in Louisiana the nineteenth century was a time that saw expansion rather than contraction in slavery, a trend mirrored in the Deep South as a whole. However, while the expansion of slavery in Senegal was closely associated with both imperialism and colonialism, in the United States it took place in a country that had recently become an independent republic. Yet, although the British Empire no longer controlled North America, imperialism did not disappear from the continent. The United States did not claim to be an empire but it bore all the characteristics of imperial formations, including a process of internal colonization.[61] Independence from Great Britain did not end the local colonial situation defined by the assertion of authority and control by Euro-Americans over Native Americans, Africans, and African Americans. Many of the nineteenth-century Francophone migrants to New Orleans were, indeed, attracted by the possibility of making their fortune thanks to the slave economy of the city and its surroundings. Nevertheless, slavery was abolished in the United States in 1865 at the end of the Civil War, decades before a set of laws was promulgated in French West

Africa in 1904–1905 to repress the slave trade and slavery after the wars of conquest had come to an end. With the development of railroads and the growth of peanut production, slave labor could be replaced by forced labor. Still, it took a very long time for the abolition of the slave trade and slavery to become effective in Senegal, while the failure of Reconstruction led to the promulgation of Jim Crow laws in the United States. What characterized the empires of the modern period was not that slaving ceased to intersect with imperialism and colonialism as it had done in the Atlantic world throughout the early modern period, but that it did so in a very different way.

IMPERIALISM, COLONIALISM, AND SLAVING IN SAINT-LOUIS AND NEW ORLEANS

The three sections of this volume follow the way the interplay between imperialism, colonialism, and slaving evolved over time in both Saint-Louis and New Orleans and how it affected their connections both in practice and in imagination. The essays of part I, "Negotiating Slavery and Freedom," highlight the centrality of the institution of slavery in the urban societies of Saint-Louis and New Orleans from their foundation to the second half of the nineteenth century. They question what the two cities might have held in common in terms of the way an urban setting informed their slave systems. Population density, social mixing, physical proximity, and the needs of the urban economy tended to make the boundaries between slavery and freedom blurred and porous, which forced the authorities and masters, in particular, to develop practices and institutions that allowed for the perpetuation of the slave order. Beyond these structural similarities, these essays seek to explain the disparities that existed between the two port cities in terms of living conditions and the social position of slaves and, more generally, the structure and social hierarchy for all of the urban population. They explore, in particular, the trajectories of individuals of African or mixed origins who circulated between Saint-Louis and New Orleans for what they reveal about the different logics that governed the relationship among status, gender, and race on each side of the Atlantic.

In "The Role of Slavery in the Economic and Social History of Saint-Louis, Senegal," Martin A. Klein analyzes how local slavery was profoundly affected by engagement with the transatlantic slave trade in ways that distinguished it from what had been practiced before European encounter. Klein shows that by the seventeenth century, patterns of slave labor, ownership, and life experience in Saint-Louis bore the imprint of the rise of the transatlantic commerce in slaves. The Company relied on the labor and expertise of *laptots,* enslaved men entrusted with the management and protection of the Senegal River convoys that transported captives from the deep interior of Senegambia to the coast. In Saint-Louis itself, the enslaved provided the domestic and manual labor needed to support the requirements of the slaves in transit before the Middle Passage and of the French and the Africans who resided there. The wealthy, influential African women known as signares, and then the families they formed, owned and controlled the majority of this enslaved labor force. Because the signares and the habitants of the city who were descended from them needed their personal slaves to manage and control the captives in transit to the Americas, they granted them some rights and privileges that helped to soften and at the same time perpetuate the slave order.

The signares of Saint-Louis reveal the power that African women wielded in their homeland as slave owners, even at the eighteenth-century height of the racist slave regime that anchored the French colonial project across the ocean. Their authority and privilege, however, were specific to their place in African society and the importance of entrepôts like Saint-Louis to the success of the Atlantic enterprise. If a free African-born woman crossed into territory that was under French control, whether literally or figuratively, she exposed herself to the imposition of a set of expectations and limitations dictated by larger French imperial aspirations tied to chattel slavery. In her essay, "Wives, Soldiers, and Slaves: The Atlantic World of Marie Baude, la femme Pinet," Jessica Marie Johnson traces the itinerary of a woman whose experience exposes the centrality of locale in the operation of slavery. In their American colonies, the French could promulgate, exercise, and enforce the racial hierarchy and legal apparatus they designed to uphold the forced labor system at the center of the Atlantic economy. They could not do the same in Senegambia. Slavery and race existed in Saint-Louis and in New Orleans, but their operation in each place was markedly different, shaped by imperatives specific to the situation of each city. The life experience of Marie Baude, who left her native Senegambia to join her French husband in New Orleans, embodied the difficulty of reconciling the ways that slavery and race functioned on either side of the Atlantic.

Marie Baude's husband, a gunsmith, occupied a relatively low social status in French society. At first blush, he would seem to confirm some historians' view that whites of low status in the French Atlantic were more willing than their social betters to establish relations of solidarity with African and African-descended people, even those who were enslaved. Cécile Vidal's contribution to this volume, "The Streets, the Barracks, and the Hospital: Public Space, Social Control, and Cross-Racial Interactions among Soldiers and Slaves in French New Orleans," challenges this presumption and underlines one of the cleavages between Africa and the Americas regarding racial formation. Soldiers and slaves occupied two of the lowest rungs on the French colonial social ladder. They were often thrown into close physical proximity with each other in the crowded urban space of colonial New Orleans, a situation that some scholars suggest would likely have fostered a bond between these two groups. Vidal offers a nuanced analysis of this in a methodical study of encounters between the enslaved and French soldiers in three public or semipublic sites in New Orleans. Even though some forms of cooperation and solidarity developed between soldiers and slaves, their relationships were not devoid of tensions and violence. In the public space, soldiers often felt compelled to assert their racial superiority through physical conflicts.

The Age of Revolutions deeply transformed Atlantic dynamics. Yet slavery was maintained or reestablished in most territories despite the proclamation of the universality of human rights and the abolition of the international slave trade in 1807 for the United Kingdom, 1808 for the United States, and 1815 for France. Many American colonies became independent, including Louisiana when it was integrated into the American Republic. The advent of new political regimes and principles—republics or constitutional monarchies based, entirely or at least partially, on popular sovereignty, equality before the law, the separation of the three branches of government, and the dissociation between nationality and citizenship—transformed the way imperialism, colonialism, and/or slaving operated. In colonial and/or slave societies, those who were denied the rights associated with citizenship drew on the new political culture to claim them. The second part of this volume, "Elusive Citizenship," explores and analyzes how the notions of nationality, citizenship, and subjecthood, as well as the rights or the lack of rights associated with them, including those related to the judicial and penal systems, were mobilized, manipulated, or negotiated at key moments in the histories of each city.

As Ibra Sene demonstrates in "The Prison of Saint-Louis: French Expansion, Social Control, and the Early Development of the Penitentiary Institution in Senegal, circa 1834–1895," prisons were an integral part of the process of transforming Senegal into a genuine colony. Nineteenth-century prisons in the West aimed to replace corporal punishment and to reform and rehabilitate criminals so that they could return to society as fully participating members of their polities. In contrast, the French had no interest in preparing the indigenous population of Senegambia for full membership in their empire. Penal rehabilitation was incompatible with the new French project to impose their colonial dominance within Saint-Louis and to conquer and subjugate the populations of Senegambia outside the port city. Consequently, the penal system of the colony of Senegal was developed to serve those ends. The construction of the first prison in Saint-Louis in the 1830s was an experiment in social engineering, which the French proceeded to refine and expand in the coming decades as an effective agent of colonial control and exploitation with the development of penal labor. Penal labor was one of the means used by colonial authorities to address their workforce needs, a problem that had been amplified by the abolition of slavery in Saint-Louis.

When France abolished slavery in all of its territories in 1848, it also ruled that no one who claimed French citizenship could own slaves, whether they lived on French soil or not. This edict produced a crisis among the large number of slave owners in New Orleans and its surrounding region who claimed French citizenship. When French citizenship was officially linked to abolition, it effectively forced many to choose between French and American national allegiances. The inhabitants of Saint-Louis had no such choice, but Marieke Polfliet shows in her essay, "Citizenship and the Abolition of Slavery after 1848: Conflicts of National Allegiance among the French in New Orleans," that the two cities experienced similar challenges to their political, social, and economic landscapes. As ports on the margins of the French Empire that flourished as entrepôts for the transport of goods produced by enslaved labor forces, New Orleans and Saint-Louis were forced to come to terms with the tension between an Atlantic economy rooted in slavery and the rising tide of antislavery movements in Europe and the Americas. This was, however, a long process, and many compromises were made by French authorities in both places before the liberation of slaves became effective.

Rebecca J. Scott traces one of the discourses that informed and gave momentum to the politics of antislavery and racial equality both before and after 1848. "Asserting Citizenship and Refusing Stigma: New Orleans Equal-Rights Activists Interpret 1803 and 1848" focuses on developments at three turning points in the history of rights in New Orleans that were crucial to making the case for full black citizenship. At each juncture, Scott argues, people of African descent drew on events and ideas that played out in France, its empire, and its former colony of Saint-Domingue/Haiti to elaborate claims to citizenship on American soil. Long after New Orleans severed its formal ties to the French Atlantic, it continued to reflect and assert rights ideologies rooted in it.

Whereas obtaining effective full citizenship for black people would remain a political struggle until the second half of the twentieth century in New Orleans and elsewhere in the United States, the French National Assembly voted in 1916, in the context of World War I, to extend full French citizenship to the inhabitants of Saint-Louis and three other cities in Senegal. Notably, the law was proposed by Blaise Diagne, who was elected the first black deputy of the colony in 1914. Larissa Kopytoff's essay, "French Citizenship and Colonial Rule in Saint-Louis, Senegal," unpacks the complicated, sometimes confusing backstory to the 1916 act. The legislation applied only to the inhabitants of Saint-Louis, Gorée, Dakar, and Rufisque, and only to those who could prove that they were born in one of these cities. The logic of the geographic and natal requirements of the 1916 law is not self-evident, but Kopytoff's analysis reveals it as a product of the history of these cities as sites of what the French considered to be productive interaction with African inhabitants. The indigenous inhabitants of the hinterland, on the other hand, represented a mostly hostile and alien population to be conquered and controlled. Such a neat division of Senegal's African population made sense to the French in the abstract, but implementing and managing its application proved difficult in a territory where people moved from place to place in response to opportunities or threats.

The third and final section of this volume, "Mythic Persistence," explores the construction, reproduction, and transformation of myths and popular imagination in the colonial and postcolonial cities. It is here, in the imagined past, that New Orleans and Saint-Louis most clearly mirror one another. The essays in this section offer two examples of how historical realities have been and continue to be simplified, distorted, or obliterated to minimize the violence of the cities' common slave and colonial past in order to promote a romanticized present.

In "Transatlantic Currents of Orientalism: New Orleans Quadroons and Saint-Louis Signares," Emily Clark and Hilary Jones interrogate the trope of the exotic, beautiful, and seductive free woman of color that has long been associated with both New Orleans and Saint-Louis. At both sites, the figure was evoked to assert an essential difference between African and European that was in turn employed to construct and uphold the racial hierarchy essential to the success of slave regimes and colonialism. Clark and Jones trace the peregrinations of the stereotype from its Orientalist origins to the eighteenth-century French Antilles, to early nineteenth-century New Orleans, and finally to French colonial West Africa. The figure was a product of the same French imperial ambition that facilitated its transmission across the Atlantic from one outpost of empire to another. In its postcolonial incarnation it has been transformed in both Saint-Louis and New Orleans into the embodiment of a romanticized past stripped of the traces of racism and slavery that might undermine the cities' appeal to the tourists on whom their economies rely.

Together with the Congo, Senegal was, and continues to be, the African locale most associated with New Orleans jazz and its musicians. Whereas many seek to identify and verify unbroken links between Senegal and New Orleans, Bruce Boyd Raeburn's essay, "Reflections of Senegambia in New Orleans Jazz," suggests that a mythic past that claims a direct relationship is every bit as important to understanding the origins and evolution of jazz as is a scholarly history rooted in the empirical evidence of the archives. The imaginary quality of some of the city's ties to Africa has not diminished the power and allure of the Afrocentric image it projects about itself and its iconic music.

* * *

NOTES

1. Archives of the Archdiocese of New Orleans, St. Louis Cathedral, Volume A, Marriages 1731–1733, 03/19/1731.

2. Cécile Vidal and Emily Clark, "Famille et esclavage à la Nouvelle-Orléans sous le Régime français (1699–1769)," *Annales de Démographie historique* 122:2 (2011): 99–126.

3. This traditional form was used for the marriages of other free and enslaved people of African descent in the 1720s. After November 1731, it completely disappeared from the sacramental records. Marriage certificates that did not concern whites did not mention banns or the places of birth of the spouses anymore.

4. In the eighteenth century the term *Sénégal* was used in French sources to designate a "nation" or ethnic group, a country, the French concession, or only the island where Saint-Louis stood. It appears, for instance, in the title of famous travel accounts or histories: Jean-Baptiste Labat, *Nouvelle relation de l'Afrique occidentale, contenant une description exacte du Sénégal et des païs situés entre le Cap-Blanc et la rivière de Serrelionne [. . .]* (Paris: T. Le Gras, 1728); Michel Adanson, *Histoire naturelle du Sénégal, coquillages. Avec la relation abrégée d'un voyage fait en ce pays, pendant les années 1749, 50, 51, 52 & 53* (Paris: Jean-Claude Bauche, 1757). However, it is only during the French Revolution that the expression "colony of Senegal" became prevalent. Hence, for the early modern period, we use the category Senegambia to designate the "vast stretch of territory covering the two great river basins, the Senegal and the Gambia River valleys, understood as an inclusive region beginning at the sources of the two rivers high on the Futa Jallon plateau, and ending at their mouths on the Atlantic coast." This vast region constituted a great commercial and cultural zone. It is now divided among six different nation-states. The political dismemberment of greater Senegambia took place over the period of the Atlantic slave trade and colonization. Boubacar Barry, *Senegambia and the Atlantic Slave Trade* (Cambridge: Cambridge University Press, 1998 [1st ed. 1988]), xi.

5. Philip D. Curtin, *The Atlantic Slave Trade: A Census* (Madison: University of Wisconsin Press, 1969), 184.

6. Peter H. Wood, "The Changing Population of the Colonial South: An Overview by Race and Region, 1685–1790," in M. Thomas Hatley, Gregory Waselkov, and Peter Wood, eds., *Powhatan's Mantle: Indians in the Colonial Southeast* (Lincoln: University of Nebraska Press, 1989), 35–103; Gilles Havard and Cécile Vidal, *Histoire de l'Amérique française* (Paris: Champs Flammarion, 2008), 194–203.

7. Throughout the volume, *city* is used to translate the French term *ville* and to distinguish a kind of territory characterized by its urbanity. In the early modern French language and culture, there was no distinction such as the one existing in English between *city* and *town*, which is based on both a demographic and legal distinction. There was originally a distinction between *ville* and *cité* in French, *cité* designating a city with a cathedral (a bishopric), but this distinction became less significant in the early modern period. On the evolution of the vocabulary used to designate urban phenomena in various languages, see Laurent Coudroy de Lille, Jean-Charles Depaule, Brigitte Marin, and Christian Topalov, eds., *L'aventure des mots de la ville à travers le temps, les langues, les sociétés* (Paris: Robert Laffont, Bouquins, 2010).

8. Alain Sinou, *Comptoirs et villes coloniales du Sénégal. Saint-Louis, Gorée, Dakar* (Paris: Karthala and ORSTOM, 1993); Samuel Wilson, *The Architecture of Colonial Louisiana* (Lafayette: Center for Louisiana Studies, University of Southwestern Louisiana, 1987); Gilles-Antoine Langlois, *Des villes pour la Louisiane française: Théorie et pratique de l'urbanistique coloniale au 18e siècle* (Paris: L'Harmattan, 2003).

9. Mobile was founded before New Orleans in 1702, but the outpost was not considered an urban center by historical actors at the time, whereas New Orleans was conceived from the outset as a genuine city. See Joseph Zitomersky, "Ville, État, implantation et société en Louisiane française. La variante 'mississippienne' du modèle colonial français en Amérique du Nord," in Alain Saussol and Joseph Zitomersky, eds., *Colonies, Territoires, Sociétés: L'enjeu français* (Paris: L'Harmattan, 1996), 23–48.

10. After 1763 the eastern part of what had been French Louisiana no longer bore the name of Louisiana. The term *Louisiana* was reserved for New Orleans and the western part ceded to Spain. After 1803, only a small section of what had been Spanish Louisiana became the territory and then the state named Louisiana within the United States.

11. François Weil, "The Purchase and the Making of French Louisiana," in Peter J. Kastor and Francois Weil, eds., *Empires of the Imagination: Transatlantic Histories of the Louisiana Purchase* (Charlottesville: University of Virginia Press, 2009), 301–26.

12. Nathalie Dessens, *From Saint-Domingue to New Orleans: Migration and Influences* (Gainesville: University Press of Florida, 2007); Paul Lachance, "The Foreign French," in Arnold R. Hirsch and Joseph Logsdon, eds., *Creole New Orleans: Race and Americanization* (Baton Rouge: Louisiana State University Press, 1992), 1–130; Marieke Polfliet, "Émigration et politisation: Les Français de New York et La Nouvelle-Orléans dans la première moitié du XIXe siècle (1803–1860)," PhD diss., Université de Nice, 2013.

13. Marjorie Bourdelais, *La Nouvelle-Orléans: Croissance démographique, intégrations urbaine et sociale (1803–1860)* (Bern: Peter Lang, 2012), 128.

14. Jean-Pierre Dozon, *Saint-Louis du Sénégal—Palimpseste d'une ville* (Paris: Karthala, 2012), 5, 8.

15. Rufisque and Dakar also obtained the status of Communes in the early 1880s.

16. Mamadou Diouf, "L'idée municipale: une idée neuve en Afrique," *Politique africaine* 74:2 (1992): 18.

17. Dozon, *Saint-Louis du Sénégal;* G. Wesley Johnson, *The Emergence of Black Politics in Senegal: The Struggle for Power in the Four Communes, 1900–1920* (Stanford, CA: Stanford University Press, 1971).

18. Charles Becker, Victor Martin, Jean Schmitz, and Monique Chastanet, with the collaboration of Jean-François Maurel and Saliou Mbaye, *Les premiers recensements au Sénégal et l'évolution démographique: Présentation de documents* (Dakar: 2008), 2, accessed October 7, 2016, https://core.ac.uk/download/pdf/14520211.pdf; James Searing, *West African Slavery and Atlantic Commerce: The Senegal River Valley, 1700–1860* (Cambridge: Cambridge University Press, 1993), 227n86 (for the 1779 census); Martin A. Klein, "Slaves, Gum, and Peanuts: Adaptation to the End of the Slave Trade in Senegal, 1817–48," *William and Mary Quarterly* 66:4 (2009): 895–914 (896 for the 1819 population).

19. Paul Lachance, "The Growth of the Free and Slave Population of French Colonial Louisiana," in Bradley G. Bond, ed., *French Colonial Louisiana and the Atlantic World* (Baton Rouge: Louisiana State University Press, 1992), 204–43; Paul Lachance, "The Louisiana Purchase in Demographic Perspective," in Kastor and Weil, eds., *Empires of the Imagination,* 143–79.

20. John G. Clark, *New Orleans, 1718–1812: An Economic History* (Baton Rouge: Louisiana State University Press, 1970).

21. Elizabeth Fussell, "Constructing New Orleans, Constructing Race: A Population History of New Orleans," *Journal of American History* 94:3 (December 2007): 846–55; Clarence L. Mohr and Lawrence N. Powell, "Through the Eye of Katrina: The Past as Prologue? An Introduction," *Journal of American History* 94:3 (December 2007): 692–94.

22. On the internal slave trade, see Walter Johnson, *Soul by Soul: Life inside the Antebellum Slave Market* (Cambridge, MA: Harvard University Press, 1999); Walter Johnson, ed., *The Chattel Principle: Internal Slave Trades in the Americas* (New Haven, CT: Yale University Press, 2004).

23. On the demographic and economic growth of New Orleans, see Bourdelais, *La Nouvelle-Orléans;* Eberhard L. Faber, *Building the Land of Dreams: New Orleans and the Transformation of Early America* (Princeton, NJ: Princeton University Press, 2016). On Louisiana slavery in the antebellum period and on the expansion of slavery in the Deep South, see Robert Follett, *The Sugar Masters: Planters and Slaves in Louisiana's Cane World, 1820–1860* (Baton Rouge: Louisiana State University Press, 2005); Adam Rothman, *Slave Country, American Expansion and the Origins of the Deep South* (Cambridge, MA: Harvard University Press, 2005); Walter Johnson, *River of Dark Dreams: Slavery and Empire in the Cotton Kingdom* (Cambridge, MA: Harvard University Press, 2013).

24. Klein, "Slaves, Gum, and Peanuts," 895–914; James L.A. Webb Jr., "The Trade in Gum Arabic: Prelude to French Conquest in Senegal," *Journal of African American History* 26:2 (1985): 149–68.

25. Searing, *West African Slavery and Atlantic Commerce,* 165–66.

26. Becker et al., *Les premiers recensements au Sénégal et l'évolution démographique,* 3–7.

27. Sinou, *Comptoirs et villes coloniales du Sénégal,* 172, 197.

28. Nowadays, Saint-Louis includes around 210,000 inhabitants (in 2013), while New Orleans has not completely recovered from the consequences of Hurricane Katrina and has a population estimated at 390,000 (in 2015). Agence nationale de la statistique et de la démographie, République du Sénégal, http://sigstat.ansd.sn/sigstatv2/repertoire_localites_senegal, and United States Census Bureau, accessed October 7, 2016, http://www.census.gov/quickfacts/table/PST045215/2255000.

29. Philippe Haudrère, *La Compagnie des Indes au XVIIIe siècle* (Paris: Les Indes savantes, 2005). For a work on the Company of Senegal, see Abdoulaye Ly, *La Compagnie du Sénégal* (Paris and Dakar: Karthala and IFAN, 1993). For works on the Company of the Indies in Louisiana, see Marcel Giraud, *Histoire de la Louisiane française* (Paris: Presses universitaires de France, 1953–1974), 4 vols.; Marcel Giraud, *A History of French Louisiana. Vol. 5: The Company of the Indies, 1723–1731* (Baton Rouge: Louisiana State University Press, 1991); Erin M. Green-

wald, *Marc-Antoine Caillot and the Company of the Indies in Louisiana* (Baton Rouge: Louisiana State University Press, 2016).

30. Gwendolyn M. Hall, *Africans in Colonial Louisiana: The Development of Afro-Creole Culture in the Eighteenth Century* (Baton Rouge: Louisiana State University Press, 1992), 56–95 and 171–72; Thomas N. Ingersoll, "The Slave Trade and the Ethnic Diversity of Louisiana's Slave Community," *Louisiana History* 37:2 (1996): 133–61; Ibrahima Seck, "The Relationships between St. Louis, Senegal, Its Hinterlands, and Colonial Louisiana," in Bond, ed., *French Colonial Louisiana and the Atlantic World*, 265–90; Ibrahima Seck, "Les Français et la traite des esclaves en Sénégambie," *Dix-huitième siècle* 44:1 (2012): 49–60; Daniel H. Usner, "From African Captivity to American Slavery: The Introduction of Black Laborers to Colonial Louisiana," *Louisiana History* 20:1 (1979): 25–48.

31. Registers of the Superior Council of Louisiana 1747/05/05/01, 1747/05/05/02, 1747/05/06/04, 1747/05/06/07, 1747/05/18/01, 1747/05/18/02, 1747/05/18/03, 1747/05/18/04, 1747/05/19/05, 1747/05/19/06; 1765/10/15/01, 1765/10/16/01, 1765/10/16/02.

32. On the d'Erneville/Derneville family in Louisiana, Kimberly S. Hanger, *Bounded Lives, Bounded Places: Free Black Society in Colonial New Orleans, 1769–1803* (Durham, NC: Duke University Press, 1997), 65; Jennifer M. Spear, *Race, Sex, and Social Order in Early New Orleans* (Baltimore: Johns Hopkins University Press, 2009), 82–84, 89. On the d'Erneville family in Saint-Louis, see Hilary Jones, *The Métis of Senegal: Urban Life and Politics in French West Africa* (Bloomington: Indiana University Press, 2013), 19–20, 193.

33. Rebecca J. Scott and Jean M. Hébrard, *Freedom Papers: An Atlantic Odyssey in the Age of Emancipation* (Cambridge, MA: Harvard University Press, 2012).

34. Ibrahima Seck, "La traite négrière entre Saint-Louis du Sénégal, les Antilles et la vallée du Mississippi au XIXe siècle," in *Saint-Louis et l'esclavage. Actes du Symposium international sur « La traite négrière à Saint-Louis du Sénégal et dans son arrière-pays »* (Saint-Louis, 18, 19, et 20 décembre 1998), ed. Djibril Samb (Dakar: IFAN and Université Cheikh Anta Diop, 2000), 217–35.

35. For studies insisting on the Creole character of colonial and antebellum New Orleans and Louisiana, see Hall, *Africans in Colonial Louisiana;* Shannon Lee Dawdy, *Building the Devil's Empire: French Colonial New Orleans* (Chicago: University of Chicago Press, 2008); Hirsch and Logsdon, eds., *Creole New Orleans;* Nathalie Dessens, *Creole City: A Chronicle of Early American New Orleans* (Gainesville: University Press of Florida, 2015); Dianne Guenin-Lelle, *The Story of French New Orleans: History of a Creole City* (Jackson: University Press of Mississippi, 2016). For works on the meanings and uses of a Creole identity in contemporary Louisiana, see Virginia R. Domínguez, *White by Definition: Social Classification in Creole Louisiana* (New Brunswick, NJ: Rutgers University Press, 1986); Sara Le Menestrel, "Déclinaisons et enjeux de l'identité créole en Louisiane," in *Situations créoles. Pratiques et représentations,* ed. Carlo A. Célius (Quebec: CELAT, Éditions Nota Bene, 2006), 219–29. For works depicting Saint-Louis as a Creole city even when they insist on the importance of the African and Muslim population, see Dozon, *Saint-Louis du Sénégal;* Jones, *The Métis of Senegal;* Fernando R. Rosa, "The Creole Port City: Cosmopolitanism, Intimate Encounters and Republican Ideals in Twentieth-century Saint-Louis-du-Sénégal," *Journal of African Cultural Studies* 24:1 (2012): 89–99.

36. P. Alquier, "St-Louis du Sénégal, pendant la Révolution et l'Empire," *Bulletin du Comité d'études historiques et scientifiques de l'Afrique occidentale française* 5 (1929): 277–320 and 411–63; François Deroure, "La vie quotidienne à Saint-Louis par ses archives (1779–1809)," *Bulletin de l'IFAN* 26 (1964): 397–437. As James Searing has underlined, "these works are full of descriptions of the charm and fecundity of the *signares* and of the libertine life of European traders. They simply reproduce the popular colonial image of the islands." Searing, *West African Slavery and Atlantic Commerce,* 224n2. For a work seeking to deconstruct the myth surrounding free women of color in New Orleans, see Emily Clark, *The Strange History of the American Quadroon* (Chapel Hill: University of North Carolina Press, 2013).

37. Jean-Luc Angrand, *Céleste ou le temps des signares* (Paris: Éditions Anne Pépin, 2006); Fadel Dia, *La Raparille. Roman* (Paris: Présence Africaine, 2009); Tita Mandeleau, *Signare Anna* (Saint-Louis, Senegal: Xamal, 1998); Abdoulaye Sadji, *Nini. Mulâtresse du Sénégal* (Paris: Présence Africaine, 1957). Likewise, "the revival of the Fanal [lantern festival] is part of a burgeoning interest in Senegal's heritage of métissage and in particular of its signares, a brand of métis women known for their wealth and extravagance who dominated the social and economic life in the European trade posts of the eighteenth century." Ferdinand de Jong, "Shining Lights: Self-Fashioning in the Lantern Festival of Saint Louis, Senegal," *African Arts* (2009): 38–53.

38. In 2000, UNESCO designated the island of Saint-Louis a World Heritage site. The UNESCO website emphasizes "the magnificent 'balconied houses,' the 'gallery houses' and beautiful Signares as well as the rare 'Portuguese maisons basses'" that "give the city its aesthetic quality and identity." See the UNESCO website, accessed October 5, 2016, http://whc.unesco.org/en/list/956. See also Abdoul Adir Aïdara, *Saint-Louis du Sénégal d'hier à aujourd'hui* (Brinon-sur-Sauldre: Grandvaux, 2005). However, the work by Clément Verfaillie demonstrates that the designation "house of signares" is highly problematic because this type of architecture was not restricted to women of color and métis families. Clément Verfaillie, "Caty Miller (1760–1834), une Signare dans la ville," unpublished paper, International Conference on "Saint-Louis, Senegal and New Orleans: Two Mirror Cities, 17th–21st Century," Tulane University, New Orleans, April 22–25, 2013.

39. The conferences gathered scholars and graduate students from France, North America, and Senegal, first in Saint-Louis, then one year later in New Orleans. Papers were precirculated each time. Most of each session was devoted to collective discussions of each paper. This means that they have been written or rewritten three times. International conferences, "Saint-Louis du Sénégal et La Nouvelle-Orléans: Histoire comparée et croisée de deux cités portuaires de part et d'autre de l'Atlantique du XVIIe au XXIe siècle," June 4–7, 2012, Université Gaston Berger, Saint-Louis, Senegal, and "Saint-Louis, Senegal and New Orleans: Two Mirror Cities, 17th–21st centuries," April 22–25, 2013, Historic New Orleans Collection and Tulane University, New Orleans. Louisiana and Senegal musicians also took part in the exchange, and a concert was organized in each city. A partnership with RFI (Radio France international) led to the broadcasting of two sessions of the radio show *La marche du monde* by Valérie Nivelon on June 23, 2012, and May 11, 2013, http://www.rfi.fr/emission

/20120623-1-saint-louis-senegal-nouvelle-orleans-deux-villes-miroir and http://www.rfi.fr /emission/20130511-2-nouvelle-orleans-saint-louis-senegal-deux-villes-miroir.

40. This piece, written by Douglas Rogers, originally appeared in the May 2014 issue of *National Geographic Traveler* magazine. For the note posted on the *National Geographic* website on May 26, 2014, accessed October 5, 2016, see http://intelligenttravel.nationalgeographic.com/2014/05/26/all-jazzed-up-in-west-africa/.

41. In fact, it was an email sent in March 2009 by Marie-Caroline Camara to Cécile Vidal about the international conference she had organized with François Weil at the EHESS on Frenchness in the French Atlantic in October 2008 and suggesting that she should organize such an event in Saint-Louis, Senegal at the occasion of the three-hundred-year anniversary of the foundation of the city, which gave us the idea of organizing our series of two international conferences on Saint-Louis and New Orleans.

42. See the selective bibliography on each city at the end of the introduction.

43. For the bibliography on "colonial cities," see Gerard L. Telkamp, *Urban History and European Expansion: A Review of Recent Literature Concerning Colonial Cities and a Preliminary Bibliography* (Leiden: Center for European Expansion, 1978); Hélène Vacher, ed., *Villes coloniales aux XIXe–XXe siècles. D'un sujet d'action à un objet d'histoire (Algérie, Maroc, Libye et Iran): Essais et guide bibliographique* (Paris: Maisonneuve et Larose, 2005). For the historiography on African urban history, see David M. Anderson and Richard J. A. R. Rathbone, eds., *Africa's Urban Past* (Oxford: James Currey, 2000); Andrew Burton, "Urbanization in Eastern Africa: A Historical Overview," in Andrew Burton, ed., *The Urban Experience in Eastern Africa, c. 1750–2000* (Nairobi: British Institute for Eastern Africa, 2002), 1–28; Catherine Coquery-Vidrovitch, "The process of Urbanization in Africa from the Origins to Independence: An Overview Paper," *African Studies Review* 33:4 (1991): 1–99; Laurent Fouchard, "L'histoire urbaine en Afrique: une perspective ouest-africaine," *Histoire urbaine* 9:1 (2004): 129–44; John D. Y. Peel, "Urbanization and Urban History in West Africa," *Journal of African History* 21 (1980): 269–77.

44. Ira Berlin, "Time, Space, and the Evolution of Afro-American Society on British Mainland North America," *American Historical Review* 85:1 (1980): 44–78. For a pioneering work on urban slavery in the United States, see Richard C. Wade, *Slavery in the Cities: The South, 1820–1860* (New York: Oxford University Press, 1964). For studies of urban slavery in the Americas from the 1980s, see, among other books: Ira Berlin and Leslie M. Harris, eds., *Slavery in New York* (New York: The New Press, 2005); Herman L. Bennett, *Africans in Colonial Mexico: Absolutism, Christianity, and Afro-Creole Consciousness, 1570–1640* (Bloomington: Indiana University Press, 2003); Mariana L. R. Dantas, *Black Townsmen: Urban Slavery and Freedom in Eighteenth-Century Americas* (New York: Palgrave Macmillan, 2008); Thelma Wills Foote, *Black and White Manhattan: The History of Racial Formation in Colonial New York City* (Oxford: Oxford University Press, 2004); Jared Ross Hardesty, *Unfreedom: Slavery and Dependence in Eighteenth-Century Boston* (New York: New York University Press, 2016); Mary C. Karasch, *Slave Life in Rio de Janeiro, 1808–1850* (Princeton, NJ: Princeton University Press, 1987); Gary B. Nash, *Forging Freedom: The Formation of Philadelphia's Free Black Community, 1740–1820* (Cambridge, MA: Harvard University Press, 1988); Pedro L. V. Welch, *Slave Society in the City: Bridgetown,*

Barbados, 1680–1834 (Kingston, Miami, and Oxford: Ian Randle Publishers and James Currey Publishers, 2003).

45. For works on American port cities, see, among other books: Franklin W. Knight and Peggy K. Liss, eds., *Atlantic Port Cities: Economy, Culture, and Society in the Atlantic World, 1650–1850* (Knoxville: University of Tennessee Press, 1991); Gary B. Nash, "Special Issue: Early Cities of the Americas," *Common-Place* 3:4 (2003), http://www.common-place.org/vol-03/no-04/talk/; Guadeloupe Garcia, *Beyond the Wall City: Colonial Exclusion in Havana* (Berkeley: University of California Press, 2015); Emma Hart, *Building Charleston: Town and Society in the Eighteenth-Century British Atlantic World* (Charlottesville: University of Virginia Press, 2010); Alejandro de La Fuente, *Havana and the Atlantic in the Sixteenth Century* (Chapel Hill: University of North Carolina Press, 2008); Anne Pérotin-Dumon, *La ville aux îles. La ville dans l'île. Basse-Terre et Pointe-à-Pitre, Guadeloupe, 1650–1820* (Paris: Karthala, 2000). For works on African slave trading posts, see Mariana Candido, *An African Slaving Port and the Atlantic World: Benguela and its Hinterland* (New York: Cambridge University Press, 2013); Jean Delcourt, *Gorée, six siècles d'histoire* (Dakar: Editions Clairafrique, 1984); Mark Hinchman, *Portrait of an Island: The Architecture and Material Culture of Gorée, Sénégal, 1758–1837* (Lincoln: University of Nebraska Press, 2015); A. J. H. Latham, *Old Calabar, 1600–1891: The Impact of the International Economy upon a Traditional Society* (Oxford: Clarendon, 1973); Robin Law, *Ouidah: The Social History of a West African Slaving Port, 1727–1892* (Athens: Ohio University Press, 2005); Kristin Mann, *Slavery and the Birth of an African City: Lagos, 1760–1900* (Bloomington: Indiana University Press, 2007); Alain Sinou, *Le comptoir de Ouidah. Une ville africaine singulière* (Paris: Karthala, 1995); Randy J. Sparks, *Where the Negroes Are Masters: An African Port in the Era of the Slave Trade* (Cambridge, MA: Harvard University Press, 2014). This Atlantic history of port cities draws on an older tradition of urban studies in early North America, linked to discussions about the American Revolution. See Carl Bridenbaugh, *Cities in the Wilderness: The First Century of Urban Life in America, 1625–1742* (New York: Knopf, 1955); *Cities in Revolt: Urban Life in America, 1743–1776* (New York: Knopf, 1955); Gary Nash, *The Urban Crucible: Social Change, Political Consciousness, and the Origins of the American Revolution* (Cambridge, MA: Harvard University Press, 1979); Benjamin L. Carp, *Rebels Rising: Cities and the American Revolution* (Oxford: Oxford University Press, 2007).

46. Jorge Cañizares-Esguerra, Matt D. Childs, and James Sidbury, "Introduction," in Jorge Cañizares-Esguerra, Matt D. Childs, and James Sidbury, eds., *The Black Urban Atlantic in the Age of the Slave Trade* (Philadelphia: University of Pennsylvania Press, 2013), 1–18. The volume includes a very useful "Bibliographical Essay," 341–50.

47. John Thornton, *Africa and Africans in the Making of the Atlantic World, 1400–1800* (Cambridge: Cambridge University Press, 1992); David Northrup, *Africa's Discovery of Europe, 1450–1850* (Oxford: Oxford University Press, 2002).

48. As James Searing has underlined, "the 'door of no return' is an apt metaphor for the passageway that carried slaves across the Atlantic. Historians of the slave trade have focused their gaze in the same direction, on the slaves and commodities that left the continent. This book looks back into Africa through the same passageway, using Atlantic commerce as a win-

dow for studying change within Africa. Atlantic commerce transformed West Africa, creating a divide in its history." Searing, *West African Slavery and Atlantic Commerce,* x.

49. Bernard Bailyn, *Atlantic History: Concept and Contours* (Cambridge, MA: Harvard University Press, 2005); Alison Games, "Atlantic History: Definitions, Challenges, and Opportunities," *American Historical Review* 111:3 (2006): 741–57; Jack P. Greene and Philip D. Morgan, eds., *Atlantic History: A Critical Appraisal* (Oxford: Oxford University Press, 2009); Nicholas Canny and Philip Morgan, eds., *The Oxford Handbook of the Atlantic World,* 1450–1850 (Oxford: Oxford University Press, 2011); Cécile Vidal, "For a Comprehensive History of the Atlantic World or Histories Connected in and beyond the Atlantic World?," *Annales HSS* 67:2 (2012): 279–300.

50. Georges Balandier, "La situation coloniale: Approche théorique," *Cahiers internationaux de sociologie* 11 (1951): 44–79.

51. Searing, *West African Slavery and Atlantic Commerce,* 72.

52. Richard White, *The Middle Ground: Indians, Empires and Republics in the Great Lakes Region, 1650–1815* (Cambridge: Cambridge University Press, 1991); Daniel H. Usner Jr., *Indians, Settlers, and Slaves in a Frontier Exchange Economy: The Lower Mississippi Valley before 1783* (Chapel Hill: University of North Carolina Press, 1992); Kathleen DuVal, *The Native Ground: Indians and Colonists in the Heart of the Continent* (Philadelphia: University of Pennsylvania Press, 2006); Havard and Vidal, *Histoire de l'Amérique française.*

53. Gilles Havard, *Empire et métissages. Indiens et Français dans le Pays d'en Haut, 1660–1715* (Sillery and Paris: Septentrion and Presses de l'Université de Paris-Sorbonne, 2003); Gilles Havard, "'Les forcer à devenir Cytoyens.' État, Sauvages et citoyenneté en Nouvelle-France (XVIIe–XVIIIe siècle)," *Annales HSS* 64:5 (2009): 985–1018.

54. Arnaud Balvay, *La révolte des Natchez* (Paris: le Félin, 2008); George Edward Milne, *Natchez Country: Indians, Colonists, and the Landscapes of Race in French Louisiana* (Athens: University of Georgia Press, 2015).

55. Arnold A. Sio, "Review: *The Sociology of Slavery: An Analysis of the Origins, Development and Structure of Negro Slave Society in Jamaica* by Orlando Patterson," *Social and Economic Studies* 17:1 (1968): 96–99, esp. 96.

56. Djibril Samb, ed., *Saint-Louis et l'esclavage. Actes du Symposium international sur "La traite négrière à Saint-Louis du Sénégal et dans son arrière-pays"* (Saint-Louis, 18, 19 et 20 décembre 1998) (Dakar: IFAN and Université Cheikh Anta Diop, 2000).

57. For ideas and projects of colonizing Africa in the second half of the eighteenth century within the French Empire, see the works by Pernille Røge, "The Reinvention of French Colonial System, 1756–1802," PhD diss., Cambridge University, 2009; "'La clef du commerce': The Changing Role of Africa in France's Atlantic Empire, ca. 1777–1797," *History of European Ideas* 34 (2008): 431–38; "An Early Scramble for Africa: British, Danish and French colonial projects on the coast of West Africa, 1780s and 1790s," in Robert Aldrich and Kirsten McKenzie, eds., *The Routledge History of Western Empires* (New York: Routledge, 2013), 72–86; "L'expérimentation coloniale britannique, danoise et française sur la côte ouest africaine dans les années 1780 et 1790," in Guy Saupin, ed., *Africains et Européens dans le monde atlantique, XVe–XIXe siècle*

(Rennes: Presses Universitaires de Rennes, 2014), 217–35; Laurent Veyssière, Philippe Joutard, and Didier Poton, eds., "1763 et la reconquête française du Sénégal," in *Vers un nouveau monde atlantique: Les traités de Paris, 1763–1783* (Rennes: Presses Universitaires de Rennes, 2016), 193–200; "Rethinking Africa in the Age of Revolution: The Evolution of Jean-Baptiste-Léonard Durand's Voyage au Sénégal," *Atlantic Studies* 13:3 (2016): 389–406.

58. Georges Hardy, *La mise en valeur du Sénégal de 1817 à 1854* (Paris: E. Larose, 1921).

59. On the process of territorial appropriation and the role of treaties, see Isabelle Surun, "Sénégal et dépendances: le territoire de la transition impériale (1855–1895)" (Mémoire de recherche inédit, Habilitation à diriger des recherches, Sciences Po Paris, 2012), and "Une souveraineté à l'encre sympathique? Souveraineté autochtone et appropriations territoriales dans les traités franco-africains au XIXe siècle," *Annales HSS* 69:2 (2014): 313–48.

60. Mamadou Badji, "L'abolition de l'esclavage au Sénégal: entre plasticité du droit colonial et respect de l'État de droit," *Droit et cultures* 52:2 (2006), accessed October 10, 2016, http://droitcultures.revues.org/729; Roger Botte, "L'esclavage africain après l'abolition de 1848. Servitude et droit du sol," *Annales HSS* 55:5 (2000): 1009–37; M'Baye Guèye, "La fin de l'esclavage à Saint-Louis et à Gorée en 1848," *Bulletin de l'Institut fondamental d'Afrique noire, Série B* 28:3–4 (1966): 637–56; Roger Pasquier, "À propos de l'émancipation des esclaves au Sénégal en 1848," *Revue française d'histoire d'outre-mer* 54:194–97 (1967): 188–208; François Renault, *L'abolition de l'esclavage au Sénégal: L'attitude de l'administration française* (Paris: Société française d'histoire d'outre-mer, 1972); Denise Bouche, *Les villages de liberté en Afrique noire française, 1887–1910* (Paris: Mouton, 1968). See also the more recent Martin A. Klein, *Slavery and Colonial Rule in French West Africa* (New York: Cambridge University Press, 1998).

61. Paul A. Kramer, "Power and Connection: Imperial Histories of the United States in the World," *American Historical Review* 116:5 (2011): 1348–91.

I

NEGOTIATING SLAVERY AND FREEDOM

THE ROLE OF SLAVERY IN THE ECONOMIC AND SOCIAL HISTORY OF SAINT-LOUIS, SENEGAL

MARTIN A. KLEIN

The cities of the slave trade were almost all cities with a slave majority.[1] In fact, slavery played an important role in almost all of the cities created by expanding European powers between 1450 and 1800. This was certainly true in Saint-Louis, Senegal, where slaves were a majority of the population from several generations after it was founded in 1659 until the abolition of slavery in 1848. Slaves were important in Saint-Louis because they were available, because they were more reliable than free labor, and because they were the most efficient way that labor, both skilled and unskilled, could be provided. This does not mean that there were no other sources of labor. During the first decades of the trade, workers recruited from nearby communities were the most important source of *laptots,* the sailors on the convoys that went upriver to seek slaves and gum, but the number of slaves steadily increased, and they became an overwhelming majority by the middle of the eighteenth century. Only just before abolition in 1848, the process was reversed as free laborers began to replace slaves in the river trade. Ironically, they were men who worked on riverboats in order to buy slaves and improve their economic position in their home societies.[2] Slaves predominated because they were available in greater numbers, they were more reliable, they could be trained, and they could be more profitably exploited. Urban slavery was not as regimented or as harsh as that of the slave plantation, and it allowed the slave a much greater degree of autonomy and the possibility of accumulation. Slave plantations everywhere depended on the ability to extract labor from slaves by coercion. In the cities, slaves played diverse roles and had a greater degree of autonomy. This was especially true in Saint-Louis because of the river trading system. Slaves were, however, still property and could be exchanged, sold, or most likely given to offspring as part of a dowry.

The mouth of the Senegal River was the place where the transatlantic slave trade began in 1443 when the first Portuguese ship to get south of the Sahara kidnapped several people to show the King of Portugal what they had accomplished. The slave trade lasted there for over four centuries. Though there was not a Portuguese settlement on the Senegal River, the area from Cape Verde to Sierra Leone was peppered with Luso-African villages, which were linked to a Portuguese colony on the Cape Verde Islands. From the late sixteenth century, the English, Dutch, and French challenged the Portuguese monopoly of the slave trade. The climate and the disease environment of Senegambia were somewhat more hospitable to Europeans, and it thus became the site of several permanent installations, though the number of Europeans in these colonies was always very small, and during the eighteenth century actually became smaller.[3]

In 1659, the French settlement on the island of Saint-Louis was founded by the Compagnie du Cap Vert et du Sénégal. This was the first of a succession of charter companies which controlled Saint-Louis. Only in 1783 did the French state take over. During the seventeenth century, the convoy of ships that went upriver every year included and was controlled by French men. The different companies wanted to ship to America as many of the slaves under their control as possible. Thus, much of the labor was provided at first by French soldiers and sailors, but they experienced a high mortality and were gradually replaced by free men recruited locally. They were a majority of the workers until early in the eighteenth century, though the number of slave workers on the convoy probably began increasing early. Africans increasingly controlled the boats, and slaves did most of the work. As late as 1738, there were still 231 Europeans in Saint-Louis, Gorée, and the upriver post at Galam, but the French slave trading companies had decided by then that it was more economical to rely on African sailors and artisans and *métis* enterprise.[4] By 1835, the population of these settlements had multiplied about ten times, but there were only 151 Europeans. European soldiers, sailors, and artisans were paid more and had a much higher mortality. The slaves who replaced Europeans even in skilled and leadership roles were more knowledgeable and probably more productive. This was in part because they were given a measure of autonomy and were sufficiently rewarded that they were loyal participants in the system. By the 1740s both the annual convoy and productive activity within Saint-Louis were dominated by slaves owned mostly by women called *signares.* The signares were, and their families remained, very much a part of the French presence. More important, they were crucial to the local economy, the export economy, and the development of Saint-Louis. Saint-Louis was from early on very much an African town. By the middle of the eighteenth century, it was dominated by African enterprise, and labor was provided overwhelmingly by slaves.

Each of the European settlements in West Africa developed its own trade network.[5] Often the trade came to various slave trading entrepôts, only a few of which were under direct European control. In Saint-Louis the traders went up the river to seek slaves and other commodities. By the end of the seventeenth century, the Bambara areas of what is now western Mali were the major source of slaves for both the French and British in Senegambia.[6] In the Gambia, these slaves were brought down to British trading posts by African traders. In the Senegal River, the French developed a number of trading posts in Gajaaga in the upper river area in the 1690s, of which the most important was Fort Saint-Joseph (1698). These posts tapped the slave trade from the Bambara states of Segou and Kaarta and also tried to develop the gold trade.[7] The French also developed a trade in gum arabic, which was produced by slaves working under the direction of Mauritanian slave owners in desert areas north of the Senegal River. There were four trading posts, called *escales,* in the lower Senegal River Valley, which was accessible all year long. Gajaaga in the upper river was accessible only during the rainy season when waters were high. There were thus two trading seasons. From February to May, there were trade fairs in the escales. In June, the whole trading community moved upriver in a convoy, the boats pulled by laptots.[8] In the eighteenth century, the gum trade became as important economically as the slave trade.

The convoy was made up of different groups, free and slave, métis and black, and an occasional French trader.[9] The vast majority, however, were slaves, at least from the middle of the eighteenth century to the middle of the nineteenth. Not all of the states bordering the river were friendly. The river was shallow and marked by sandbars, which meant that local horsemen could stop ships, which forced them to move in convoy and sometimes to require protection. The French made regular payments to the rulers of the African states along the river to keep the river open and tried, not always successfully, to influence the politics of the river.[10] The convoy finally returned to Saint-Louis in October, an event that was one of the most festive of the year. The convoy bought slaves and gum for export, but also gold, wax, ivory, and hides. Grain and other foodstuffs were also purchased in the middle and lower Senegal River area and sold to the Moors or used to feed Saint-Louis and supply oceangoing vessels that stopped in Saint-Louis. Much of the commercial activity in the lower river was in the hands of *marigotiers,* slaves or ex-slaves who worked the creeks and bought grain, products of local artisanship, and salt from Gandiole.

The slave trade was thus part of a vibrant Senegal River trading system. During the late eighteenth century, gum was actually more important than slaves. Gum had long been traded on the Mauritanian coast, but from the late seventeenth century, demand increased with the growth of European textile industries. The gum-producing areas used the gum to buy slaves, grain, and cloth.[11] The gum and slaves were largely for export, but much of the trade was also for local consumption. Gold was much desired by Europeans, but the local demand for gold jewelry was such that relatively little gold found its way onto French, British, or Portuguese ships. The river commercial system existed long before the French arrived, but the existence of Saint-Louis and its demand for African products stimulated its growth. Thus, salt, jewelry, textiles, livestock, and agricultural produce were traded back and forth within the river economy. The vibrancy of this economic system was rooted in the diversity of commodities produced and the links between the export trade and trade between different riverine peoples.

The slave trading companies were monopoly companies, but regularly failed because of interlopers and European wars. They were not eager to create a large costly establishment, but they found it difficult to control the growth of the colony or the behavior of men they sent out to Africa. Central to that growth was the signares that company officials cohabited with.[12] Company employees were suspected of using their partners to trade and of providing these women with the best merchandise. Employees were forbidden to trade on their own. None of the companies, however, could control either their employees or the local population. Men were prohibited from bringing their

French wives until the 1720s, but even after that, French women were rare in the colony. European males wanted sexual partners, but not solely for sex. They also wanted meals, companionship, care when sick, and trading partners. The importance of care is illustrated by the story of Antoine Feuiltaine, a French soldier who spent forty-seven years in Senegal. His story has been told by a descendant, Sylvain Sankalé. Sankalé's book describes Feuiltaine being nursed when feverous by the woman who became his wife. She used a range of African remedies including herbs and amulets. This woman was not a signare, at least not yet, but was able to use Senegalese pharmacopeia to heal the man who became her husband. Feuiltaine became an officer and his wife, Marie, became a trader, whose income was valuable when the English occupation left her husband with very limited income.[13] French men often boarded with African women, but the most important institution was *mariage à la mode du pays,* an institution that had long existed with the Portuguese.[14] The term *signare* was derived from the Portuguese *senhora.*

Men courted women, paid a bride price, promised fidelity, and were "married" in a public ceremony, which was followed by a wedding feast.[15] The signare knew her partner's language, his customs, and the foods he liked. Signares had a reputation as jealous lovers who did not tolerate the promiscuity that sometimes characterized the sexual interface of empire. They also provided tender care to partners ill with tropical diseases, as Antoine Feuiltaine discovered. Not all of the signares married European men, but for those who did, the high mortality rate of Europeans was a source of wealth. Since their trading relations were illegal and therefore secret, it was often difficult for the man's French family to get their hands on whatever he accumulated. Other men returned home, but left property or a bequest to their African wives and families. Not all were wealthy, but by the middle of the eighteenth century, there were thirty to forty important families, all with the names of their French progenitors and Christian first names.[16] More modest Europeans such as artisans and soldiers (like Feuiltaine) also formed relationships, mostly with slave women. Karen Amanda Sackur suggests that many of these women wanted to become signares, but lacked the necessary skills and connections. Her point is well taken, but Feuiltaine's marriage to Marie indicates that careers were open to talent. While both European and African societies were hierarchical, enterprising men and women were able to exploit opportunities.[17] The signares had a reputation for charm and elegance, but what is important about them is their success at converting those charms into economic power, which involved control of slavery in Saint-Louis.[18]

Some company directors were unhappy about the signares, both because their male partners gave them access to company resources and because their unions were not sanctioned by the Catholic Church. Michel Jajolet, Sieur De La Courbe, director of the Compagnie du Sénégal in the mid-1680s, railed against the immorality and tried to set up a company mess and a company laundry.[19] Most of his successors, however, including several members of his family, enjoyed the pleasures of Senegalese family life, and they discovered that the signares were more efficient at providing services the company needed: feeding its employees, providing them with laundry services, supplying wood and water, and eventually, providing artisans and slaves for Saint-Louis's annual convoy. Renting slaves from the signares thus made more economic sense than relying on company slaves, and the signares also seem to have been more efficient at using the labor time of the slaves during the off-season. The company, and later the colonial regime, became dependent on the signares, and then, as they transformed themselves into a conservative métis elite, on the métis families they created. The result was that the signares were the wealthiest people in Saint-Louis.[20] In 1848 some women were still among the largest slave owners. They owned most of the slaves and most of the boats that participated in the annual convoy. In the 1770s, almost two-thirds of households were female-headed. This was even more striking among the top families. In 1774, eighteen of the twenty-two largest slave owners were female. In 1776, they owned forty-five of the seventy registered plots of land.

Eventually, a Catholic, French-speaking, male-headed community emerged, but it was a slow process.[21] When the British occupied Saint-Louis in 1758, they found between thirty and forty influential families through whom they could best manage the economy. From the time of British occupation, there were "*maires*" (mayors) in both Saint-Louis and Gorée. They were generally men of wealth and influence. Sackur argues that by the late eighteenth century, the wealthier métis families were no longer providing light brown-skinned women for visiting French officials but were marrying each other. Although métis merchants had difficulty competing with a new class of French merchants in the nineteenth century, they remained powerful and controlled housing and jobs until late in the nineteenth century.[22] Samuel Swan, an American visitor, described Saint-Louis elite households in 1815. The larger households had high walls with a slave who controlled access. Inside were two-story houses, slaves, and storerooms on the ground floor, with family apartments and a large hall on the floor above: "Each house may in fact be considered a Fortress where the master on his sofa views & directs from the piazza his numerous slaves below. These all have their huts ranged around the wall within the yard & it is not uncommon to see carpenters, coopers, Blacksmiths, weavers, Tailors, &c. all in operation at their respective works belonging to the same yard."[23]

In the larger households, slaves sometimes lived in separate compounds or in huts along the outer wall. According to Swan, slaves were well fed, had full family lives, and enjoyed singing and dancing in the evening. Senegalese historian M'Baye Guèye speaks of master-slave relations being characterized by "great familiarity and a certain cordiality."[24] This cordiality was rooted in the relatively small size of holdings and the mutual dependence of slave and owner. Half of the year, many of the slaves were away from the city, representing their owners from afar. Half of the year, they were living and working in close proximity. The owners could not afford to be too harsh, though when emancipation approached in the 1840s, they fought hard to protect their property rights. It is unlikely that they saw any contradiction.

In spite of the efforts of France and the monopoly companies, Saint-Louis in the late eighteenth century was dominated by the signares and their dependents. They provided the infrastructure for the slave trade; developed the gum trade; bought grain, which fed both the producers of gum and the town of Saint-Louis; traded for gold, wax, and hides; and also were involved in local exchange networks. In all of this, slave enterprise was important. By 1839, there were 160 boats in the flotilla, most of them between ten and twenty tons and with a crew of ten to twelve men and a *pileuse,* a woman who pounded the millet and prepared meals. There were also smaller boats that worked the creeks, and even after the level of the river dropped, they worked areas closer to Saint-Louis. The salinity of some areas near Saint-Louis meant that they were not major sources of grain, but the saltworks of Gandiole, controlled by the nearby kingdom of Kajoor, were a source of sea salt. In the nineteenth century, there was a growth of agriculture in areas near Saint-Louis. These settlements made it possible for African merchants and entrepreneurs to avoid French antislavery measures. These settlements were by and large not staffed with Saint-Louis slaves, but with more recent imports. After 1848, Saint-Louis became an island of liberty in a servile sea.

THE NATURE OF THE SLAVE COMMUNITY

Three things marked the slave community. First, many of the enslaved people were highly mobile, moving freely in and out of the city in the service of their owners. During the 1820s, there were about 1,200 laptots working the annual convoy. Over 85 percent of them were slaves. They often ran operations. In 1821, forty-four of sixty-one captains were slaves. So too were many of the *maîtres de langues,* who handled relations with African traders and political authorities. Though steam navigation had been introduced, most boats were still pulled up the river. This means that in the post-Napoleonic era, over 1,000 slaves went up the river every year for four to six months. This was between one-third and one-half of the male slave population. If we deduct children, the old, and the sick, it means that the vast majority of able-bodied male slaves participated in the river trade. Many of them were from upper river areas or the Bambara states. Many undoubtedly knew people and had kin upriver. Their owners had to be confident that they would not flee. They were, however, paid, they were fed, and they could trade for themselves. Life in Saint-Louis was probably more secure, and even for slaves, probably better than their options elsewhere. Though there is some evidence of slave flight, the laptots tended to be loyal. They could be recruited for defense or even for permanent militia positions and were used to guard slaves or protect merchant households, but they sometimes acted in their own interests. When British vessels entered the Senegal River in 1758, laptots blockaded the fort until the British signed a written agreement guaranteeing their protection.[25]

Second, a large percentage of the slaves were skilled, particularly the men. I have not seen an occupational census from Saint-Louis, but there was one from the smaller island town of Gorée taken in 1847.[26] It is safe to assume that the occupational breakdown was similar. Of the 983 male slaves, fewer than 10 percent were listed as laborers, and under 5 percent as "sans profession." Almost one-third were sailors and the rest were masons, weavers, ship's carpenters, cooks, servants, blacksmiths, and traders. It is probable that in Saint-Louis, a higher percentage of the slaves had artisanal skills because of the seasonal nature of the Saint-Louis trade and a desire to fully exploit the labor potential of slaves during the off-season. The female slaves were less specialized. Sixty-eight percent were pileuses and 19 percent were laundresses. That does not mean that pileuses did nothing but pound millet. They could be used for different tasks, for example, spinning thread. It generally took about eight hours to spin enough thread to keep a weaver busy for an hour. If the 107 weavers were working full-time, almost all of the pileuses were spending a large percentage of their time spinning, probably more than they spent pounding. They also worked as servants. When wealthier signares went out, they were often accompanied by a servant with an umbrella and followed by several others. French officials were often bothered by the money and labor time spent on extravagant display, particularly when they faced a labor shortage, but the signare-dominated households continued to accumulate wealth. Training of slaves in various crafts not only gave their owners higher revenues, but allowed men to be fruitfully used even during the off-season. And cloth production could use both male and female slave laborers even as they aged and were no longer suited to the strenuous river voyage.

The third point is that the slaves lived in households and were involved in constant face-to-face relationships with their owners' families. Most of the signares were not very rich. Only ten households on Gorée and seventeen on Saint-Louis had more than fifty slaves. The biggest in 1779 was a signare with sixty-nine slaves. They rarely got any bigger. The vast majority of slave-owning households had under ten slaves, and many had only one or two. Generally, slaves seem to have been acquired from the 1,000 to 2,000 slaves destined for export every year. The number kept in any year was probably small and mostly children young enough to be trained. A skilled slave was valuable. In 1828, a healthy slave with no skills cost about 300 francs and could be rented out for sixty to ninety centimes a day. A skilled slave could cost as much as 1,500 francs and was hired out for up to three francs sixty centimes a day. The slaves kept half of what they earned.[27] Slave owners had different strategies, depending on their own economic activities and plans. Marie Legrose, for example, owned thirty-nine slaves, of whom nine were laundresses. In addition, there were three pileuses, four masons, three carpenters, two cooks, a sailor, and a dressmaker. Others invested heavily in pileuses. Michael David Marcson cites a household which had five pileuses and six children among seventeen slaves. Another clearly had a clothing operation: three tailors and seamstresses and a cloth dyer in a household of only thirteen.[28]

Some slaves earned enough money to buy slaves or to buy their own freedom. Male slaves in the river trade were sometimes able to buy their freedom and a boat. They could rent slaves and start out as marigotiers. Even pileuses managed to buy slaves of their own. Like other workers on boats, pileuses could trade. Guèye has suggested that some also worked as prostitutes.[29] I have seen no evidence of this, but certainly a solitary woman on a crew of ten to twelve men might have been able to profit from the sex ratio. Slaves were sometimes manumitted with a commitment to serve for several years before becoming free. The rate does not seem to have been very high, though it was increasing during the last years of slavery. Five hundred slaves were freed during the decade before 1848, but this may have simply been recognition that emancipation was imminent.[30]

When emancipation took place in 1848, it happened rather smoothly because most slaves were already in the wage economy. The skilled slaves, in particular, were able to earn a good living. They no longer had to share their wages with their masters, though some continued to live with their former masters and many remained as clients. The quality of slave life does not mean that slaves liked being slaves. Contemporary observers like Samuel Swan often tell us how well slaves were treated, but they were still slaves. They were owned, and were sometimes treated harshly, particularly by smallholders. There was, for example, Mariam Kamata, who was owned by a Wolof woman. In 1848, when she was listening to a griot chanting about the emancipation of slaves, she was told: “Yes, they are talking about liberty, but it is liberty for others and not for you.” She was held in chains, smuggled out the city, sold, kept in chains for three months, then sold again. She managed to escape, made it back to Saint-Louis, and was freed.[31]

The day of emancipation, many of the freed slaves went down to the sea for what seems to have been a symbolic ritual cleansing. They then gathered in front of government offices to dance and sing praises of the government.[32] About two hundred in Saint-Louis had no means of support and were housed temporarily in tents.[33] The ability of the rather small island town to expand was limited in Saint-Louis until a bridge to the mainland was opened in 1865. The slaves were freed at a time when the town's prospects were improving both because of the development of peanut exports since the 1840s and the colonial ambitions of the French military since the 1850s. It is clear that some of the Muslim traders, who eventually became more important than the métis, were of slave origins. In 1848, Samba Agui, a former slave himself, owned eighty-seven slaves and was very assertive in defending his property rights. Samba Agui's story demonstrates the fluidity of the Saint-Louis social structure and the ability of a man with determination, ability, and perhaps a little luck to rise out of slavery and become wealthy. Many of those who fanned out across the French Empire as traders and in subaltern roles within the colonial administration were of slave origin.[34]

LIFE CYCLES WITHIN SLAVERY

Reconstructing the life cycles of slaves in Saint-Louis is especially difficult; there are many silences in the historical record and gaps in the scholarship. Métis have often been reluctant to talk about slavery or about the sexual arrangements of their ancestors. Some historians who have studied them have been more interested in them as an African elite than as slave masters. Similarly, studies of the increasingly important Muslim community of Saint-Louis have looked at the development of commerce, the development of Muslim learning, and the *habitants* as a politically important group.[35] It thus is necessary to approach key questions by inference from limited evidence and from an analysis of the situation in which slaves and slave owners found themselves.

The first problem is childhood and education. Most slaves were either born in the coastal towns or integrated into the society there when young. The signares often had among their servants young boys called *rapasses* or girls called *raparcilles*.[36] Children were probably preferred because they could be taught to accept their status. This was not a big house and slave quarter culture. These children probably mixed when young with free children and then were increasingly separated as the free children were educated. The master tried to educate the slave to accept his or her role, and then, because a skilled slave was worth so much more than an unskilled one, would have decided what kind of training would be appropriate. The master or mistress would have seen the child grow up and would have had some idea of how to best use the child's abilities to maximize wealth.

A window into the operation of household slavery is offered by a system of adoption set up by Governor Baudin in 1849 and then reformed by Faidherbe in 1857. Worried about minor children among the ex-slaves and fearing the emergence of a rootless population, Baudin planned to place these children either into "good" families or into apprenticeship programs. Supervision was poor and people continued to buy children, mostly small girls.[37] Under the system as reformed by Faidherbe, children could be purchased on condition that they were freed and registered within twenty-four hours of being brought into Saint-Louis. Supervision remained poor, but the system persisted until 1904, when it was finally perceived as a disguised version of the slave trade: some children disappeared. It persisted partly because all social groups used these children: colonial administrators, métis, and Muslims.

Faidherbe's critique of the original system could be a critique of the system he created. Faidherbe charged that the children were almost all girls between seven and ten bought to be used as household drudges, and two or three years later, their youth was "abused" or they were resold into marriage.[38] Bernard Moitt, who has studied the system, cites some cases of sexual abuse and argues that some were forced into prostitution.[39] I think that Faidherbe's original remark is very suggestive. With the exception of some boys purchased by artisans and taught the artisan's craft, the children were almost all young girls.[40] I do not think that they were purchased for sex. If they were, teenage girls would have been purchased. It is more likely that they were purchased as servants. Young girls were and are often still used as servants. Baudin and Faidherbe were almost certainly responding to the demand among habitants, both métis and Muslim, for child servants and for dependents, who increased the flexibility of the larger households because they could grow into a variety of roles.

Evidence is limited, but it is probable that as girls matured, they were sometimes drawn into sexual relations, particularly when they were isolated and surrounded by men. Were these occasional affairs or was concubinage common? I cannot say. In Muslim families, a young girl could easily become someone's wife. Further, some métis men were known to be polygamous. Technically, the young girls were free at eighteen, but in an African city, freedom was not always attractive. I believe that they were probably married off. I would not use the term *resold,* but that remark by Faidherbe reflects the French perception that paying a bride price involved a sale. I would guess that many households pursued a marriage strategy, and young female dependents could be used to attract clients, to keep slaves happy, or to keep former slaves as dependents; in some cases, they became partners or wives for younger sons. Most of the girls were brought in young enough to have integrated themselves into the urban culture of Saint-Louis. Those who did so successfully were most valuable in any marriage strategy. It is also interesting that métis' first marriages tended to be with other métis, but if a wife died, the male partner often took a black woman as his second wife.

In African slavery, and not only in the cities, women were always more numerous than men. I have argued elsewhere that women formed the backbone of the social order, that elite men took the prettiest women, that slave warriors depended on their wives to farm, and that there were always enough women to serve as partners for male slaves. I see no reason to think that the towns were different from the rural areas. The household was inevitably influenced by sexuality and involved with reproduction. I am thus hypothesizing for female slaves a trajectory from child servant to wife and worker. If widowed, she could depend on her children or return to the household as a servant, a spinner, or a nanny. Slave women were useful at almost all ages, and even at ages when they were no longer formally defined as slaves. For male slaves, their life trajectory involved not sex but work. They started working within the household from a very young age, possibly like the girls, as servants. Most would have begun working as apprentices to senior craftsmen, and would have begun sailing in the convoys up the Senegal River in their early teens. Many of the craftsmen would have continued taking part in the annual expedition, though that probably depended mostly on their craft. Housing construction generally took place in the off-season. Artisans were also capable of working into old age, though with decline and illness they undoubtedly reached a point where they were totally dependent.

A major question in slave systems was the ability of slave owners to use the slave's labor time for almost all of the year. It is this that made the exploitation of slave labor within relatively small family-based units more flexible than a system based on company slaves. The companies clearly preferred relying on métis households. In Saint-Louis, the position of slaves was based on commerce, but the métis households were also effective production units. We see this not only in the construction of boats during the off-season, but also in the development of a textile industry. In order to use the thread the women produced, métis households acquired or trained weavers. The cloth they produced was useful in producing clothing both for themselves and for the river trade.

I have written elsewhere that in all slave systems flow-through and amelioration were important to the functioning of the system. By flow-through, I mean the progression of a slave through a series of stages from captive through to integration in a social system and eventually to manumission. The percentage manumitted in Saint-Louis does not seem to have been very high. If it were high, the slaves would not have remained a majority of the population until 1848. The possibility of manumission was, nevertheless, important to the morale of slaves, particularly the most ambitious like Samba Agui. In Saint-Louis, manumission was probably less important than amelioration, which meant access to more privileged positions within slavery. There were slave ship captains, slaves who traded for their masters, and maîtres de langues, who worked as interpreters and diplomatic agents on the commercial expeditions. Slaves who worked in such positions could accumulate wealth but had to also maintain the confidence of their owners. In town, there were also positions of authority held by people who directed the work of others. There were always confidential roles in which the slave's knowledge and advice were important, such as ship captains who were responsible for merchandise and for buying and selling. There are numerous other cases in African commercial societies where slaves counseled their masters, undertook missions on their behalf, and were more important and trusted than sons.[41]

When students of slavery describe either elite slaves or slaves who have significant autonomy, they are often asked whether that is slavery. In fact, it is. The slave chief in his finery and the ship captain with his comfortable income are still slaves. They are owned, can be deprived of their privileges, and enjoy their privileges only as long as they remain loyal. Slavery is a social relationship full of ambiguities. Slaves are in theory things that have no rights or privileges, but they are constantly pushing against the boundaries of their enslavement and are often successful because of their value to their owners. Because they have no rights, they are dependable. This process of pushing the boundaries of their enslavement and exploiting opportunities within slavery was probably more important than resistance. Why was slave labor so important? It has sometimes been suggested that slave labor was so important on the frontiers of empire because free labor was not available. It seems, however, that free labor was available. There was a significant amount of free labor in the early years, though never enough, and there remained some free labor throughout the history of slavery in Senegal. During the last decades of slavery, the number of free laptots was increasing because wages attracted nobles from the very market-oriented Soninke society.

Relying on free labor would probably have been costly. Also, free labor was not always dependable. Free men often wanted to be back home during the growing season and were loyal to their native communities. Slaves, on the other hand, were part of Saint-Louis. Their well-being depended on operating within the system. Owners could profit from training them. The accumulation of slaves also was strategic for signares, who were able to leverage their situation into a dominant economic role by accumulating land, houses, boats, and slaves. They owned the vast majority of slaves in Saint-Louis. The slave trade companies, and into the mid-nineteenth century the state, had to deal with them.

The signares and the métis families they created were not the whole picture. Mamadou Diouf has suggested that even in the eighteenth century, during the "age of the Signares," Saint-Louis was a Muslim city. Who were these Muslims, and what was their overall position in the city? Not much research has been done, but certainly some things are clear. The societies of the Senegal River basin—Fulbe, Moors, Soninke, and Wolof—were all Muslim societies. The free laborers and most of the slaves were Muslim. By the nineteenth century, Saint-Louis became a good place for Muslim traders and religious leaders. Some of the Muslim traders were probably of slave origin, men who started as laptots and became ship captains or marigotiers.[42] Others moved into Saint-Louis because they saw opportunities there or because of conflicts upriver. They had ties with the métis firms, but also with the interior. Bou el-Mogdad, the French-approved *cadi* in the mid-nineteenth century, was the landlord for Moorish caravans coming to Saint-Louis. The more successful probably had households that operated in some ways like the signare households, but the Muslim household economy has not been studied. One difference was probably that many slave women were assimilated as wives and concubines. The abolition of slavery in 1848 forced the increasingly important Muslim petty trader community to relocate their slave trade and slavery-based activities outside the city or run the risk of their clandestine activities being prosecuted.

What we have here is a confluence of social, cultural, and economic factors that produced a slave economy controlled by local entrepreneurs, who had an interest in an economy freer and more open than most agricultural slave societies. When a signare apprenticed a young male slave to a carpenter or a mason, she was quadrupling his potential income, and thus increasing her own. The nature of this society was not a product of any ideological agenda, but of the way different actors related to the system of production and exchange. The nature of the slavery that resulted contrasted to the harsher regimes that harvested gum or produced grain upriver. To understand the form slavery took, we must understand the way slavery fit into the mode of production.

NOTES

1. While I have done archival work on nineteenth-century Saint-Louis, this essay depends heavily on a handful of books and unpublished theses. See James Searing, *West African Slavery and Atlantic Commerce: The Senegal River Valley, 1700–1850* (Cambridge: Cambridge University Press, 1993); Michael David Marcson, "European-African Interaction in the Precolonial Period: Saint Louis, Senegal, 1758–1854," PhD diss., Princeton University, 1976; Karen Amanda Sackur, "The Development of Creole Society and Culture in Saint-Louis and Gorée, 1719–1817," PhD diss., School of Oriental and African Studies, University of London, 1999; Hilary Jones, *The Métis of Senegal: Urban Life and Politics in French West Africa* (Bloomington: Indiana University Press, 2013); Mamadou Kane, "L'esclavage à St. Louis et à Gorée à travers les archives notariées, 1817–1848," Mémoire de maîtrise, Université de Dakar, 1984; Ibrahima Ka, "L'évolution à St. Louis du Sénégal du XIXe siècle au début du XXe siècle," Thèse de 3e cycle, Université de Dakar, 1981; Djibril Samb, ed., *Saint-Louis et l'esclavage* (Dakar: Université Cheikh Anta Diop, 1998). I have also benefited from conversations with Lindsay Gish, a graduate student at Michigan State University doing research on early Saint-Louis, Senegal.

2. Francois Manchuelle, *Willing Migrants* (Athens: Ohio University Press, 1997).

3. On the early Portuguese settlements, see Toby Green, *The Rise of the Transatlantic Slave Trade in West Africa 1300–1589* (Cambridge: Cambridge University Press, 2012). Though mortality rates were high, some Europeans adapted to the disease environment. One was Paul Benis, an illiterate French artisan, who learned Wolof, became a successful trader, and had children with nine different women. See also Peter Mark and José da Silva Horta, *The Forgotten Diaspora: Jewish Communities in West Africa and the Making of the Atlantic World* (Cambridge: Cambridge University Press, 2011).

4. Searing, *West African Slavery and Atlantic Commerce,* 103–4. During the first century of French activity in Senegal, there were seven different chartered slave trading companies. The reliance on African enterprise and African labor was, in part, a result of the fragile nature of these companies. The slave trade was profitable, but the vicissitudes of war, weather, and competition led to the failure of many companies.

5. Philip Curtin, *Economic Change in Precolonial Africa: Senegambia in the Era of the Slave Trade* (Madison: University of Wisconsin Press, 1975).

6. Bambara became a catchall term for both slaves and non-Muslims from the upper Senegal and upper Niger, most of whom spoke Mande languages. The largest percentage, however, was from Bamana-speaking areas. See Richard Roberts, *Warriors, Merchants and Slaves: The State and Economy in the Middle Niger Valley, 1700–1914* (Stanford, CA: Stanford University Press, 1987).

7. The gold found in the upper Senegal and upper Niger valleys was a major attraction of Senegambia to Europeans, though the trade was never up to their hopes. Xavier Guillard, "Un commerce introuvable: L'or dans les transactions du XVe au XVIIIe siècle," in Jean Boulègue, ed., *Contributions à l'histoire du Sénégal* (Paris: Karthala, 1987), 31–75; Philip Curtin, "The Lure of Bambuk Gold," *Journal of African History* 14:4 (1973): 623–32; Curtin, *Economic Change,* 198–206.

8. The term comes from the Wolof word for sailor. It came to be used for different types of workers in the service of the French. J. Malcolm Thompson, "In Dubious Service: The Recruitment and Stabilization of West African Marine Labor by the French Colonial Military, 1659–1900," PhD diss., University of Minnesota, 1989.

9. Curtin, *Economic Change,* 117–21.

10. The politics of these river states are fully discussed in Makhroufi Ousmane Traore, "Marge de manoeuvre, négociations et pouvoir de décision: les souverains de la Sénégambie dans le système de relations internationales transatlantiques et dans l'évolution du capitalisme moderne du XVe au XVIIIe siècle," PhD diss., Université de Paris-Sorbonne, 2009.

11. James Webb, *Desert Frontier: Ecologic and Economic Change along the Western Sahel, 1600–1850* (Madison: University of Wisconsin Press, 1995).

12. Sackur, "The Development of Creole Society and Culture in Saint-Louis and Gorée," 55–57.

13. Sylvain Sankalé, *À la mode du pays: Chroniques saint-louisiennes* (Paris: Riveneuve, 2008). Sankalé's book is a history in novel form. There are parts that are clearly based on his researches into the life of his ancestor, but it is sometimes difficult to tell when it is history

and when it is fiction. His description of Feuiltaine's treatment rings true. On the relationship between African and European medicine on the Gold Coast, see Jonathan Roberts, "Medical Exchange in the Gold Coast during the 17th and 18th Centuries," *Canadian Journal of African Studies* 45:3 (2011): 48–523.

14. Marcson, "European-African Interaction in the Precolonial Period." On the signares, see George Brooks, *Eurafricans in Western Africa: Commerce, Social Status, Gender and Religious Observance from the Sixteenth to the Eighteenth Century* (Athens: Ohio University Press, 2003), 212–20; George Brooks, "The Signares of Saint-Louis and Gorée: Women entrepreneurs in 18th Century Senegal," in Edna Bay and Nancy Hafkin, eds., *Women in Africa* (Stanford, CA: Stanford University Press, 1976), 19–44.

15. Brooks, *Eurafricans in Western Africa.*

16. Marcson, "European-African Interaction in the Precolonial Period," 38–46.

17. Sackur, "The Development of Creole Society and Culture in Saint-Louis and Gorée"; see also Brooks, *Eurafricans in Western Africa,* 212–13. Brooks suggests that having a relationship with a soldier or an artisan was a way for a woman to learn French and the customs of French men.

18. The mystique of the signares is rooted in the accounts of contemporary observers, but has been elaborated by some of their descendants. See Sankalé, *À la mode du pays,* and Jean-Luc Angrand, *Céleste, ou le temps des Signares* (Sarcelle: Editions Anne Pépin, 2006). Angrand's publisher has the name of a well-known signare. On this mystique, see the article in this volume by Hilary Jones and Emily Clark.

19. Searing, *West African Slavery and Atlantic Commerce,* 98.

20. The signares were not unique. Similar women were found up and down the coast. On the Guinea coast, there were the Portuguese Nhara and Anglophone Mammies. See George Brooks, "A Nhara of the Guinea-Bissau Region: Mae Aurelia Correia," in Clare Robertson and Martin Klein, eds., *Women and Slavery in Africa* (Madison: University of Wisconsin Press, 1983), 295–319. In Angola, such women were called Dona. See Mariana Candido, *An African Slave Port in the Atlantic World: Benguela and Its Hinterland* (New York: Cambridge University Press, 2011). Even when the men did not die, signares could use the connection to accumulate wealth. On Gold Coast female entrepreneurs during the nineteenth century, see Kwabena Adu-Boahen, *Post-Abolition Slave-holding in the Gold Coast: Slave Mistresses of the Coastal Fante, 1807–1874* (Saarbruck: Lambert, 2011).

21. The métis early defined themselves as Catholic, but Hilary Jones sees the crucial stage as the adoption of Catholic marriage around 1870, when it was useful in defining themselves as French and establishing boundaries between themselves and other Africans. See Hilary Jones, "From *Mariage à la Mode* to Weddings at Town Hall: Marriage, Colonialism and Mixed Race Society in Nineteenth Century Senegal," *International Journal of African Historical Studies* 38:1 (2005): 27–37. There were a handful of church weddings as far back as the 1820s, but what was happening around 1870 was the full adoption of French Catholic marriage.

22. Mohamed Mbodj, "The Abolition of Slavery in Senegal, 1820–1890: Crisis or Rise of a New Entrepreneurial Class?" in Martin A. Klein, ed., *Breaking the Chains: Slavery, Bondage, and Emancipation in Modern Africa and Asia* (Madison: University of Wisconsin Press, 1993),

197–214. Control of work and housing meant that many of the slaves freed in 1848 found it desirable to remain clients of the major métis families.

23. "Samuel Swan's Journal of a Voyage Along the West Coast of Africa, 1815–18," in Norman R. Bennett and George E. Brooks Jr., eds., *New England Merchants in Africa: A History through Documents 1802–1865* (Boston: Boston University Press, 1965), 65.

24. M'Baye Guèye, "La fin de l'esclavage à Saint-Louis et à Gorée en 1848," *Bulletin de l'Institut fondamental d'Afrique noire, Série B* 28:3–4 (1966): 637–67.

25. Brooks, *Eurafricans in Western Africa,* 217.

26. Archives Nationales du Sénégal, Dakar, Senegal (hereafter ANS) 13 G 1/124. Piece 2, 1847.

27. Marcson, "European-African Interaction in the Precolonial Period," 27–28.

28. Ibid., 28. A fuller exploration of notarial records would be desirable. For a discussion of these records, see Saliou Mbaye, "L'esclavage domestique à St. Louis à travers les archives notariées (1817–1848)," in Samb, ed., *Saint-Louis et l'esclavage,* 139–58.

29. Personal communication.

30. Kane, "L'esclavage à St. Louis et à Gorée," 64.

31. Deposition of Mariam Kamata, Archives Nationales d'outre mer, Aix-en-Provence, France (hereafter ANOM), Sénégal XIV 15a.

32. Governor to Minister, 23 August 1848, ANOM, Sénégal XIV 15a. See also Guèye, "La fin de l'esclavage à Saint-Louis et à Gorée en 1848," 641–45; Roger Pasquier, "À propos de l'émancipation des esclaves au Sénégal en 1848," *Revue françaises d'histoire d'outre-mer* 54:194 (1967): 188–208.

33. Governor to Minister, 8 September 1848, ANOM, Sénégal, XIV 15a.

34. The traders are explored in Boubacar Barry and Leonhard Harding, eds., *Commerce et commerçants en Afrique de l'Ouest. Volume 1: Le Sénégal* (Paris: Harmattan, 1992). See especially Mamadou Diouf, "Traitants ou négociants? Les commerçants saint-louisiens. Hamet Gora Diop (1846–1910): Étude de cas," 105–54.

35. David Robinson, in *Paths of Accomodation: Muslim Societies and French Colonial Authorities in Senegal and Mauritania* (Athens: Ohio University Press, 2000), discusses Bou el Mogdad. He was the cadi, but he was also the landlord-broker for Mauritanian traders. Many illegal slave transactions were probably negotiated there. On a transaction that took place in Bou el Mogdad's compound, see Martin Klein, *Slavery and Colonial Rule in French West Africa* (Cambridge: Cambridge University Press, 1998), 61.

36. Brooks, *Eurafricans in Western Africa,* 214. I am grateful to Vanessa Oliveira, Mariana Candido, and Jose Curto for discussion of these terms.

37. Bernard Moitt, "Slavery, Flight and Redemption in Senegal, 1819–1905," *Slavery and Abolition* 14 (1993): 70–86.

38. Minutes of Conseil d'Administration, 5 December 1857, ANOM, Sénégal XIV 15a.

39. Moitt's source was a remark made by Georges Deherme, who was sent to Africa by the French Colonial Office to study the problem of slavery. See Georges Deherme, "L'esclavage en Afrique occidentale française: étude historique, critique, et positive (1906)," in Paul Lovejoy

and Alexander Sydney Kanya-Forstner, eds., *Slavery and Its Abolition in French West Africa* (Madison: African Studies Program, University of Wisconsin, 1994), 111–206. Moitt is now working on a book on the adoption system.

40. In the first years after emancipation, it involved many boys. Between 1857 and 1862, 433 persons were freed. About half were under the age of eighteen, and of these, 70 percent were girls. Some were freed with relatives, usually a mother, but 77 percent were assigned to the guardianship program. The report also lists "free foreign orphans," who were mostly boys. Of the eighty-eight in this group, fifty-six were boys and thirty-two girls. The boys were almost all apprenticed to various crafts: ten masons, twelve woodworkers, seven carpenters, etc. In later years, it was overwhelmingly young girls. Report of F. Carrère on Conseil de Tutelle, October 1862, Archives Nationales du Sénégal.

41. See G. I. Jones, *Trading States of the Oil Rivers: A Study of Political Development in Eastern Nigeria* (London: Oxford University Press, 1963); Bruce Hall and Yacine Daddi Addoun, "The Arabic Letters of the Ghadames Slaves in the Niger Bend, 1860–1900," in Alice Bellagamba, Sandra E. Greene, and Martin A. Klein, eds., *African Slavery/African Voices* (New York: Cambridge University Press, 2013), 485–500.

42. On the development of this Muslim commercial community, see Barry and Harding, eds., *Commerce et Commerçants en Afrique de l'Ouest,* 35–190.

WIVES, SOLDIERS, AND SLAVES

The Atlantic World of Marie Baude, la femme Pinet

JESSICA MARIE JOHNSON

La Galathée est arrivée à l'embouchure du fleuve le 18 de ce mois avec 260 nègres restant de 400 qu'elle a pris à Gorée.

(*La Galathée* has arrived at the mouth of the river, the 18th of this month, with 260 slaves of the 400 that it took from Gorée.)

—JACQUES DE LA CHAISE to the minister of the navy, New Orleans (1729)

The displacement of difference, geographic domination, transatlantic slavery, and the black Atlantic Ocean differently contribute to mapping out the real and imaginative geographies of black women; they are understood here as social processes that make geography a racial-sexual terrain.

—KATHERINE MCKITTRICK, *Demonic Grounds: Black Women and the Cartographies of Struggle* (2006)

In early 1729, a Senegal woman arrived in New Orleans, a muddy Gulf Coast outpost on the Mississippi River. Like so many Africans crossing the Atlantic during the first decades of the eighteenth century, she embarked from the Senegambia *comptoirs* (trading forts) of Saint-Louis and Gorée aboard a French *négrier* (slave ship) in the company of hundreds of shackled men, women, and children. However, unlike the majority of Africans making the same voyage from Saint-Louis or Gorée to New Orleans, she did not arrive enslaved. Marie Baude was a slave-owning free woman of African descent traveling of her own volition.[1] Her husband, Jean Pinet, a Company of the Indies employee, awaited her arrival in Louisiana. Neither property nor free status protected Marie Baude from the everyday uncertainties of the early Atlantic world. Alongside sailors and slaves, she endured a grueling journey many did not survive. When she arrived on the Gulf Coast, trading company agents detained her, claiming she owed the Company duties on her slaves for transporting them from Gorée.[2] Marie Baude's husband appealed on her behalf, but the slaves were sold with others arriving on the same ship. Propertyless and living in New Orleans, la femme Pinet's freedom, marital status, and racial designation took on a different meaning.

Marie Baude's journey constructs an Atlantic biography, articulating the myriad ways sex, status, race, and violence unfolded during these years.[3] Her journey from Saint-Louis to New Orleans occurred as the dramatic forces creating the early French Atlantic began to transform the lives of women of African descent along the Atlantic littoral. She was the wife of a white artisan and trading company employee. She was born in West Africa and enjoyed free status in both Africa and the Americas. She owned property while living in coastal Senegambia, only to lose it upon arrival in Louisiana. She traveled the "wider Atlantic community" connecting continental African societies to maritime commercial networks, and maritime commercial networks to the Americas.[4]

As exceptional as she was, Marie Baude typified the collision of imperialism, patriarchy, and bondage in the lives of women of African descent. Marie Baude moved through an Atlantic world of African wives, company soldiers, and chattel slaves. Her latitude extended horizontally from Saint-Louis, Senegal, through the Middle Passage, to New Orleans. Her longitude climbed vertically through chattel slaves marked for sale, other forms of coerced labor, and marital status, to administrators, governors, and royalty. When Marie embarked from Senegambia, she left behind a cohort of women of similar race, wealth, and status and a multiethnic, polytheistic community of traders, property owners, and cultural brokers. Although she was not enslaved, Marie's status as spouse, and as a spouse of African descent married to a white man, evoked a history of sex across the color line and the intimate ties binding the crossroads of empire.[5] Her migration from Saint-Louis was precipitated by an act of violence perpetrated by Jean, her husband, that led to his eventual deportation to a relatively new colonial venture—New Orleans, Louisiana.

This essay chronicles Marie Baude as she shifted with her longitude and latitude, and takes a nonlinear approach to her story. The first section describes the journey of Marie Baude as *la mulâtresse passagère,* an unnamed half African, half European female passenger who travels by slave ship from Senegambia to Louisiana and survives. The second section moves back in time to place Marie Baude a "native of Joal," the daughter of a French "Sieur," with her husband at Saint-Louis, Senegal. The third section returns to Louisiana through Jean's deportation to encounter Marie Baude as "la femme Pinet and her slaves," a mixed-race wife with no name who experiences the loss of her slaves within days of her arrival.

LA MULÂTRESSE PASSAGÈRE

In 1728, a mulâtresse passagère boarded the slave ship *La Galathée* at Gorée. *La Galathée* had embarked from Lorient in May of that year, arriving at Saint-Louis near the end of June. The frigate moored without incident and loaded approximately one hundred thirty-one "*nègres, négresses,* and *négrillons*" before proceeding to Gorée. When it arrived, the appearance of a new passenger with enslaved property in tow caused the captain to write in the margins of his ship log, "Took on one mulâtresse passagère bound for 'Mississippi.'" Slave ships were the connective tissue of the Atlantic world. Technological innovations of the early modern period, slave ships were peculiar creations, combining "war machine, mobile prison, and factory," with complex racial-sexual landscapes.[6] Ships were also "cultural and political units," maritime territories ruled by captains, and populated by heterogeneous crews, occasional passengers, and enslaved Africans seized for sale across the Atlantic. For the majority of Africans crossing the ocean in the eighteenth century, encountering the Atlantic world began on slave ships and along their itineraries. *La Galathée* was no different. La mulâtresse passagère may have been the only woman of African descent on the ship who was not enslaved. Traveling with slaves, she would have been even more conspicuous.

Of the twenty-three slave ships to travel from West Africa to the Gulf Coast during the French period, *La Galathée*'s journey was especially fraught. By October 1728, when *La Galathée* embarked for Louisiana, one of the sailors had drowned and a male slave had already died of unspecified causes. Two days into the journey, death began to stalk the ship. Scurvy, drowning, and an unspecified, general illness killed several slaves and much of the crew. On average, a slave or crew member died for nearly every day of travel between Gorée and the first stop, Les Cayes on Saint-Domingue's southern coast. It arrived in December. At Les Cayes, the captain expressed concern that "all of the crew are ill and in the Company building with all of the sick blacks." *La Galathée* rested at Les Cayes for several days, hiring sailors and laborers living at the port as emergency crew. In the end, forty-five slaves and seven of the crew remained in Saint-Domingue, too sick to continue. By mid-December, *La Galathée* was back at sea, but by the time the ship arrived on the Gulf Coast, some ninety slaves had died, including several women.

If la mulâtresse passagère or her slaves experienced any illness, there is no record of it. Women's misery aboard slave ships was acute. At least nine of the thirty-three slaves who died between Gorée and Les Cayes were female. Ship-wide illnesses like scurvy caused everyone distress, but scurvy in women may also have been "misdiagnosed as a condition relating to menstruation."[7] Along with illness, the ocean offered a considerable threat. Drowning claimed the life of at least one négresse. Children succumbed to the terrors of the Middle Passage. At least two deaths were suckling infants, a loss that would have had a deep impact on everyone on board, women included. The mulâtresse passagère survived the worst of the scourge, but she was luckier than many others on board.

In January 1729, *La Galathée* dropped anchor at Balize, a French fort at the mouth of the Mississippi River. At Balize, officials processed merchandise brought for sale into the colony, including captive Africans, and secured it for the journey upriver. Days could pass while captains, passengers, crews, and bondspeople waited for trading company officials to meet them by riverboat. When officials finally arrived, concern for the health of the slaves initially distracted them from the presence of one mulâtresse and her enslaved property.[8] Louisiana's governor, Étienne Périer, lamented the loss of so many slaves to scurvy and placed the sickest ones on the first sloop to New Orleans while the rest waited at Balize. All of the slaves, sick and well, would go to auction within three days. When attention did turn to the mulâtresse, confusion appears to have ensued. At first, she was detained. Officials levied a tariff of one hundred twenty *livres* on each of her slaves. Eventually, authorities confiscated them, "leaving her with only a petite Négritte," about five or six years of age. The mulâtresse was then forwarded "hastily" to New Orleans.[9]

No testimony exists from this passenger on the particulars of her experience as a free woman of African descent on a slave ship. The mechanics of her journey remain a mystery. Although la mulâtresse passagère represented one of many connections between Senegal and Louisiana, it is unknown whether she felt anxiety as the ship embarked from one location and disembarked at the other, fear as sickness enveloped the ship, or pleasure as the frigate approached its destination; these emotions continue to be lost to time. Upon arrival in New Orleans, the unnamed mulâtresse passagère of *La Galathée* transformed into la femme Pinet, the unpropertied wife of a Company employee. A change occurred as she crossed the Atlantic, one with profound implications for her life in a new place.

MARIE BAUDE, LA FEMME PINET

Four years earlier, Marie Baude stood before a clerk, the current Company director, and the governor of Saint-Louis, Senegal. It was 1724, a June afternoon, and these venerable French men called her before them to discuss a murder that had occurred the night before. According to several witnesses, her husband, Jean Pinet, a gunsmith for the Company stationed at Saint-Louis, killed a mulâtre sailor named Pierre LeGrain in their home the night before.[10] Testimony varied, but the broad outline of the evening was clear. While at the house drinking with a couple of sailors, Jean was joined by Pierre LeGrain, a "half a bottle of eau de vie" in his hand.

At some point during the evening, tempers ran high and conversation between Jean and Pierre grew heated. The conflict culminated in Pierre making a sexual boast or threat against Marie Baude and her sister, still living at Gorée. The two fought, Jean "kicking" Pierre several times before taking up a sword and striking the sailor down. Jean left Pierre for dead "in the doorway of his forge" while he relocated with his guests to the hospital "to continue drinking." André, a twelve-year-old "Christian and Portuguese Nègre," and Jean Pinet's slave offered the most colorful testimony. André testified that Pierre LeGrain "told Pinet, in the presence of the two sailors, he intends to f— his wife and f— his sister-in-law at Gorée."[11] When asked if Pinet knew before he left that Pierre LeGrain was dead or dying, André stated: "He heard Pierre LeGrain cry out, 'My God, I am dead,' at the same time Pinet left the house for the hospital with the two sailors. LeGrain said it once more then stopped responding. Another witness testified that he came across the body when he went to visit the house later that night. He rushed to find Jean at the hospital, informing him, 'there is a dead person sprawled in door of his forge.' According to the witness, Jean retorted, 'It is just a mulâtre, I'm not very bothered by it.'"[12]

Unlike other witnesses, Marie Baude offered few such clarifying details. Her most revealing answers constitute her autobiography. For the record, Marie stated her full name, that she was "the wife of the said Pinet," twenty-three years old, and from Joal, an *escale* (trading post) down the coast from Gorée. She did not describe herself as a mulâtresse. Marie Baude stated she had gone to bed before the murder occurred and had slept through most of the night's events. She repeated this claim throughout the interrogation. She offered no clear information about the timing of events and the nature of the violence that had occurred, although André's testimony suggests she was awake.[13] When asked if Marie Baude wished to oppose her husband, André stated she did wish to but Jean paid her no mind. She claimed not to know her husband had killed anyone or anything about any injuries he incurred. She also claimed to know nothing about the individuals involved. She was aware an insult had been offered, but described the comment made against both her and her sister as a "a matter of little consequence."

Marie Baude's autobiography and recalcitrant testimony situate her within a community of women of African descent descended from European-African unions occurring in the decades before and during French trade on the coast. Trading company officials attempted to institutionalize racial and sexual differences through regulations that prevented white Company employees from socializing with employees of color and prohibited marriage between white employees and African women.[14] Nonetheless, on the ground, where Company employees desired food, clothing, and intimate companionship, African women played a central role in commercial and social life at the comptoirs. Atlantic trade at Saint-Louis and Gorée provided access to new forms of social capital that women on the coast often accessed by embodying or securing coveted status as wives, as négresses and mulâtresses, as *libres* (free) and not enslaved, or as property owners. However, neither free nor marital status shielded African women from inequalities inherent to the Atlantic societies in which they lived.

Jean Pinet hailed from Rochefort, France, one of several French towns to become active, Atlantic hubs during the late seventeenth and early eighteenth centuries. His service with the Company brought him to the islands of Saint-Louis and Gorée on the Senegal coast. Jean first found work at Gorée, where his training as an artisan earned him a modest income and some small distinction within the island's labor hierarchy.[15] Jean was also the only gunsmith employed at Gorée, a lucrative position that may have played a role in the connection he made with a young woman named Marie Baude, described only as "the daughter of S. Baude."[16] By 1721, thirty-two-year-old Jean was married to eighteen-year-old Marie in a ceremony at Gorée.[17] While details about S. Baude remain to be uncovered, Marie Baude's father was wealthy enough to give the officiant a fourteen-year-old slave named Gabriel Manuel "in recognition of the celebration of the marriage of his daughter with le. Sr. Jean Pinet, gunsmith."

Over the next few years, Jean Pinet and Marie Baude moved from Gorée to Saint-Louis, where Jean continued to serve as gunsmith. An island at the mouth of the Senegal River, Saint-Louis was flanked on one side by a long sandbar and on the other by the coast. Trading companies based their Senegal headquarters at Saint-Louis but did not exercise hegemony over the island. The Wolof kingdoms of Kajoor, Bawol, and Waalo claimed jurisdiction over Saint-Louis and other trading points along rivers and the coast.[18] The *damels* or rulers controlled trade in the region and blocked French merchants from extending their influence beyond the coast and rivers. Wolof officials rented the islands of Saint-Louis and Gorée to trading companies, charging at all of the trade posts for provisions like millet, water, and firewood. Intermediaries exacted annual tribute and duties on individual goods, including slaves. Gorée too fell under Wolof administration. From Gorée, merchants traded with the coastal escales or unfortified posts at Rufisque, Portudal, and Marie's native Joal. The escales bordered the Wolof principalities of Kajoor, Bawol, and the neighboring Serer state of Siin, all connected through economic and social ties to administrators, traders, and residents at the other comptoirs and escales.

African women and women of African descent played a central role in the formation of African Atlantic society at Saint-Louis. A cohort of residents, descended from generations of trade and kinship between Portuguese traders and African women, made the island their home. These long-established families peddled their knowledge of the terrain and commercial contacts to the French. Transatlantic trade brought a new influx of European officials, soldiers, and traders to the islands. Flouting regulations, Company employees and soldiers eschewed lodging in the humid, drafty fort to live with African women in much cooler straw cabins around the island. The labor and hospitality of African women was such an important part of military life that soldiers mutinied when Company officials attempted to expel African wives and domestics from the island or enforce the Company ban on cohabitation.[19] Employees hired women from the mainland to work as domestics, cooks, laundresses, and millet pounders. African women appeared on census rolls as bakers, gardeners, cooks, and healers.[20] While the Company purchased some provisions from the damels and received meager supplies from France, African women formed impromptu markets near the main fort and in villages around the island.[21]

Marie Baude was not the first Saint-Louis resident with kinship ties to Gorée and the coastal escales. Networks of trade, intimacy, and bondage brought seemingly disparate peoples together as residents and workers. In 1720, Marie Thereze Yacam Semaine worked for the Company at Saint-Louis. She was the négresse widow of Joseph de Gorée, but she and her son, Michel de Gorée, lived and worked at Saint-Louis. The same year Paula, the widow of Saint-Louis resident S. Charles Cavillier, lived at Gorée.[22] Paula was originally from Rufisque.[23] Employees had families who lived and worked at the comptoirs. African women and men began to appear on trading company employee rolls. In 1720, the Company of the Indies paid François Aubin, a mulâtre carpenter, 160 livres for work completed.[24] In 1724, Antoine Le Bilan, nègre libre, worked for the Company as a caulker while Malietal and another man, both nègres libres, were employed as translators.[25] After Pierre Charron, a sailor working for the Company at Saint-Louis, passed away, his daughter, Marie Charron, mulâtresse, received his wages. Marie Thereze Yacam Semaine, négresse, received back wages after her husband, Joseph de Gorée, a *maître de barque,* passed away.[26] Some employees, like Michel de

Gorée and Dominique, Christian nègres, worked for the Company at Saint-Louis and traveled back and forth to France as laborers and passengers.[27] By 1724, Jean and Marie lived in a house with a forge where Jean could do his work, and owned at least two slaves—a twelve-year-old boy named André, described as a Christian and Portuguese nègre, and a twenty-two-year-old slave named Basil, described as from "Gambia."[28]

It is possible that Marie Baude's testimony accurately reported the night in question—in bed and asleep, she perhaps did not realize an altercation had occurred until the next morning. More poignant, it is interesting to consider how and whether Marie Baude could have reported events differently. The ambiguity of Jean Pinet's act of violence, with his casual reference to the dead body of a mulâtre, and the precariousness of Marie Baude's status as "the wife" in an Atlantic African society of kinship bonds and boundaries (itself ominously connected to Atlantic slaving and American bondage), all may have forced the narration of an impossible event.[29] Yet her very silence, as witness and wife, articulated slavery, race, and sex.

In the aftermath of the investigation, Jean was found culpable for LeGrain's death. He expressed some protest over the proceedings by refusing to sign his testimony, but signature or not, Jean was deported from Saint-Louis on *L'Esperance.* He was consigned to prison in Nantes. In an official document, the Company director at Saint-Louis expressed sympathy for his role in the affair. Claiming Jean would not have resorted to such violence outside of the insult given his wife and sister-in-law, the interrogators recommended a king's pardon on Jean's behalf.[30] Signing their names, they sent their request ahead to Nantes.

In 1728, why Marie Baude chose to accompany her husband remains a mystery. She was not found culpable for LeGrain's death or formally deported. But Jean's action and his exile charted Marie Baude's path to Louisiana.

PINET'S WIFE (AND HER SLAVES)

Near the end of January 1726, Jean Pinet, still imprisoned in Nantes, received notice of a "*brevet de rémission*" commuting his prison sentence with conditions. The provisions seemed simple. Once again, he was to be employed as a gunsmith for the Company. Only this time, he was required to "serve the rest of his days at the garrison in Louisiana." The king's decision was an act of mercy and pragmatism. The "nomination" occurred at the request of Company officials in New Orleans, the colony's capital. The garrison was in dire need of his skills.[31] Jean's leave required him to take an apprentice. For his service he would receive 300 livres a year.

The king commuted Jean's sentence during the nadir of French migration to Louisiana. Between 1717 and 1720, under the aegis of the Company of the West (later the Company of the Indies), a labor stream of some seven thousand French men, women, and children flowed from France to the Louisiana colony.[32] A majority were forced deportations and bonded laborers, many of them French men and women indentured to the Company.[33] In 1718, the Company founded New Orleans on a crescent strip of land on the Mississippi River, a location meant to facilitate trade and travel to French colonies in the Caribbean and the metropole. The rugged outpost quickly became a comptoir of prisoners, orphans, and poor persons forcibly deported from cities who rapidly died or disappeared.[34] Poverty, death, and desertion likewise claimed lives and drove settlers back to France. A number of inhabitants, men in particular, shunned life at the outposts, lodging instead among the Indian villages, marrying indigenous women. The Company's financing, particularly for its Louisiana ventures, remained tied to an investment mechanism engineered by John Law, the unwieldly "Mississippi Bubble." In 1720, financiers attempted to withdraw their investments, demanding their shares in gold the Company did not have. The bubble popped—and with it financial support and enthusiasm for migration to the Gulf Coast.[35] After 1721, when the Company's resources disappeared, French migration to Louisiana slowed to a trickle.[36] Fewer than two thousand European colonists remained.[37] Jean's exile to Louisiana filled a vacancy left by the last gunsmith, "the man named Gamian."

French relocation to the colony may have slowed, but African migration had not, and for Jean, the scene might have been familiar, if dissonant. Beginning in 1719, African slaves had been arriving in the colony from the continent, purchased by landowners eager to begin staple production in the region.[38] The import population was overwhelmingly Senegambian. The Company of the Indies held a crown monopoly on the French slave trade to Louisiana.[39] Throughout the 1720s and 1730s, captive Africans embarked on slave ships like *La Galathée,* bound for the port of New Orleans. Of the twenty-one to arrive, sixteen purchased or loaded their slaves at either Gorée or Saint-Louis, often both.[40] Their immediate and concentrated arrival created a critical mass of Bamana, Wolof, and Mandingo slaves. Slaves at New Orleans and Mobile were put to work constructing buildings, reinforcing fortifications, and maintaining the levees that protected the towns from flooding. Although several large landowners requested slaves to grow indigo and rice on surrounding concessions, subsistence work took precedence over plantation work.

Instead of trade with Wolof intermediaries and brokers, African women and men participated in a frontier-exchange economy with voyageurs, who were French-Canadian fur traders, and members of Native nations. Like so many other Company employees, settlers, and bonded laborers, Jean Pinet entered a region long settled and occupied by Gulf South Native nations such as the Choctaw, Natchez, Chickasaw, and Houma.[41] Selling goods along the levee and itinerant peddling encouraged residents to form economic ties across race and status. But the majority of people of African descent remained enslaved to and at the mercy of French slave owners and colonial officials—a stark difference from Saint-Louis, Senegal. The provenance of African power brokers within and surrounding Saint-Louis made enforcement of race as status an impossibility. The same could not be said for New Orleans. At New Orleans, unlike in Saint-Louis, the promulgation of regulations like the 1724 Code Noir and its enforcement through force and law signaled early and institutional enforcement of bondage and race along the Gulf Coast.[42]

Nonetheless, as early as 1722, a free presence of African descent existed in New Orleans.[43] The Louisiana Code Noir prohibited slave owners from manumitting slaves without official approval, but Africans escaped bondage in a range of ways.[44] As in Saint-Louis, Africans and people of African descent found employment with the trading company. But in New Orleans, employment could accompany manumission. In 1725, Louis Congo was appointed the colony's executioner in return for his freedom, land, rations of alcohol, and "full time use" of his wife "who remains a slave of the Company of the Indies."[45] In 1727, in New Orleans, Thérèse, wife of Jean Mingo, was also on the path to freedom. Her husband contracted to work off her price himself.[46] Jean Mingo, a nègre libre, asked slave owner Jonathan Darby for permission to marry the négresse slave Thérèse, and for any children of the union to be declared free. Mingo agreed to work in exchange.[47] Manumission for service also occurred on an individual level. Slave owners petitioned the Superior Council for permission to formally manumit their enslaved property.[48] Many justified their decision by citing the "good and agreeable services" slaves had performed for them. Occasionally, a free person of color like la femme Pinet arrived in New Orleans as a passenger and traveler. Slave owner and shipmaster Étienne Larue, a Senegal mulâtre, was one of these.[49]

Some slaves were granted manumission in exchange for extraordinary service to the colony. In 1729, to help curb the Natchez Uprising, the governor offered freedom to slaves who fought on behalf of the French.[50] One official encouraged these manumissions, suggesting that doing so "will give others a great desire to deserve similar favors by material services."[51] Some fifteen men were freed and, in the decades to follow, free men of color continued to find work for the colony as soldiers and militiamen.[52] Marie Aram's husband, François Tioucou, won his freedom helping the French subdue the Natchez and indentured himself to the hospital for seven years to secure her freedom. Venus's husband, Jean Baptiste Marly, did the same. Military work provided many free men of color the support needed to help free their own loved ones—and it also may have raised their social standing as potential suitors.[53]

Company employees of color and others who secured their freedom began to establish themselves within Gulf society through the acquisition of property. By 1727, Louis Congo lived with his wife and another couple on Bayou Road.[54] In 1731, Marie, a négresse, owned property on Bourbon Street, between Anne and Dumaine.[55] Another free person of color, Xavier, is listed as living on Bourbon a year later. Simon and Scipion, free men of color, owned property along the banks of the river just outside of town.[56] Others resided in households adjoining their employers. A domestic of M. Duoy secured ownership of a residence on Rue Royale.[57] Finally, as in Gorée and Saint-Louis, some slaves lived with the independence of free people of color. A slave belonging to Mezelliers inhabited property on Rue Royale, down the street from the domestic of Monsieur Duoy. By 1731, colonial officials counted eight mulâtres who owned property in New Orleans.[58] These may have been free people of color, who were not counted separately in the censuses, and this may also be an underestimation of the free population of color.[59] Counted or undercounted, the free population of color continued to grow and play a role in the city's development.

At some point between 1726 and 1728, Jean Pinet asked the Company for permission to bring his own free African wife and slaves to Louisiana from Senegal. Company officials consented, but required the slaves to also work for the Company to pay the price of the voyage. Jean Pinet agreed and waited for Marie Baude to arrive. However, when she arrived with her bondspeople in tow, the three slaves were taken to satisfy the "tariff of Gorée." Jean complained but the governor stalled in resolving the matter, claiming he required guidance from Company directors in Paris. After a year, Jean petitioned the Superior Council again for a decision on the slaves. With no word from France, the Superior Council responded that the slaves had been placed by accident among those taken from the ship and sold at auction. In light of the mistake, the Superior Council agreed to compensate Jean for half the value of the slaves.[60] Jean, angered, demanded the Company finance the voyage of another group of his slaves. It remains unclear whether or not the Company agreed.

Settled in New Orleans, Marie Baude was no longer a propertied, free, African woman in a community of women of similar wealth, race, or status. She was also not the nameless, propertyless mulâtresse passagère traveling to "Mississippi" for undisclosed reasons. She became something in between, la femme Pinet, the unpropertied wife of a French artisan in an overseas colony where the majority of people of African descent were enslaved and where slavery was linked to perpetual bondage and servitude. In 1731, census documents record a Jean Pinet living downriver from the city with an unnamed wife, five black slaves or servants, and one white servant.[61] He died in 1737. There is no record of what became of Marie Baude.

Marie Baude's life at Saint-Louis, journey across the Atlantic, and arrival in New Orleans reveal ways women of African descent interacted with forces creating the Atlantic world. At Saint-Louis, women of African descent saw their networks expand as geographies of social responsibility and customary relations exploded across the ocean. Forming unions with European soldiers, sailors, traders, and artisans integrated women into networks of commerce and kin stretching back towards France and to Louisiana. At New Orleans, something similar occurred among women of African descent, but enslavement was more prevalent, widespread, and institutionalized than at Saint-Louis. As a result, Marie Baude's shifting geographies accompanied new forms of subject-hood. Chattel slavery and French colonial authority in New Orleans reinforced the importance of free status and left even free women of African descent's position as wives, daughters, and colonial subjects vulnerable to the intrusions of property, bondage, and empire.

Marie Baude's journey from Saint-Louis to New Orleans illuminates ways women of African descent in the Atlantic world found their freedom and autonomy to be continually shaped by their status, race, and sex. As she moved, slavery, sex, marriage, and property took on new meanings. Agents of empire and systems of slavery interceded on and influenced her everyday life and countless lives of enslaved and free women of African descent. African women as cultural brokers, social engineers, and household managers shaped the formation of slave-holding society at Saint-Louis. African women and women of African descent likewise escaped slavery and built new property and kinship networks that shaped the formation of colonial society in New Orleans. At both locations, French men and men of African descent were often cast as real or presumed masters, while people of African descent, including women, slave and free, navigated the lower tiers. However, only at New Orleans could French authority be institutionalized as custom and law, reinforced by an ongoing trade in Africans as chattel slaves. In the end, African women and women of African descent at both locales navigated encounters in a social climate structured to their disadvantage and predicated on men's presumed access to their labor and bodies. Considering the experience of Marie Baude, an African woman swept into the Atlantic circuit, however, further illuminates the ways slave trading and plantation slavery changed the terrain of interaction, had an impact on both sides of the Atlantic, and offered women of color possibilities both fruitful and dangerous.

NOTES

Note to first epigraph: Archives Nationales d'Outre-Mer, Fonds des Colonies, Aix-en-Provence, France (hereafter ANOM COL), C13A 11, f. 315–16, January 30, 1729, Étienne Périer and Jacques de La Chaise to the Minister of the Navy.

1. Marie Baude was first introduced into the scholarly record as "la femme Pinet," the mulâtresse wife of Jean Pinet, by Gwendolyn Midlo Hall. Since then, she's been mentioned in work by Peter Caron, Shannon Lee Dawdy, and Jennifer Spear. This is the first attempt at a gendered, transatlantic analysis of her world at the time she made her journey across the Atlantic from Senegal to New Orleans. See Gwendolyn Midlo Hall, *Africans in Colonial Louisiana: The Development of Afro-Creole Culture in the Eighteenth Century* (Baton Rouge: Louisiana State University Press, 1995), 128; Peter Caron, "'Of a Nation Which the Others Do Not Understand': Bambara Slaves and African Ethnicity in Colonial Louisiana, 1718–1760," *Slavery & Abolition* 18:1 (1997): 11–12; Jennifer M. Spear, *Race, Sex, and Social Order in Early New Orleans* (Baltimore: Johns Hopkins University Press, 2008), 80, 90.

2. Archives Nationales, Paris (herafter AN), 4JJ 16 f. 13, November 21, 1728, Cdt. Préville-Quinet, Journaux de bord de *La Galathée*. All of the information on the crossing of the Galathée comes from these journaux de bord. See also Voyages Database, 2010. Voyages: The Trans-Atlantic Slave Trade Database, accessed April 4, 2016, http://slavevoyages.org/voyage/32905/variables.

3. See also Rebecca J. Scott and Jean Hébrard, *Freedom Papers: An Atlantic Odyssey in the Age of Emancipation* (Boston: Harvard University Press, 2012); James H. Sweet, *Domingos Alvares, African Healing, and the Intellectual History of the Atlantic World* (Chapel Hill: University of North Carolina Press, 2011); Daniel L. Schafer, *Anna Madgigine Jai Kingsley: African Princess, Florida Slave, Plantation Slaveowner* (Gainesville: University Press of Florida, 2010); Randy J. Sparks, *The Two Princes of Calabar: An Eighteenth-Century Atlantic Odyssey* (Cambridge, MA: Harvard University Press, 2004).

4. Robin Law and Kristin Mann, "West Africa in the Atlantic Community: The Case of the Slave Coast," *William and Mary Quarterly* 56:2 (1999): 307, 311. See also John K. Thornton and Linda M. Heywood, *Central Africans, Atlantic Creoles, and the Foundation of the Americas, 1585–1660* (New York: Cambridge University Press, 2007); Toyin Falola and Matt D. Childs, eds., *The Yoruba Diaspora in the Atlantic World* (Bloomington: Indiana University Press, 2004).

5. The phrase "sex across the color line" gained wide usage thanks to Martha Hodes. Martha Hodes, *Sex Across the Color Line: White Women and Black Men in the Nineteenth-Century American South* (Princeton, NJ: Princeton University, 1991). See also Ann Laura Stoler, "Tense and Tender Ties: the Politics of Comparison in North American History and (Post) Colonial Studies," in Ann Laura Stoler, ed., *Haunted by Empire: Geographies of Intimacy in North American History* (Durham, NC: Duke University Press, 2006); Joseph C. Miller, "Domiciled and Dominated: Slaving as a History of Women," in Gwyn Campbell, Suzanne Miers, and Joseph C. Miller, eds., *Women and Slavery: The Modern Atlantic* (Athens: Ohio University Press, 2007), 284–312; and Hilary Jones, *The Métis of Senegal: Urban Life and Politics in French West Africa* (Bloomington: Indiana University Press, 2013).

6. Marcus Rediker, *The Slave Ship: A Human History* (New York: Viking Press, 2007); Paul Gilroy, *The Black Atlantic: Modernity and Double Consciousness* (Cambridge, MA: Harvard University Press, 1993), 16. See also Simone Brown, *Dark Matters: On the Surveillance of Blackness* (Durham, NC: Duke University Press, 2015).

7. Sowande' Mustakeem, "'I Never Have Such a Sickly Ship Before': Diet, Disease, and Mortality in 18th-Century Atlantic Slaving Voyages," *Journal of African American History* 93:4 (2008): 485. See also Sowande' M. Mustakeem, *Slavery at Sea: Terror, Sex, and Sickness in the Middle Passage* (Urbana: University of Illinois Press, 2016).

8. ANOM COL C13A 11, f. 315–6, January 30, 1729, Périer and de La Chaise to the Minister of the Navy.

9. Ibid.

10. ANOM COL E 336ter, no. 32, June 15, 1724, Pinet (Jean), armurier au Sénégal, Affaire Criminelle. All of the information on the murder comes from these testimonies, hereafter Pinet, Affaire Criminelle.

11. Pinet, Affaire Criminelle, f. 11–12. The missing word is *foutre,* slang for sexual intercourse. The verb André used is *vouloir,* which makes it difficult to read the level of aggression in LeGrain's words. Translated here as "intends to," it could also be read as a "wish," a "desire," or a "will," depending on the level of the threat. None of these nuances change the fact that LeGrain made a sexually violent remark directed at Marie Baude and meant to be understood as at the expense of Jean Pinet.

12. Pinet, Affaire Criminelle, f. 7–9.

13. Pinet, Affaire Criminelle, f. 4–5. When officials asked André if Marie Baude "protested" her husband's behavior, André affirmed that she did, before he struck LeGrain down.

14. ANOM COL C6 6, March 14, 1721, and March 8, 1721, Pierre de Salvert, "Règlements de la Compagnie royalle du Senegal et Costes D'Affrique"; Delcourt, *La France et les établissements français,* 95, 98. Drinking, socializing, and quarreling between the white Company employees and African inhabitants of Saint-Louis and Gorée was prohibited. These prohibitions failed. On Company officials attempting to have the ban on marriage lifted, see ANOM COL C6 8, f. 5, May 25, 1724, Julien Dubellay to Messieurs le Directeurs de la Compagnie des Indes; ANOM COL C6 11, f. 22, August 2, 1737, Conseil Supérieur to Messieurs les Directeurs de la Compagnie des Indes; Delcourt, *La France et les établissements français,* 123.

15. ANOM COL C6 6, f. 4, April 20, 1720, André Brue, "État des appointements qui sont dus aux employés de la Compagnie des Indes à la Concession du Sénégal par les comptes arrêtés par M. Brüe Directeur et Commandant général." The Company listed "Jean Pinet, armurier" at Gorée as due a credit of 177 livres and ten *sols.* Pinet's credit was comparable to that of other masons, blacksmiths, and other artisans on the island (whose credit ranged from 87 to 400 livres, and much higher than many sailors and cabin boys (35 livres). For comparison, it is possible to situate Pinet's credit at this time against the 8,000 livres due then-governor of Gorée, François Duval.

16. Another hint to the status both Baude and Pinet enjoyed is use of the appellation "Sr" in official documentation. "Sr" or "S" was short for "Sieur," an honorific reserved for men of property, wealth, or social status.

17. ANOM COL C6 6, f. 16, May 24, 1721, Nicolas Deprès de St. Robert to Messieurs les Directeurs de la Compagnie des Indes.

18. James F. Searing, *West African Slavery and Atlantic Commerce* (Cambridge: Cambridge

University Press, 1993), 93–164; Boubacar Barry, *Senegambia and the Atlantic Slave Trade* (Cambridge: Cambridge University Press, 1998), 78; George E. Brooks, *Eurafricans in Western Africa: Commerce, Social Status, Gender, and Religious Observance from the Sixteenth to the Eighteenth Century* (Athens: Ohio University Press, 2003), 61. For the later period, see Jones, *The Métis of Senegal,* 2012.

19. ANOM COL C6 6, March 8, 1721, and March 14, 1721, "Règlements de la Compagnie royale du Sénégal et côtes d'Afrique"; Michel Jajolet de la Courbe, *Premier voyage du sieur de la Courbe fait a la coste d'Afrique en 1685* (E. Champion, 1913), 25–26, 28, 105; Carson Ritchie, "Deux textes sur Le Sénégal (1673–1677)," *Bulletin de l'Institut fondamental d'Afrique noire* 1 B (1968): 294–98.

20. Abdoulaye Ly, *La Compagnie du Sénégal* (Paris: Karthala, 1993), 263–64. ANOM COL C6 11, May 1, 1736, "Rôle général des Blancs et Nègres au service de la Compagnie des Indes à la concession du Sénégal le 1er mai 1736"; Searing, *West African Slavery and Atlantic Commerce,* 93.

21. Courbe, *Premier voyage,* 26, 28.

22. ANOM COL C6 6, f. 2–3, April 30, 1720, Saint-Robert, "État de ce que les dits employés doivent à la dite Compagnie par les comptes attestés par le dit Sieur Brue le 30 Avril 1720."

23. Ibid. Paula is the earliest instance I have found in French documents of a woman being described by the honorific "signare." Forthcoming work by Lindsey Gish may uncover earlier references.

24. Ibid.

25. ANOM COL C6 8, f. 3, August 20, 1724, "Facture des marchandises, ustensiles et autres effets chargés du magasin du Sénégal par ordre de Monsieur Julien Dubellay, Directeur et Commandant général sur le brigantin *Le Fier* Capitaine Mr. La Rue pour porter à Arguin et remettre au Sr Delamotte garde magasin au d. lieu"; ANOM COL C6 8, f. 2, October 28, 1724, "Facture des marchandises chargées du magasin du Sénégal par ordre de Monsieur Julien Dubellay, Directeur."

26. ANOM COL C6 6, f. 3, April 30, 1720, André Brue, "État des appointements qui sont dus aux employés de la Compagnie des Indes à la Concession du Sénégal par les comptes arrêtés par M. Brüe Directeur et Commandant général le 30 Avril 1720 dont le montant a été porté à leur crédit par Mr. de Saint Robert dans leurs comptes nouveaux."

27. ANOM COL C6 8, f. 2, November 16, 1724, Julien Dubellay, "Rôle des passagers venus de France par la frégate Le Prothée commandée par Monsieur Hautier arrivée au Sénégal."

28. Pinet, Affaire Criminelle, f. 13.

29. Saidiya V. Hartman, "Venus in Two Acts," *Small Axe* 12:2 (2008): 10. Hartman asks, "What is required to imagine a free state or to tell an impossible story?" See also Christopher Miller, *The French Atlantic Triangle: Literature and Culture of the Slave Trade* (Durham, NC: Duke University Press, 2008); Michel-Rolph Trouillot, *Silencing the Past: Power and the Production of History* (Boston: Beacon Press, 2012).

30. Pinet, Affaire Criminelle, f. 1–2.

31. ANOM COL C13A 9, f. 329, January 26, 1729, "Délibérations du Conseil Supérieur de la Louisiane."

32. In 1718, the French Crown granted the colony of Louisiana to the Company of the West. Two years later, the Company of the West was absorbed, with several other French trading companies, into the Company of the Indies. Cécile Vidal, "French Louisiana in the Age of the Companies, 1712–1731," in Louis H. Roper and Bertrand Van Ruymbeke, eds., *Constructing Early Modern Empires: Proprietary Ventures in the Atlantic World, 1500–1750* (Leiden: Brill, 2007), 148.

33. Jerah Johnson states some 2,462 who made the journey were indentured servants. Jerah Johnson, "Colonial New Orleans: A Fragment of the Eighteenth-Century French Ethos," in Arnold R. Hirsch and Joseph Logsdon, eds., *Creole New Orleans: Race and Americanization* (Baton Rouge: Louisiana State University Press, 1992), 12–57.

34. Lawrence N. Powell, *The Accidental City: Improvising New Orleans* (Cambridge, MA: Harvard University Press, 2013); Hall, *Africans in Colonial Louisiana,* 5; Johnson, "Colonial New Orleans," 32–33. See also Marcel Giraud, *A History of French Louisiana,* vols. 1–3 (Baton Rouge: Louisiana State University Press, 1993).

35. Although John Law was rumored to have stolen from the Company he created, there is no evidence he was anything more than impractical, if bold and idealistic. See Powell, *The Accidental City.*

36. For more on John Law's Company, see Mathé Allain, *Not Worth a Straw: French Colonial Policy and the Early Years of Louisiana* (Lafayette: University of Southwestern Louisiana Press, 1988).

37. ANOM G1 464, f. 11, 1726, "Recensement général des habitations et habitants de la colonie de la Louisiane."

38. When one is discussing the French slave trade to Louisiana, figures gathered by Jean Mettas and put into further context by Gwendolyn Midlo Hall provide the best summaries of numbers and origins. Jean Mettas, Serge Daget, and Michelle Daget, eds., *Répertoire des expéditions négrières françaises au XVIIIe siècle* (Paris: Société française d'histoire d'outre-mer, 1984), vol. 2; Hall, *Africans in Colonial Louisiana.* It is important to note these figures do not take into account private sales of any individual slaves arriving on smaller ships from British mainland North America or transshipped from the Caribbean. See Thomas N. Ingersoll, "The Slave Trade and the Ethnic Diversity of Louisiana's Slave Community," *Louisiana History* 37:2 (1996): 137–39.

39. After 1725, the monopoly was lifted and private traders were allowed to participate in slave-trading activities. However, only one ship financed entirely by private traders arrived in Louisiana during the French period, and it was funded by Louisiana slave traders. It, too, embarked from Saint-Louis and Gorée. See voyage #32170, Saint Ursin, arrived in Louisiana in 1743. Voyages Database, 2010. Voyages: The Trans-Atlantic Slave Trade Database.

40. Voyages Database, 2010. Voyages: The Trans-Atlantic Slave Trade Database, accessed November 7, 2016, http://slavevoyages.org/voyages/gJg89pyd.

41. For more on Gulf South Native nations in colonial Louisiana, see Spear, *Race, Sex, and Social Order*; Daniel H. Usner Jr., *American Indians in the Lower Mississippi Valley: Social and Economic Histories* (Omaha: University of Nebraska Press, 2004); Daniel H. Usner Jr., *Indians, Settlers, and Slaves in a Frontier Exchange Economy: The Lower Mississippi Valley before 1783*

(Chapel Hill: University of North Carolina Press, 1992); Sophie White, *Wild Frenchmen and Frenchified Indians: Material Culture and Race in Colonial Louisiana* (Chapel Hill: University of North Carolina Press, 2012).

42. Hans W. Baade, "The Gens de Couleur of Louisiana: Comparative Slave Law in Microcosm," *Cardozo Law Review* 18:2 (1996): 54. In 1723, Governor Bienville signed a peace treaty with the Natchez that required them to return a free black taking refuge among them, dead or alive. ANOM COL F3 24, f. 153–4, November 26, 1723, "Relation de la punition des Natchez en 1723."

43. Laroze, a "free negro," was convicted of stealing from Company stores. He was punished with flogging and imprisoned for six years. "Conviction and Sentence of Flogging and Incarceration, September 13, 1722," Records of the Superior Council of Louisiana, *Louisiana Historical Quarterly* (hereafter RSCL, *LHQ*) 7:4 (1924): 678; see also Donald E. Everett, "Free Persons of Color in Colonial Louisiana," *Louisiana History* 7:1 (1966): 24, who may be misidentifying him as the free nègre Raphael Bernard.

44. Article 50, "Le Code Noir, ou Édit du Roi, servant de règlement pour le gouvernement et l'adiminstration de la justice, police, discipline et le commerce des esclaves nègres, dans la province et colonie de la Louisianne; donné à Versailles au mois de Mars 1724," in *Le Code Noir, ou, recueil des règlements rendus jusquà présent: concernant le gouvernement, l'administration de la justice, la police, la discipline & le commerce des nègres dans les colonies françoises, et les conseils & compagnies établis à ce sujet* (Paris: Chez L. F. Prault, 1742), 321.

45. ANOM COL C13 A, f. 267–8, October 24, 1725, "Délibérations du Conseil Supérieur de la Louisiane."

46. "Marriage License, Free Negro and Slave," November 18, 1727," RSCL, *LHQ* 4:2 (1922): 236; "Promissory Note," November 28, 1727, ibid., 236; "Agreement for Hire of Free Negress," 4:3, 355.

47. "Decision between Mingo and Darby, 25 November 1730," RSCL, *LHQ* 5:1 (1924): 103.

48. Thomas N. Ingersoll, "Slave Codes and Judicial Practice in New Orleans, 1718–1807," *Law and History Review* 13:1 (1995): 37; "Emancipation Paper, 1 October 1733," RSCL, *LHQ* 5:2 (1922), 250; "Petition to Emancipate Slave, 11 July 1737," RSCL, *LHQ* 5:3 (1922): 403; "Manumission, 28 March 1736," RSCL, *LHQ* 8:2 (1925): 287.

49. For documentation in English on Étienne La Rue, see Heloise Cruzat, "The Documents Covering the Criminal Trial of Étienne La Rue, for Attempt to Murder and Illicit Carrying of Arms," *LHQ* 13:3 (1930): 377–90. See also Shannon Lee Dawdy, *Building the Devil's Empire: French Colonial New Orleans* (Chicago: University of Chicago Press, 2008), 131, 174; Ibrahima Seck, "Cultures africaines et esclavage dans la basse vallée du Mississippi d'Iberville à Jim Crow," PhD diss., Université Cheikh Anta Diop, 1999, 60.

50. "Proposal to Free Negroes, Memorial of M. de La Chaise," May 16, 1730, in Heloise H. Cruzat, ed., "New Orleans under Bienville: Sidelights on New Orleans in Bienville's Time," *LHQ* 1:3 (1917): 132–133; ANOM COL C13A 12, f. 37, Étienne de Périer, "Relations du massacre des Natchez arrivé le 28 novembre 1729"; RSCL, Louisiana Historical Center, May 13, 1730; Jean-François-Benjamin de Montigny, "History of Louisiana," in B. F. French, ed., *Historical Memoires of Louisiana* (New York: Lamport, Blakeman & Law, 1853), 99–102.

51. Thomas N. Ingersoll, *Mammon and Manon in Early New Orleans: The First Slave Society in the Deep South, 1718–1819* (Knoxville: University of Tennessee Press, 1999), 365n.

52. Donald E. Everett, "Free Persons of Color in Colonial Louisiana," 28–29, 31–33; Dawdy, *Building the Devil's Empire,* 178–80. However, forthcoming work by the editors of this volume may challenge the view of enslaved men's access to milita labor.

53. "Petition of the Directors of the Charity Hospital of New Orleans to Grant Freedom to Maria Aram, a négresse slave, 6 March 1744," RSCL, *LHQ* 7:3 (1924): 552. See also Henry P. Dart, ed., "Emancipation of Marie Aram, a Slave," *LHQ* 3:4 (1920): 551–53; "A Free Negro Agrees to Serve as Cook," RSCL, *LHQ* 14:3 (1931): 594.

54. "Census of New Orleans as reported by M. Périer, Commandant General of Louisiana, July 1, 1727," in Charles R. Maduell, ed., *Census Tables for the French Colony of Louisiana* (Baltimore: Genealogical Publishing, 1972), 2:A-27–14. Louis Congo likely lived on land he had secured as part of his appointment as the colony's "negro executioner." This position, unseemly as it was, would have warranted a parcel of land outside of the city.

55. Bienville and Salmon, "Plan de La Nouvelle-Orléans telle qu'elle était au mois de décembre 1731," December 1731, [map], 1974.25.18.135, Historic New Orleans Collection; "List of Property Owners of New Orleans on the Map Published by Gonichon in 1731," *Census Tables,* 3: A-31–1-5.

56. "Census of Inhabitants along the River of the Mississippi Dated 1731," *Census Tables,* B-31–8.

57. Ibid.

58. ANOM G1, December 1731, "Plan de la Nouvelle Orleans telle qu'elle estoit au mois de dexembre 1731"; in Maduell, Census Tables, "List of Property Owners of New Orleans on the Map Published By Gonichon in 1731," 113–53.

59. Free people of color were not counted separately in censuses until 1763.

60. ANOM COL C13A 11, f. 349–50, June 29, 1729, "Déliberations privées en l'Assemblée des Directeurs."

61. Maduell, Census Tables, "Census of Inhabitants along the River of the Mississippi Dated 1731," 138. Maduell lists two Pinets: one named Yves in the city and living with his brother, and the second an inhabitant listed simply as "Pinet," a gunsmith living along the river. The exact relationship between the two remains unclear, but given the unique surname, they were certainly related. My forthcoming work on Marie Baude and free African women in New Orleans's Atlantic world delves further into these kinship ties and archival silences.

THE STREETS, THE BARRACKS, AND THE HOSPITAL

Public Space, Social Control, and Cross-Racial Interactions among Soldiers and Slaves in French New Orleans

CÉCILE VIDAL

In June 1731 the only known slave conspiracy in French Louisiana was uncovered.[1] The plot was revealed by an altercation between an enslaved woman and a serviceman. In his travel account, Antoine-Simon Le Page du Pratz recounted: "A Negress attached to the brick factory, although she belonged to the Company, came back at noon for dinner. A soldier who needed wood tried to force her, by paying her, to look for some for him; she refused to go, as she was pressed for time. The lazy soldier got very mad, & slapped her so violently that the Negress claimed in her anger that the French would not strike the Negroes for long. Those of the French who heard these threats arrested her & brought her to the governor who ordered to throw her in jail."[2] Although the precise site of the incident is not mentioned—it might have taken place in the streets of the Louisiana capital—we know for sure that it happened in public in front of many witnesses, including several whites. The reason for the conflict was closely related to the two protagonists' social status. In this slave society, people of African descent furnished most of the labor force, whereas soldiers were characterized as a social group by the fact that, except for a few exceptions, they were non-slaveholders. The social preeminence associated with mastery was inaccessible to most servicemen, who could not benefit from the slave workforce unless they hired and paid enslaved laborers. Since the slave system strengthened the social stigma traditionally associated with manual work in what was also an ancien régime society, this situation could only reinforce the contempt felt for the military. When the enslaved woman refused to obey the soldier, she implicitly reminded him of his precarious social position. It was all the more inacceptable in his view as she humiliated him in public. Consequently, he used violence in order to restore what he saw as the right racial and gender order. Whatever she felt about him, the woman knew that she could not fight back. She very likely revealed the plot because she found herself powerless in front of his demonstration of force. Indeed, the racial divide was based on the imposition by whites of their monopoly on physical violence.

Over the last two generations, the history of slavery in the United States has mainly evolved into a history of slaves.[3] In contrast, the incident that led to the aborted slave revolt in the New Orleans region highlights the need to develop a relational history of slavery among all social actors, and to take into account masters and slaves, as well as non-slaveholders. It has been argued that one of the main factors differentiating slave systems in the Americas was the size and origins of the necessary intermediary group of non- or small slaveholders that developed between masters and slaves, either free people of color or poor whites.[4] In French Louisiana, soldiers constituted a crucial component of this category of whites of the lower sorts. The same was true in all slave societies under French sovereignty since the strong presence of troops in every colony was a distinctive feature of the French Empire, particularly in comparison with British North America.

Focusing on the interactions between the enslaved and the military is also important to better understand the specificities of racial slavery in an urban environment. While servicemen were not found on plantations except when military expeditions were sent to the countryside to track down runaways, soldiers and slaves lived together both in the city and in every colonial outpost with a garrison. What makes their interactions interesting to study within New Orleans is the importance of the public space in the urban setting. What defines any city is the "culture of the public arena" ("*culture de la place publique*").[5] The public space is characterized by both its accessibility and its visibility. The passersby are also spectators. They form the necessary audience to the urban scene where the representations associated with the city can coalesce because people not only interact, but also observe one another.[6] In ancien régime societies, this practice of watching one another in the public space was of crucial importance. Since these societies were highly unequal, and worked mainly through oral communication, they were characterized by an exacerbated "culture of appearances."[7] Public buildings and spaces (public in the sense of open to the public) served as sorts of theatrical stages on which social actors projected their vision of the social order, negotiated their social position, and displayed their power struggles with a finely tuned sense of representation. Their behavior and interactions in public were conditioned by the fact that they were under other people's scrutinizing gaze.

This essay adopts a micro-sociological approach to analyze the forms, circumstances, and places of the daily interactions between soldiers and slaves in public and semipublic spaces.[8] While it uses the administrative correspondence and series D on colonial troops in the Colonial Archives to explore the demographic and social position of the military and the enslaved in relation to each other, it is based mainly on a systematic analysis of all the trials, found in the Records of the Superior Council of Louisiana, that concerned conflicts between soldiers and people of African descent—slaves most of the time and a free man of color in one case. In the interrogatories and testimonies, judges oriented the oral statements by asking questions, but they let the defendants or witnesses speak freely and at great length. Although their discourses were shaped by the judicial circumstances in which they were pronounced, their stories reveal how soldiers and slaves interacted in their daily lives and how they viewed these relationships. The goal is to study how historical actors used the public space both to give a symbolic meaning to their interactions and to negotiate the power dynamic within their relationships.

In so doing, this essay seeks to complicate the ways the relationships between the military and the enslaved have been described. The historians who make the strongest claims about the disorder that is believed to have prevailed in French Louisiana often underline solidarities among the lower social groups, soldiers and slaves in particular. While they mention cases of verbal and physical violence, they overemphasize a shared sociability around alcohol, a common criminality, and joint attempts at escaping. They explain these phenomena, arguing that enslaved and enlisted men found themselves in a similar position, as they assimilate the military condition to a kind of bondage and stress the fact that servicemen were exploited, mistreated, and despised. Class solidarities are claimed to have been stronger than race antagonisms.[9] In contrast, this essay will insist as much on tensions as on cooperation between soldiers and slaves who shared the bottom rungs of the social ladder but were separated by status and race. In addition to many other phenomena, the complicated relationships that the military and the enslaved maintained demonstrate that New Orleans society was deeply shaped by race from the outset.[10]

THE SOCIAL STATUS OF SERVICEMEN WITHIN NEW ORLEANS

Slaves and soldiers were the two largest status groups within Louisiana colonial settlements, although the former quickly outnumbered the latter until the arrival of massive reinforcements at the end of the Seven Years War.[11] However, it is more difficult to evaluate the precise number of troops than the size of the slave population. In New Orleans, the enslaved accounted for 261 (252 were of African and 9 of Native American descent) out of 884 civil inhabitants (29.5%) in 1731 at the time of the retrocession of the colony by the Company of the Indies to the king, just before the slave trade from Africa nearly ceased. Slaves became the majority with 989 (963/26) out of 1,748 inhabitants (56.6%) in 1737. They still amounted to 1,135 (1,098/37) out of 2,449 inhabitants (46.9%) in 1763 at the end of the French Regime, just before the cession of the colony to the English and the Spanish.[12]

Within the colony, New Orleans had an important geopolitical role as the only port and gateway to navigation on the Mississippi, but its defensive function was limited. As a result, the Louisiana capital always housed a relatively small garrison, though it could be temporarily expanded by soldiers who stopped by on their way to or from the metropole.[13] During the French Regime, the number of *compagnies franches de la Marine* (navy's companies) garrisoned in the city constantly evolved.[14] After the Company's withdrawal, the king sent new recruits to fill four companies in 1731–1732. In theory, each company comprised fifty men, but they were often incomplete because of disease, death, and desertion. Already in May 1732, there were only 99 men left in the four companies instead of 200.[15] From the early 1750s, in wartime, the number of compagnies franches de la Marine rose to six.[16] Yet in 1760, Commissaire-ordonnateur Vincent-Gaspard Rochemore reported that there had never been more than 600 soldiers garrisoned in New Orleans, and that they were reduced to 150 at the time.[17] In addition to these compagnies franches de la Marine, there were also one or two units of Swiss companies garrisoned in the capital. After the retrocession, new Swiss troops were drawn from the Karrer Regiment.[18] In 1732, they gathered 140 Swiss soldiers.[19] Finally, additional troops from either the navy or the army were also sent temporarily in times of Native American or imperial wars. At the end of the Seven Years War, for instance, after the capture of Havana by the British in 1762, when the Crown expected New Orleans to be the next target of the British Navy, the Angoumois Regiment with ten companies was ordered to join Louisiana.

Because we have both a census and a precise account of the soldiers garrisoned in New Orleans for the year 1732, we can compare their numbers: 258 slaves, among whom 105 men, against 239 French and Swiss servicemen. The ratio was not so unbalanced at the time, but the gap grew over the years. This demographic imbalance became a preoccupation for local authorities. In 1733, Jean-Baptiste Le Moyne de Bienville tried to convince the minister of the navy to send new recruits to New Orleans out of fear of a slave rebellion: "however, I have the honor to observe to My Lord, that, although this capital is not very much exposed to Native attacks, it can have more dangerous enemies such as Negroes, and even the unhappy French who cannot leave this country where they have much to suffer, one could wish that the Swiss company would be complete. An increase of fifty men of such a good troop would fortify this garrison."[20]

The use of soldiers to prevent any criminal activity by patrolling and serving as sentinels in the gatehouses around the city, especially at night, to pursue runaway slaves, and to arrest slaves accused of criminal behavior, may have fueled social antagonism between them. Not only may the enslaved have resented troops as the power instrument used by authorities and masters to impose their force over them, but servicemen may also have been angry because their police function was seen as a dishonorable activity, contrary to military service. When Commissaire-ordonnateur Honoré Michel de Villebois de La Rouvillière tried to justify his proposal to create a *maréchaussée* (a rural police force) in 1751, he argued:

> Troops should give a helping hand, but they are not accustomed to do so, and they are extremely reluctant to accomplish this kind of service. If order has to be enforced and we ask the troops for assistance, soldiers secretly warn the innkeepers and other culprits; if arrests have to be car-

ried out there are always some arguments; soldiers are happy to bear arms but none of them want to have anything to do with criminal matters for fear of losing their honor. Every day we have runaway slaves who gather together in the woods around the city, they insult passers-by, and often come out at night to raid plantations that they ransack. If it is necessary to track them down in their hiding place, the soldiers retort that it is not their role, that at least they have to be paid, and indeed it has always been done that way.[21]

The reluctance of troops to fulfill policing duties combined with the lack of soldiers explains why local authorities had to ask civilians to guard the city. In the early 1730s, they organized three guard units, each composed of forty servicemen and settlers chosen from among workers of European descent.[22] Then, in the early 1760s, militiamen, who until then had only been mobilized in wartime, started to assist soldiers in policing the city against slave unrest.[23]

Servicemen may have also resented having to work alongside slaves. Local authorities employed both enslaved and enlisted men for all public works such as the erection and maintenance of fortifications and levees and in the convoys that circulated between the capital and the Illinois Country. Construction work and rowing up the river were hard and grueling tasks. Hence, the author of a memorandum on Louisiana, Redon de Rassac, reported that at the English Turn the officers "used [soldiers] as negroes or galley slaves."[24] Nevertheless, unlike slaves, servicemen were paid to do this work or received a bonus. In 1724, for instance, soldiers complained against their wages, as they were much better remunerated when they were employed by private settlers.[25] In the same way, officials employed slaves in the military campaigns against the Natchez and the Chickasaw in the 1730s, but they only armed them against the Natchez, and then preferred to use them to row the boats, dig trenches, and build defensive military positions during the expeditions against the Chickasaw.[26] Moreover, troops expressed their resentment against having to serve alongside slaves in these expeditions by abusing them. In 1739, the planter Joseph Chaperon presented a request to the Superior Council because he had given two enslaved laborers to serve against the Chickasaw. One fell ill; the other was dying from the lack of food and the constant blows soldiers inflicted on him on the road.[27]

Yet, like slaves, servicemen had to face difficult material conditions. The state was supposed to provide for their material needs, but metropolitan or local authorities did not hesitate to cut costs at their expense. Soldiers were often badly dressed, as replacements were not sent frequently enough and the quality of the uniforms was poor.[28] In order to earn money, they sometimes tried to sell their apparel, and it was often slaves who wore these illicitly sold garments.[29] Instead of being a sign of military and masculine pride, uniforms in rags reflected the low status of soldiers. Likewise, at times, the governor and commissaire-ordonnateur did not scruple to give troops rice bread or bread made with half wheat, half rice in their rations despite the king's order to feed them with wheat bread.[30] Even though servicemen were not the only ones, among the population of European descent, who had to eat rice because of the frequent wheat flour shortages, they were prompt to show their discontent.[31] In 1760, when Commissaire-ordonnateur Rochemore had no choice but to feed troops with rice bread because wheat flour was lacking, he decided to give them one pound of meat every day for free in order to maintain peace and tranquility.[32] Not only did wheat bread suit the soldiers' taste better, it also allowed them to distinguish themselves from slaves who were fed with locally produced rice and corn.

Judicial repression is another phenomenon that could have contributed to reducing the social distance between soldiers and slaves although they were not tried in front of the same institution—a military court for the former and the Superior Council for the latter. Throughout the French Regime, the military formed the social category that, with the enslaved, suffered the most from repression by royal justice. While cases of individual insubordination against an officer or sergeant and collective mutinies were rare, desertion was the most common crime for which soldiers were prosecuted and punished.[33] The phenomenon was widespread, although it does not seem to have been more marked in Louisiana than in the metropole or in other colonies: between 1744 and 1770, almost 9 percent of all servicemen deserted in the Mississippi colony.[34] Soldiers and slaves sometimes chose to flee together, but enslaved laborers were on occasion kidnapped and forced to follow deserters. Moreover, runaways and soldiers could have conflicting relationships.[35]

When servicemen were tried, military justice was characterized by great leniency most of the time, but extreme severity when authorities thought that they ought to make an example. Among the 1,819 soldiers stationed in Louisiana between 1744 and 1770 for whom we have information, 18 were tried in absentia, 7 were expelled out of the navy, 10 were sentenced to the galleys for life, and 26 to the death penalty (most were shot to death, but a few were hanged or broken on the wheel).[36] For the same offense committed by several soldiers on the same occasion, the nature of the punishment also varied. In 1751, for instance, three deserters were caught together. One chosen at random had his head broken in front of the troops, and the other two were sent to the galleys.[37] In time of war, general amnesties were occasionally promulgated in order to reinforce the troops.[38]

In addition to these phenomena, which set the military apart from the civilian population of European descent, the way soldiers were recruited should have made them transient and extraneous members of the local community, but many succeeded in becoming well integrated into the society. For Louisiana, the Crown's policy was to recruit men in the metropole, not in the colony. Contrary to most slaves who were destined to stay and die there, soldiers were supposed to go back to France at the end of their time. This difference increased over time with the creolization of the slave community after the quasi-ending of the slave trade from Africa in 1731: in the last decades of the French Regime, more and more slaves were natives of the colony, whereas servicemen were always born in the metropole. Their recruitment was both voluntary and coercive: they were a mixture of criminals or deserters condemned to serve in the colonies, poor wretches who tried to escape misery, and voluntary migrants who took advantage of military service to try their luck overseas. Most of them were in their late teens or early twenties and came from Paris or maritime provinces, Brittany in particular. A majority had a trade or craft of some sort, while a minority came with their wife and sometimes children.[39] Hence, the geographical and social origins of many soldiers were not so different from those of civilian migrants, indentured servants in particular.[40]

Furthermore, for economic reasons, officials tried to convince servicemen to reenlist after they had served their time by giving them an allowance, and many agreed.[41] Consequently, they remained in service for a long period of time: in 1759, 82 percent of all Louisiana soldiers had served for more than six years, the average time being nine years.[42] In 1753, Governor Louis Billouart de Kerlérec even listed a dozen sergeants, corporals, and soldiers who asked for their leave with half-pay after they had been in service for between fifteen and twenty years for the majority and thirty years for a few of them.[43] Although the compagnies franches de la Marine had from time to time to move from one outpost to another depending on the policy of the governor, they were able to create and maintain relationships with the local civilian population.[44] Some even shared the life of the urban settlers: for those who were married, their wives maintained their own households within the city (in the 1727 New Orleans census, for instance, 19 out of 361 households were headed by a woman married to a soldier); servicemen with a craft worked in their spare time for local tradesmen.[45]

Local authorities also sought to convince soldiers to establish themselves as settlers.[46] In 1750, Governor Pierre de Rigaud de Vaudreuil and Commissaire-ordonnateur Michel explained to the minister of the navy that among the new recruits that had just arrived forty-two servicemen were married and came with their wives (although one died) and children. They believed that it made more sense to place them on plantations or in the city than to leave them in the troops: "As most of these married men have some craft, and so have their wives too, we hope that, by this means and by their industry, they will get themselves out of misery as soon as they have adapted to the climate."[47] Other soldiers were very likely discharged once they got married in the colony. In the sacramental records, there were 34 marriages in which the groom was a serviceman out of a total of 441 unions from 1720 to 1733, and 36 out 227 from 1759 to 1768.[48] This rate of marriage, which was far from negligible in comparison with the military's demographic weight within the population of European descent, reveals that soldiers were not social outcasts.

These few pieces of evidence about the military career and social backgrounds of soldiers throughout the French Regime complicate their sociological portrait as young, unruly, and uprooted single men. Even though most of them remained single, the long duration of their service in Louisiana allowed them to put down roots. A minority also arrived already married or succeeded in marrying in the colony. They managed to become socially integrated and to experience some kind of social mobility. After their discharge, these integrated soldiers chose not to go back to the metropole.

Consequently, New Orleans's population was composed of many former servicemen, as local authorities acknowledged.[49] Hence, the social distance between the civil and military populations was probably less significant than in other places. This social proximity might have developed to the detriment of the military esprit de corps, but should have made it easier for civilian whites of the lower sorts and soldiers to unite and identify with each other. Their shared policing duties against slave unrest might have played the same role. The construction of whiteness among all whites of lower-class backgrounds very likely influenced the relationships between the military and the enslaved.

THE MAINTENANCE OF VERTICAL RELATIONSHIPS AT CHURCH, IN TAVERNS, AND IN THE MARKETPLACE

Soldiers and slaves had many occasions to interact in public. During the early modern period, public sociability that was not reserved to the elites took place in three main places of every city: the church, the taverns, and the marketplace. However, for both slaves and soldiers, we have very little information about their Christian religious practices. We only know that in 1751 local authorities felt obliged to rule that "All the Negroes and other slaves who go to church will hear, in the morning, the first mass, those of the countryside will be taken there by the driver of each gang, who will then take them back to their master's. And if there are some enslaved domestics who are in the habit of following their masters to the other masses, they will withdraw to the church door to wait for them, on pain of punishment."[50] Such an article means that racial segregation within the church was probably not well enforced.

Unfortunately, there are no traces of slaves' and soldiers' encounters within the church, except for one marriage and for dozens of baptismal records of enslaved infants or adults of African or Native American descent. In 1725, the priest of Saint-Louis church solemnized the only recorded mixed union found in the archives, between a free black man and the daughter of a white drummer. This military family had probably just arrived from the metropole and did not yet share the racial prejudice that was already common to most white people in the colony. They must have also been anxious to find a spouse for their daughter.[51] Other than this exceptional union, the documentation includes very few traces of interracial sexuality among enlisted men and enslaved women. The only other allusion was found in the birth certificate of an enslaved infant, born to a Native slave, in which the priest mentioned that the father was a soldier named Ratine.[52] This does not mean that servicemen did not have sex, forced or consented, with enslaved or free women of African descent; they very likely did, but they did not publicly acknowledge these furtive or long-lasting unions not formalized by the Catholic Church or the law.

More commonly, soldiers served as godfathers for slaves, and when they did the godmother was always, except for a few baptisms, a white woman, even when enslaved infants' godparents were increasingly chosen among people of African descent from the late 1740s on.[53] Some servicemen, sergeants and corporals in particular, were practicing Catholics and had close relationships with the Capuchins who did not hesitate to ask them to serve as godparents in slaves' baptisms. In so doing, soldiers behaved as benevolent and patronizing whites. Even without the solicitation of the priests, they might have voluntarily sought to serve as godfathers for people of African descent in order to mimic the elites' behavior and display their social superiority in public. For public religious practices, the military and the enslaved did not interact as if they belonged to the same social world.

While some urban dwellers attended mass on Sundays, others preferred to spend the Sabbath in taverns. Consequently, local officials continuously promulgated legislation to regulate the number of inns and taverns and their opening hours (they were supposed to remain closed on Sundays and holidays). They also tried to segregate places where alcohol was sold to the military and the civil population, and forbade the sale of alcohol to slaves and Indians.[54] Despite various measures taken to implement their prohibitions, local officials could not completely prevent the opening of clandestine taverns. Some of them were run by soldiers, because selling alcohol was a very profitable and easy trade. When the judge accused a slave named Jean, who was suspected of theft, of being drunk frequently on Sundays and holidays, the defendant admitted that "he goes with some friends to drink some pints of rum at Fabre the Swiss sergeant's and at Dabouc the soldier's who lives in a house which previously belonged to Joupillon."[55] However, the court records include many cases that took place in taverns and inns, and all of them give the impression that they were sites of an exclusively white masculine sociability.[56] Fearing that they could be caught, the enslaved probably came to authorized taverns to buy alcohol, but did not spend time there.[57] Sometimes, they did not even dare to go themselves. When François alias Cariton, who was accused of having killed another slave with whom he was fighting playfully while intoxicated, was asked by the judge where he got his alcohol—the trial took place just after officials had promulgated a new ordinance on the subject in 1751—he replied that he had not purchased any alcohol "since the prohibitions to buy some at La Carpentras, La Gautreau and at Perrot" and that he drank only what was given to him. The magistrate then asked him "if he did not use some soldiers or sailors to go to the taverns to get some drink for him, since he did not dare to go himself" or "through the means of some Negress," which François denied.[58] While it was difficult for slaves and soldiers to share a common sociability in taverns, some forms of cooperation existed between them.

The last important public space where the military and the enslaved could meet was the marketplace that was situated on the levee. The levee was a ridge of earth completed in 1724 to protect the city against the flooding of the Mississippi. It quickly became the economic and social core of New Orleans: it was used as a promenade where the urban dwellers of all backgrounds came to go for a walk, show off, have a chat and gossip; it was also the port and the site of the marketplace. In 1744, a slave named Jupiter alias Gamelle was tried for thefts committed in the city. He explained to the judge that his master, a former military officer and planter named Jean de Pradel, sent him every day from his plantation to New Orleans to sell herbs, vegetables, and milk with the help of a group of enslaved children. He was chastised if he did not sell everything he brought to the city, even if he had too many goods, and had started to steal in order to have enough money to give back to his master. Several witnesses testified that they knew Jupiter for having seen him on the levee selling his products. Among them were Antoine Jolly, a Swiss sergeant, and his wife Anne Françoise. The marketplace was an important place of contacts and exchanges among soldiers and slaves as among all social groups.[59]

The maintenance of trading relationships, however, did not necessarily reduce the social distance between them. People of African descent like Jupiter often took part in a system of pawnbroking with soldiers and other poor whites. In 1743, for instance, a free black named Jean-Baptiste, who worked as an indentured servant for a military officer heavily involved in all kinds of commercial activities, acknowledged that he had pawned shirts for 40 *livres* to a soldier because he needed money.[60] Pawnbroking was a common practice among the lower sorts in European cities. It was an operation of credit that worked through sale and repurchase: the person who needed money sold a commodity at a price below its value and committed him/herself to buy it back some time later at a price which corresponded to the capital plus interest. Since the buyer/creditor was in a position of imposing a lower price, the seller/debtor was in a position of dependency towards him/her that was not only a relationship of economic, but also of moral dependency.[61] At first sight, soldiers and slaves in New Orleans may have appeared socially close as they were often engaged in pawning relationships. However, far from representing a form of solidarity, the practice helped the military to maintain their social superiority over people of African descent, because the latter were obliged to them.

FROM COOPERATION IN THE BARRACKS AND AT THE HOSPITAL TO STREET FIGHTS

More than in the church, the taverns and the marketplace, it was in the barracks and the hospital that soldiers and slaves could engage in relations of cooperation that overlooked racial boundaries. In the metropole, the idea of building barracks instead of billeting soldiers with the local population was difficult to put into practice during the eighteenth century, but officials immediately resorted to this solution in the two colonial cities created ex nihilo in the first decades of the eighteenth century, Louisbourg and New Orleans.[62] While the Swiss troops had their own barracks built in wood very early on, it was not the case for the French soldiers before the early 1730s. As they were quickly falling into ruin, their barracks were replaced by new ones erected in bricks between 1737 and 1739. The buildings were located on the two sides of the Place d'Armes (the main square) in the center of the city. At the end of the Seven Years War, as the barracks were once again in very bad shape, most of the troops were then lodged in the new Hôtel de Mars, destined to serve as a hospital for officers, and in the new military hospital for soldiers.[63]

Besides health, the other main argument put forward by local authorities in favor of the construction of the new barracks in the late 1730s was surveillance and discipline.[64] Yet the buildings could not serve as places of confinement if circulation into and out was not controlled. Contrary to what seems to have happened in Louisbourg, where "civilians never ventured in one of the strictly military zones—the guardhouses, barracks, or parade squares," slaves could easily enter the barracks in New Orleans.[65] The enslaved children who helped Jupiter sell his baskets of herbs and vegetables often came into the buildings to sell or to offer for free their merchandise to the troops. In return, servicemen gave them pieces of bread or bacon, and let them stay all day to keep warm. Apparently, Jupiter felt that he could not do the same and did not venture into the barracks himself.[66] However, in another case, an enslaved man named Sozie entered the rooms where soldiers slept to buy some shirts. This was typical of the illicit exchange economy around clothes that developed among the lower classes, including, very often, between the military and the enslaved.[67] The transaction never took place because Sozie, who promised to give the money later, was known among the servicemen as a "rascal." Sozie then stole a blanket that he later tried to sell on the levee before being arrested.[68]

The fact that not all exchanges between soldiers and slaves took place in a spirit of cooperation and that some forms of solidarity could quickly be followed by antagonism, competition, and conflict is confirmed by another case that occurred in the Natchez fort. Usually, slaves only passed by the barracks, but the trial concerned a runaway who had been caught by Native Americans, lived temporarily in the guardhouse, and was employed at digging canals with troops. Pierre alias Jassemin was accused of having assaulted a soldier with an iron tool. He justified himself by pointing out the continual mistreatments he suffered from the serviceman when they were working together. He claimed that he had only tried to defend himself against the soldier who was trying to impede him from going to the officers to complain against the abuse. In his defense, the serviceman, who had to give his testimony lying in his bed in the New Orleans hospital, explained that the slave had no reason to be mad at him and that he and his comrades often gave him food. The two contradictory versions of the story are in fact not so incompatible: soldiers could feel some sympathy for a slave and give him some food, while also asserting their superiority by abusing him physically as they worked together.[69] It is not surprising that food and work played such a role in this conflict. Since both soldiers and slaves were underfed, they had to struggle to supplement their diet. Sometimes, this led to cooperation, sometimes to competition between them, as in the case of the murder of a young soldier by a teenage slave outside New Orleans; these two young men had fought over access to hunting grounds.[70] Moreover, asserting their superiority over slaves might have been all the more important for servicemen since they were themselves caught in a highly hierarchical relationship with officers who had the power of disciplining and punishing them.[71] Being themselves in a subordinated position, they had to oppress another social group to regain some measure of social dignity.

The importance of both status and race is also revealed by two other cases that took place at the hospital. A Company's and then king's hospital was very quickly established in New Orleans to accommodate and treat troops not only from the New Orleans garrison, but from all the colony's outposts.[72] Because they lived in a communal setting and were underfed and overworked, servicemen were extremely vulnerable to health problems. In 1750, for instance, Commissaire-ordonnateur Michel complained that there were no less than ninety to one hundred sick men at the hospital.[73] Soldiers and slaves had occasions to interact there. The Company's and then king's slaves were also treated at the hospital, although in separate rooms or buildings.[74] Most of all, over time, the French nurses who worked there were assisted, and then probably completely replaced, by enslaved women and men.[75] At one point, the king's hospital even employed a slave named Jean-Baptiste as a surgeon. According to Le Page du Pratz, he might have been the teenager first trained as a surgeon on the Company's plantation when he was the director, and who helped him look for the culprits of the 1731 slave plot.[76]

The fact that these slaves took care of sick soldiers created an intimate relationship between them, which was, however, not always strong enough to erase all racial antagonism. In 1752, a serviceman named Pierre Antoine Pochenet was convicted for having attacked several slaves in the street while he was drunk. Among them were several enslaved women from the convent and the hospital who were busy washing laundry in the Mississippi near the barracks. They had refused to wash a handkerchief for him and apparently rejected his sexual proposals. Pochenet also fought an enslaved man from the hospital who rushed up to help the women, who had cried for help. The rescuer was the enslaved surgeon Jean-Baptiste, and one of the women, very seriously injured, was his wife Louison, who also worked at the king's hospital. The soldier knew them well: although he was garrisoned in the Arkansas outpost, he had spent a long time at the New Orleans hospital when he was sick. During his trial, he admitted that "those Negresses were not his enemies, on the contrary while he was sick at the hospital they took care of him." He also said that he was "sorry for having hit Jean-Baptiste because he owes him a great deal for having saved his life several times at the hospital." However, as he was intoxicated and unable to recognize enslaved women and men he personally knew, he felt he could attack any slave who refused to execute his orders in the street. For once, the elites took the soldier's side. The Ursulines who owned Louison refused to take part in the case: they told the judge that if they could save Pochenet's life they would do it, and that they even preferred to lose their slave than to do something against charity towards their fellow human being. The serviceman was only condemned to the galleys and not to the death penalty.[77]

Alcohol was the source of another conflict between three sick soldiers who were taking a walk in front of the king's hospital and Étienne Larue, who presented himself to the judge as being "born in Senegal, from the Roman and apostolic Catholic religion, around twenty-two years old, a pilot on the ship *L'Unique* come to this colony from St. Louis on the coast of St. Domingue, the natural son of Sr. Larue, a free Negro commandant of the vessels of the Company of the Indies." During his stay in New Orleans, Larue had crossed the path of the three men on the quay near the hospital. He politely raised his hat to them in greeting. The servicemen were offended by this gesture, which failed to acknowledge the subaltern position of the free man of color and suggested that he considered himself equal to them. One of the soldiers ironically retorted with a "*Bonsoir seigneur négritte*" ("Good evening, Mi'lord Pickaninny"). The insult struck a blow at the free black man's masculinity and was intended to lower him socially, but Larue did not allow himself to be moved and replied with a "*Bonsoir seigneur jeanfoutre*" ("Good evening, Mi'lord Bugger").[78] The soldiers slapped him in the face and a fight followed. Larue's speech and behavior reveal that, because of his origins and life, he had a very high idea of himself, a far cry from how the three servicemen perceived him. They had quickly judged this unknown man of color whom they had met by accident in the streets of New Orleans. In their testimonies the three men explained the defendant's behavior by the fact that he was drunk. They implied that without alcohol Larue would not have behaved the way he did and that his pretensions toward equality could not be understood any other way. No doubt because his father served the Company of the Indies and because the plaintiffs were only soldiers, Larue was not sentenced to any corporal punishment. However, since during his arrest he had fired several shots in order not to be jailed with loaded pistols in his pockets, he had to be admonished in the Court's chamber, pay a 100-livres fine to the poor and 10 livres to the king, and have his pistols confiscated.[79]

CONCLUSION

Each of these cases of conflict among soldiers and slaves (or a free man of color), although unique and circumstantial, constitutes a highly meaningful micro-event.[80] One case in itself might not be enough to dismiss the historical thesis describing New Orleans society as an unracialized society with color-blind and unruly lower classes, but their accumulation in the historical and sociological context in which they took place demonstrates that the relationships between the military and the enslaved were made of both circumstantial cooperation and racial tensions. Daily interactions between soldiers and slaves favored solidarity in places theoretically restricted to the troops. While the king's hospital was the site of intimate relationships between the military and the enslaved because white authorities chose to rely on slave labor to take care of patients, servicemen and slaves illicitly turned the barracks into a semipublic place, subverting the strict separation of soldiers from civilians, including slaves, that the state tried to impose, because they needed to exchange goods and services away from the public eye. However, cooperation could quickly turn into conflict.

Moreover, the streets of New Orleans were the site of many public confrontations related to race in which servicemen were involved. Those incidents seemed to have multiplied from the late 1740s. It is possible that the rise in the number of slaves and the massive influx of troops in 1750 and then again in 1762 in time of war created racial tensions. As the object of social contempt, the military might have been all the more inclined to use violence against slaves in public as their only claim to social respect, honorability, and power was their virility as men of war. They were also in competition with enslaved men for the sexual favors of black women. The violence of non-slaveholders, soldiers in particular, against slaves was such that local authorities felt compelled to legislate on the subject and to distinguish it from vigilantism. In their 1751 ruling, they added one last article that sought to curb the propensity all whites displayed for punishing slaves even when they did not belong to them:

> We have just exposed all the obligations and the deference that negroes need to show towards whites, masters in particular. It is a good thing to instruct the public that this does not apply to everybody indiscriminately. A private individual, a soldier or anyone else, does not have the power to abuse a negro who has done nothing to him and is not disrespectful towards him. He can arrest him in some circumstances and ask for justice, as the negro is only subjected to that of his master and that of the police. Consequently, and following the king's orders, we forbid anyone to take these liberties, on pain of punishment chosen according to what the cases require.[81]

The inclusion of this article had been motivated by a conflict between a rich planter and soldiers who had taken revenge against him by attacking one of his most valued enslaved laborers.[82] It sought to resolve the tensions between the necessary solidarity among all whites on which white hegemony was based and the defense of property owners.

The social diversity that characterized the urban milieu, the demographic and social importance of male non-slaveholders, including troops, among whites in particular, complicated the way the system of racial slavery worked in the city in comparison with on plantations. When slaves and white non-slaveholders interacted in the public space, three or four parties were really involved in the relationship because behind every slave there was a master, and local authorities were never far away. The interests of the state, of the slave owners, and of the non-slaveholders could contradict one another. When local authorities and the elite tried to subjugate both the military and the enslaved and to defend the rights of property owners, they undermined the cohesion of the white community. As soldiers were deprived of the attributes that made the elite's authority—marriage, property and mastery over other human beings—, they also put into tensions competitive models of white masculinity.[83] Yet, although all whites did not benefit in the same way from the system of racial slavery and did not have the same individual motivations and interests, they all shared the same commitment to the perpetuation of the racial order. They may have disagreed on the way white supremacy should be achieved, but they all sought to enforce the racial divide in the public space. While the historiography often emphasizes the role of officials and elite in the racialization of slave societies, the study of the interactions between soldiers and slaves demonstrates that racial formation was both a top-down and a bottom-up phenomenon.

NOTES

1. Gwendolyn Midlo Hall, *Africans in Colonial Louisiana: The Development of Afro-Creole Culture in the Eighteenth Century* (Baton Rouge: Louisiana State University Press, 1992), 96–118.

2. *The History of Louisiana or of the Western Parts of Virginia and Carolina . . . Translated from the French of M. Le Page Du Pratz, . . . A new Edition* (London: T. Becket, 1774), 77.

3. The title of Philip Morgan's comparative history between the slave systems of the Chesapeake and the Lowcountry is typical of this long-lasting historiographical trend emphasizing the slaves' perspective. Philip Morgan, *Slave Counterpoint: Black Culture in the Eighteenth-Century Chesapeake and Lowcountry* (Chapel Hill: University of North Carolina Press, 1998). See also Cécile Vidal, "Des marges au centre: L'esclavage dans l'historiographie nord-américaine de la période coloniale," in Cécile Vidal and François-Joseph Ruggiu, eds., *Sociétés, colonisations et esclavages dans le monde atlantique moderne: Historiographie des sociétés américaines des XVIe–XIXe siècles* (Bécherel: Les Perséides, 2009), 191–241.

4. Philip D. Morgan, "British Encounters with Africans and African-Americans circa 1600–1780," in Bernard Bailyn and Philip D. Morgan, eds., *Strangers within the Realm: Cultural Margins of the First British Empire* (Chapel Hill: University of North Carolina Press, 1991), 157–219.

5. Daniel Roche, *La France des Lumières* (Paris: Fayard, 1993), 595.

6. Isaac Joseph, *La ville sans qualités* (La Tour d'Aigues: Éditions de l'Aube, 1998).

7. I borrow the expression from Daniel Roche, who used it for clothing and material culture, but it can be extended to all sorts of symbolic expressions of social distinction. Daniel Roche, *La culture des apparences: Une histoire du vêtement, XVIIe–XVIIIe siècle* (Paris: Fayard, 1989).

8. Erving Goffman, *Relations in Public: Microstudies of the Public Order* (New York: Basic Books, 1971).

9. Hall, *Africans in Colonial Louisiana,* 19–27, 146–79; Shannon Lee Dawdy, *Building the Devil's Empire: French Colonial New Orleans* (Chicago: University of Chicago Press, 2008), 93, 147–50, 174–75, 185–86, 200–213, 287n40; Daniel H. Usner Jr., *Indians, Settlers, and Slaves in a Frontier Exchange Economy: The Lower Mississippi Valley before 1783* (Chapel Hill: University of North Carolina Press, 1992), 219–43.

10. For a comprehensive study of the process of racialization in French New Orleans, see Cécile Vidal, *Caribbean New Orleans: Empire, Race, and the Making of a Slave Society* (Chapel Hill: University of North Carolina Press, 2019).

11. For general studies on slaves and slavery, in addition to Hall, see also Thomas N. Ingersoll, *Mammon and Manon in Early New Orleans: The First Slave Society in the Deep South, 1718–1819* (Knoxville: University of Tennessee Press, 1999); Jennifer M. Spear, *Race, Sex, and Social Order in Early New Orleans* (Baltimore: Johns Hopkins University Press, 2009).

12. Archives Nationales d'Outre-mer (hereafter ANOM) COL G1 464, "Recensement général de la ville de la Nvelle Orléans [. . .] fait au mois de janvier 1732"; Archivo General de Indias, Audiencia de Sto Domingo, Luisiana y Florida, Años 1766 a 1770, 2595–589, "Recensement général 1763"; Paul Lachance, "The Growth of the Free and Slave Populations of French Colonial Louisiana," in Bradley G. Bond, ed., *French Colonial Louisiana and the Atlantic World* (Baton Rouge: Louisiana State University Press, 2005), 204–43.

13. ANOM COL C13A 35, f. 328v, July 20, 1750, Michel to the Minister.

14. René Chartrand, "The Troops of French Louisiana, 1699–1769," *Military Collector and Historian* 25, no. 2 (1973): 58–65; S. G. Lemann, "The Problem of Founding a Viable Colony: The Military in Early French Louisiana," in J. J. Cooke, ed., *Proceedings of the Sixth and Seventh Annual Meetings of the French Colonial Historical Society, 1980–1981* (Washington: University Press of America, 1982), 27–35; Bernard Lugan, *Histoire de la Louisiane française, 1682–1804* (Paris: Perrin, 1994), 165–81, 244–49; Carl A. Brasseaux, *France's Forgotten Legion, A CD-ROM Publication. Service Records of French Military and Administrative Personnel Stationed in the Mississippi Valley and Gulf Coast Region, 1699–1769* (Baton Rouge: Louisiana State University Press, 2000); Arnaud Balvay, *L'épée et la plume: Amérindiens et soldats des troupes de la marine en Louisiane et au Pays d'en Haut (1693–1763)* (Sillery: Presses de l'Université Laval, 2006).

15. ANOM COL D2C 51, f. 81–83, December 2, 1731, "Compagnies détachées de la Marine, garnison de la Nvelle Orléans"; ANOM COL D2C 51, f. 92–95r, May 4, 1732, "La Louisiane, revue de mai 1732, Garnison de la Nvelle Orléans."

16. ANOM COL D2C 52, f. 88, "Revue générale des Compagnies franches de la Marine en garnison à La Nouvelle-Orléans durant l'année 1759."

17. ANOM COL C13A 42, f. 118v–119r, June 23, 1760, Rochemore to the Minister.

18. David Hardcastle, "Swiss Mercenary Soldiers in the Service of France in Louisiana," in Alf A. Heggoy and James J. Cooke, eds., *Proceedings of the Fourth Meeting of the French Colonial Historical Society, April 6–8, 1978* (Washington, DC: University Press of America, 1979), 82–91; Khalil Saadani, *La Louisiane française dans l'impasse 1731–1743* (Paris: L'Harmattan, 2008), 200–201.

19. ANOM COL C13A 15, f. 160rv, July 16, 1732, Salmon to the Minister.

20. ANOM COL C13A 16, f. 275, July 25, 1733, Bienville to the Minister.

21. ANOM COL C13A 35, f. 207v–209r, May 18, 1751, Michel to the Minister.

22. ANOM COL C13A 13, f. 8–25, December 5, 1731, Périer and Salmon to the Minister.

23. Records of the Superior Council of Louisiana (hereafter RSCL) 1764/07/10/02, 1764/07/13/01, 1764/07/21/02.

24. ANOM COL C13A 43, f. 378r–379r, August 15, 1763, "Plan pour rendre la Louisiane la plus riche et la plus puissante de toutes les colonies françaises, par Redon de Rassac." For other testimonies about the exploitation of soldiers by their officers, see ANOM COL C13A 13, f. 112r, December 1, 1731, Salmon to the Minister; RSCL 1743/06/18/01; Dumont de Montigny, *Regards sur le monde atlantique, 1715–1747* (Sillery: Septentrion, 2008), 143–44.

25. ANOM COL C13A 9, f. 324r, January 5, 1726, Deliberations of the Council. Officers also used soldiers in their own private service.

26. Roland C. McConnell, *Negro Troops of Antebellum Louisiana: A History of the Battalion of Free Men of Color* (Baton Rouge: Louisiana State University Press, 1968), 16–17; Roland C. McConnell, "Louisiana's Black Military History, 1729–1865," in Robert R. Macdonald, John R. Kemp, and Edward F. Haas, eds., *Louisiana's Black Heritage* (New Orleans: Louisiana State Museum, 1979), 32–62.

27. RSCL 1739/12/21/01.

28. See, for instance, ANOM COL C13A 13, f. 110v, December 1, 1731, Salmon to the Minister; ANOM COL C13A 17, f. 23, February 1, 1733, Salmon to the Minister.

29. ANOM COL A 23, f. 36v, "Ordonnance des directeurs de la Compagnie du 29 août 1722 qui défend d'acheter des hardes et des armes des soldats"; RSCL 1744/03/05/01.

30. ANOM COL C13A 13, f. 112, December 1, 1731, Salmon to the Minister; ANOM COL C13A 15, f. 111v, January 15, 1731, Salmon to the Minister; ANOM COL C13A 28, f. 109–111r, July 20, 1743, Salmon to the Minister.

31. For the trial of a soldier for insubordination because he violently protested against the bad quality of the bread in his ration, see RSCL 1745/07/12/01, 1745/07/13/01, 1745/07/13/02, 1745/07/13/03, 1745/07/13/04, 1745/07/13/05, 1745/07/13/06, 1745/07/13/07, 1745/07/13/08, 1745/07/14/01, 1745/07/14/02.

32. ANOM COL C13A 42, f. 128v, July 12, 1760, Rochemore to the Minister.

33. ANOM COL D2C 54, 1744–1770, "Rôle général des troupes de la Louisiane." See also RSCL 1745/07/12/01, 1745/07/13/01, 1745/07/13/02, 1745/07/13/03, 1745/07/13/04, 1745/07/13/05, 1745/07/13/06, 1745/07/13/07, 1745/07/13/08, 1745/07/14/01, 1745/07/14/02; ANOM COL C13A 37, f. 97–99r, September 18, 1753, Kerlérec to the Minister; ANOM COL C13A 38, f. 69–70v,

June 21, 1754, Kerlérec to the Minister; ANOM COL 38, f. 168–169, July 15, 1754, D'Auberville to the Minister.

34. ANOM COL D2C 54, 1744–1770, "Rôle général des troupes de la Louisiane"; André Corvisier, *L'armée française, de la fin du XVIIe siècle au Ministère de Choiseul* (Paris: Presses universitaires de France, 1964), 693, 738; Boris Lesueur, *Les troupes coloniales d'Ancien Régime: Fidelitate per Mare et Terras* (Paris: SPM, coll. Kronos, 2014), 194–95, 197, 208; André Lachance, "La désertion et les soldats déserteurs au Canada dans la première moitié du XVIIIe siècle," *Revue de l'Université d'Ottawa* 47, no. 1–2 (1977): 151–61.

35. RSCL 1739/10/10/01, 1765/09/09/02, #11.

36. ANOM COL D2C 54, 1744–1770, "Rôle général des troupes de la Louisiane."

37. ANOM COL C13A 35, f. 205–210r, May 18, 1751, Michel to the Minister.

38. ANOM COL C13A 31, f. 30–32, March 18, 1747, Vaudreuil to the Minister; Vaudreuil Papers L0150, November 11, 1748, Maurepas to Vaudreuil; ANOM COL F3 243, f. 185–86, April 16, 1760, "Ordonnance portant amnistie pour les soldats déserteurs."

39. Corvisier, *L'armée française,* 720, 738; Ingersoll, *Mammon and Manon in Early New Orleans,* 14–16; Lesueur, *Les troupes coloniales d'Ancien Régime,* 165–69.

40. Marcel Giraud, *Histoire de la Louisiane française* (Paris: Presses universitaires de France, 1966–1974), III, 154–283, IV, 120–95.

41. ANOM COL D2C 51, f. 137 (July 10, 1738), f. 163 (June 25, 1738), f. 167–68, f. 169, f. 180 (June 22), various lists of soldiers who reenlisted.

42. Lesueur, *Les troupes coloniales d'Ancien Régime,* 198.

43. ANOM COL D2C 51, f. 245, November 25, 1753, "Signalement des sergents, caporaux et soldats hors d'état de service et qui demandent la demi-solde."

44. On the policy of moving companies between outposts, see Cécile Vidal, "Les implantations françaises au Pays des Illinois au XVIIIe siècle," PhD diss. (Paris: EHESS, 1995), 169–73.

45. ANOM COL G1 464, "Recensement général des habitants [. . .] de la Nouvelle Orléans qui s'y sont trouvés au 1er juillet 1727." A judicial case for suicide shows that a chair turner employed a Swiss soldier in his workshop. ANOM COL F3 242, f. 265–90, May 28, 1738, "Audience criminelle du Conseil Supérieur de la province de Louisiane."

46. On this policy of military peopling, see Vidal, "Les implantations françaises au Pays des Illinois au XVIIIe siècle," 173–77.

47. ANOM COL C13A 35, f. 56–59r, August 20, 1750, Vaudreuil and Michel to the Minister.

48. St. Louis Cathedral, Baptisms/Marriages/Funerals, Vol. A; Baptisms/Marriages, Whites/Free People of color/Slaves, Vol. IV and V; Marriages, Vol. A and B.

49. ANOM COL C13A 12, f. 329v, August 1, 1730, Périer to Ory; ANOM COL C13A 24, f. 168–69, October 10, 1739, Salmon to the Minister.

50. ANOM COL F3 243, f. 84–89, "Observations sur le règlement de police de Ms. de Vaudreuil et Michel du 6 mars 1751, publié et affiché à la Louisiane les 28 février et 1er mars."

51. St. Louis Cathedral, Marriages, Vol. A, 06/30/1725.

52. St. Louis Cathedral, Baptisms, Whites/Free People of Color/Slaves, Vol. III, Part II, 05/02/1757.

53. St. Louis Cathedral, Baptisms, Whites/Free People of Color/Slaves, Vol II and III, 12/05/1744, 04/06/1744, 26/07/1744, ??/07/1744, 23/01/1746, 14/08/1746, 31/08/1746, 11/05/1747, 18/11/1747, 03/03/1748, 05/05/1748, 01/06/1748, 23/10/1748, 17/11/1748, 07/07/1749, 26/09/1749, 23/11/1749, 01/12/1750, 07/03/1751, 12/04/1751, 07/05/1752, 22/10/1752, 16/03/1754, 05/01/1758, 06/08/1758, 13/10/1758; St. Louis Cathedral, Baptisms/Marriages, Whites/Free People of Color/Slaves, Vols. IV, V, and VI, 11/08/1760, 16/08/1761, 01/02/1763, 07/01/1764, 27/06/1765, 02/03/1766, 19/09/1768. On slaves' evangelization, see Emily Clark and Virginia Meacham Gould, "The Feminine Face of Afro-Catholicism in New Orleans, 1727–1852," *William and Mary Quarterly* 59, no. 2 (2002): 409–48.

54. RSCL 1725/10/05/01, 1728/06/05/01, 1746/08/24/01; ANOM COL A 23, f. 58 (April 11, 1725), f. 79v–80 (October 5, 1726), f. 84 (March 29, 1727), f. 111v (March 26, 1733), f. 114v (December 19, 1733), f. 122 (December 7, 1736), f. 125v–6 (January 7, 1741), f. 151v–2, (August 19, 1746), various rulings and ordinances promulgated by the Superior Council or by the governor and/or commissaire-ordonnateur about the sale of alcohol and the running of taverns.

55. RSCL 1744/02/22/02.

56. RSCL 1725/11/01/01, 1725/12/21/01, 1737/07/24/01, 1740/11/07/01, 1743/09/16/01, 1747/08/24/01; 1767/11/06/01, 1767/11/06/02, 1767/11/08/01, 1767/11/09/02.

57. RSCL 1766/11/14/02.

58. RSCL 1751/04/14/01.

59. RSCL 1743/11/30/01, 1744/01/25/01, 1740/02/15/03, 1744/02/26/01, 1744/02/29/01, 1744/03/02/01, 1744/03/03/01, 1744/03/05/01, 1744/03/07/02, 1744/03/11/01, 1744/03/11/02, 1744/03/12/01, 1744/03/12/02, 1744/03/13/01, 1744/03/14/01, 1744/03/14/02, 1744/03/16/01, 1744/03/17/01, 1744/03/18/01, 1744/03/18/02, 1744/03/10/01, 1744/03/21/01, 1744/03/21/02, 1744/03/21/03, 1744/03/21/04, 1744/03/21/05, 1744/03/23/01, 1744/03/24/01, 1744/10/03/01.

60. RSCL 1743/08/19/03.

61. Laurence Fontaine, *L'économie morale: Pauvreté, crédit et confiance dans l'Europe pré-industrielle* (Paris: Gallimard, nrf essais, 2008), 101–33.

62. On the history of barracks in the metropole, see François Dallemagne, *Les casernes françaises* (Paris: Picard, 1990).

63. ANOM COL 4DFC 74A (December 24, 1726), C78C (March 30, 1729), 79C (March 30, 1729), C77B (March 31, 1729), 95bsB (July 25, 1734); ANOM COL F3 290, 29 (October 26, 1732), 30 (October 26, 1734), various maps or drawings of the barracks; ANOM COL C13A 7, f. 22–23 and 34, March 8, 1724, La Chaise to the Company's Directors; Historic New Orleans Collection (hereafter HNOC), "Plan de La Nouvelle Orléans telle qu'elle était le 1er janvier 1732"; ANOM COL C13C 1, f. 98r, "Mémoire pour servir à l'établissement de la Louisiane"; ANOM COL C13A 46, f. 47–49, "Inventaire précis des emplacements, terrains et bâtiments appartenant au roi en cette ville de La Nouvelle-Orléans, joint à la lettre de M. Foucault du 2 avril 1766."

64. ANOM COL C13A 16, f. 50–91v, May 12, 1733, Bienville and Salmon to the Minister.

65. For the Louisbourg's barracks, see A. J. B. Johnston, *Control and Order in French Colonial Louisbourg* (East Lansing: Michigan State University Press, 2001), 174.

66. RSCL 1744/04/24/01.

67. Sophie White, "Slaves and Poor Whites' Informal Economies in an Atlantic Context," in Cécile Vidal, ed., *Louisiana: Crossroads of the Atlantic World* (Philadelphia: University of Pennsylvania Press, 2013), 87–102.

68. RSCL 1764/07/17/01, 1764/07/17/02, 1764/07/18/02, 1764/07/19/01, 1764/07/19/02, 1764/07/20/01, 1764/07/28/01, 1764/07/28/02, 1764/07/28/06, 1764/07/28/07.

69. RSCL 1742/01/09/04, 1742/01/09/05, 1742/01/13/01, 1742/01/14/02, 1742/01/14/05, 1742/01/16/01, 1472/01/16/03, 1742/01/16/04, 1742/01/16/06, 1742/01/20/01, 1742/01/20/02, 1742/01/20/03.

70. RSCL 1748/01/03/07, 1748/01/04/01, 1748/01/05/01, 1748/01/05/02, 1748/01/05/03, 1748/01/05/04, 1748/01/05/05, 1748/01/05/06, 1748/01/05/07, 1748/01/05/08, 1748/01/05/09, 1748/01/06/01, 1748/01/06/02, 1748/01/08/01, 1748/01/08/01, 1748/01/08/02, 1748/01/08/03, 1748/01/08/04, 1748/01/08/05, 1748/01/08/06, 1748/01/10/01, 1748/01/10/02, 1748/01/10/03, 1748/01/10/04.

71. For a judicial case showing how harsh this discipline was, see RSCL 1747/04/19/02, 1747/04/20/01, 1747/04/20/02, 1747/04/20/03, 1747/04/21/01, 1747/04/21/02, 1747/04/22/01, 1747/04/22/02, ND # 116 April 20, 1747; ANOM COL C13A 31, f. 93, May 16, 1747, Vaudreuil to the Minister.

72. Marcel Giraud, *A History of French Louisiana* (Baton Rouge: Louisiana State University Press, 1991), V, 216–23, 250, 304–5, 310, 438.

73. ANOM COL C13A 35, f. 328, July 20, 1750, Michel to the Minister.

74. ANOM COL F3 242, f. 56–57, July 25, 1725, "Ordonnance pour les nègres domestiques de la Compagnie"; ANOM COL C13A 28, f. 343–45, December 31, 1744, "Marché avec les Dames religieuses ursulines pour les malades de l'Hôpital du roi à La Nouvelle-Orléans"; HNOC, "Relation de Voyage de la Louisianne ou Nouv^lle^ France fait par le Sr CAILLOT en l'année 1730," 103; ANOM COL C13A 46, f. 131–278, 1766, "Inventaire général et estimation de toute l'artillerie, armes, munitions, effets, magasins, hôpitaux, bâtiments de mer appartenant à sa majesté très chrétienne dans la colonie de la Louisiane."

75. ANOM COL G1 464, "Recensement général [. . .] au premier janvier 1726"; ANOM COL G1 464, "Recensement général de la ville de la Nvelle Orléans [. . .] fait au mois de janvier 1732"; ANOM COL C13A 28, f. 346–51, December 31, 1744, "Inventaire général de tous les meubles et ustensiles appartenant à l'hôpital du roi à La Nouvelle-Orléans"; ANOM COL C13A 29, f. 116–118r, October 17, 1745, Lenormant to the Minister; RSCL 1765/10/30/01; ANOM COL C13A 42, f. 66–67, "État des nègres, négresses, négrillons et négrittes du roi au 1er janvier 1760."

76. Antoine-Simon Le Page du Pratz, *Histoire de la Louisiane* (Paris: De Bure l'aîné, la veuve Delaguette, Lambert, 1758), III, 227–28, 306–8.

77. RSCL 1752/06/08/01, 1752/06/08/02, 1752/06/12/01, 1752/06/12/02, 1752/06/13/01, 1752/06/12/05, 1752/06/13/02, 1752/06/17/01, 1752/06/17/02, 1752/06/19/01, 1752/06/20/01, 1752/06/26/01, 1752/06/26/02, 1752/06/28/01; ANOM COL C13A 36, f. 237, January 27, 1752, Michel to the Minister.

78. Shannon Lee Dawdy, "'La ville sauvage': Enlightened Colonialism and Creole Improvisation in New Orleans, 1699–1769," PhD diss., University of Michigan, Ann Arbor, 2003), 300.

79. RSCL 1747/05/05/01, 1747/05/05/02, 1747/05/06/04, 1747/05/06/07, 1747/05/18/01, 1747/05/18/02, 1747/05/18/03, 1747/05/18/04, 1747/05/19/05, 1747/05/19/06.

80. Arlette Farge, *Le goût de l'archive* (Paris: Seuil, 1989), 97–105.

81. ANOM COL C13A 35, f. 50r–51v, February 28–March 1st, 1751, "Règlement sur la police pour la province de la Louisiane," article 30.

82. ANOM COL 34, f. 333v–343v, September 29, 1750, Michel to the Minister.

83. On competitive models of masculinity in colonial and slave societies, see Thomas A Foster, Mary Beth Norton, and Toby L. Ditz, eds., *New Men: Manliness in Early America* (New York: New York University Press, 2011).

II
ELUSIVE CITIZENSHIP

THE PRISON OF SAINT-LOUIS

French Expansion, Social Control, and the Early Development of the Penitentiary Institution in Senegal, circa 1834–1895

IBRA SENE

Saint-Louis has attracted attention among historians of French colonialism for many valid reasons. The history of the city is critical to our understanding of various aspects of the colonial and postcolonial history of Senegal. This literature has provided us with an invaluable insight into the complex operation of the colonial society in Saint-Louis, by focusing, among other things, on famous French colonial administrators, the elite *originaires,* particularly the *métis,* other affluent Africans, and various political, social, and religious aspects of the history of the city.[1] However, this scholarship has routinely overlooked some important actors in this history, namely the socially marginalized groups in the city. Yet, the ways in which these groups developed, their respective historical trajectories, the manner in which the colonizers dealt with them, and their impact on the evolution of the colonial project are all factors that are critical in our understanding of the history of Saint-Louis and the role the city played in the colony of Senegal and the French colonial domain in West Africa.

This essay addresses the early development of the penitentiary institution in Senegal as a way to shed light on this poorly documented facet of the history of French colonization. Through the history of the prison of Saint-Louis, this essay tries to uncover the different stages of the formation of the penitentiary, from the 1830s to the 1890s. It argues that imprisonment was the keystone of the penal system, and that the development of the penitentiary was a byproduct of and a crucially important tool for the colonial enterprise. The history of imprisonment, like that of the struggles over citizenship and the abolition of slavery, is the history of many competing and conflicting expressions of belonging and allegiance. Although shaped by the local contexts where they took root, these expressions of belonging and allegiance had far-reaching implications that resonated across the French Empire.[2] In this essay, I first analyze the evolution of colonial imprisonment in Senegal in light of the larger historiography of colonialism and penal institutions around the world. Then, I turn to the different attempts at organizing colonial imprisonment by the colonial authorities based both in Paris and in Saint-Louis. Finally, I focus my attention on the organization and operation of the prison of Saint-Louis, which illustrates the narrowly defined mission of colonial imprisonment.

MAKING SENSE OF THE DEVELOPMENT OF IMPRISONMENT IN COLONIAL SENEGAL

Beginning in the late eighteenth to early nineteenth century, imprisonment became the dominant form of punishment in Western Europe and the New World, with the theoretical mission of transforming the deviant into a law-abiding citizen by forcing him or her to compensate the community for their wrongdoing. This punishment was supposed to be proportionate to the deviant acts committed. According to Emile Durkheim, punishment is a social institution that offsets the moral harm caused by the offender to others, restores trust between the two parties, and, as a consequence, maintains the solidarity that is vital to the harmony of any given human society. For Durkheim, the birth of the prison in Europe and the New World was a response to the breakdown of the traditional methods of punishment that were no longer operational for society.[3]

David Rothman, in his book *The Discovery of the Asylum,* makes a similar point about the origins of the American prison system. He argues that the revolution that accompanied the Jacksonian era challenged the Calvinist perception of criminality, insanity, delinquency, and poverty and the confidence in the disciplining power of a hierarchical society. This situation triggered, among intellectuals and civil society groups, a debate over the best formula for social control, the outcome of which informed the emergence of the current American penitentiary institution.[4] In *Discipline and Punish,* Michel Foucault posits that the birth of the modern prison was not a wholesale humanitarian crusade for the sake of the deviant, but rather an extension of the control of the bourgeoisie over society. Nevertheless, he challenges judicial violence and suggests that the ultimate goal of justice should not be to take revenge, but to punish in order to reform the deviant.[5]

In nineteenth-century Senegal, instead of the Western model of punishment that theoretically aimed at reforming the deviant for their own good and that of society as a whole, imprisonment pursued a different mission. The penitentiary institution followed in the path left by the French military conquest and was one of the central pillars of the colonial enterprise. The exploitative and destructive nature of the conquest, through repressive institutions such as forced labor and special legal instruments like the *Code de l'Indigénat*, were core elements of colonization and deeply influenced imprisonment.

Marc Ferro likens the methods of French colonialism to totalitarianism, and Anne Applebaum suggests that both colonial regimes and totalitarian regimes "establish a social ideal, and then seek to eliminate or reeducate everyone who doesn't fit into it."[6] Peter Zinoman makes a similar suggestion in his book *The Colonial Bastille: A History of Imprisonment in Vietnam, 1862–1940*. He observes that "colonial officials tended to conceptualize imprisonment in terms of repression rather than rehabilitation" and that this "repressive orientation launched the colonial prison on an institutional trajectory that would continue to influence its development until the end of the colonial era."[7] All these conceptions were quite similar to what the French did with the penitentiary institution in colonial Senegal. It was an important tool in the repression of the colonized populations to impose the model of society that the French sought to implement in their colonies.[8]

A number of factors would get in the way of this plan, however, because the colonizers lacked the financial means and human resources required. Most importantly, the colonized populations never accepted the institution, never trusted it, and permanently fought against it. Within the prison space, detainees developed a subculture that the French could not apprehend, which would deeply impact the penitentiary institution. Lauren Benton captures nicely how the tensions that divided colonizers and colonized people shaped many legal systems around the world.[9] Specifically about colonial Africa, Florence Bernault's edited volume, *A History of Prison and Confinement in Africa*,[10] is probably the first work to even consider the question of punishment at the continental level. Among other studies, Caroline Elkins's

Imperial Reckoning: The Untold Story of Britain's Gulag in Kenya and David M. Anderson's *Histories of the Hanged: Britain's Dirty War in Kenya and the End of Empire* provide good accounts of colonial punishment in East Africa.[11]

Donald Fyson's important work, synthesized in his book *Magistrats, police et société: La Justice criminelle ordinaire au Québec et au Bas-Canada (1764–1837),* touches on the relationships between the state, law, and the wider colonial society in French Canada.[12] The various conflicts over the meaning and legitimacy of the fledgling judiciary certainly echo the situation in the early stages of the exploitation of other French territories. In New Orleans, the French sent criminals, incarcerated debtors, and even prostitutes released from prison to help get the settlement off the ground. Although this aspect of French colonization in the Americas is not well documented, we know a little bit more about the history of French penal colonies. Stephen Toth's *Beyond Papillon: The French Overseas Penal Colonies, 1854–1952* is a history of the *bagne* in which he questions Foucault and suggests that physical violence, instead of receding, was a major factor of colonial punishment. However, Toth neglects to show that an important number of prisoners from Africa were also sent to these penal colonies and that the prison of Saint-Louis was a major transit point for prisoners bound for French Guyana or New Caledonia.[13]

In Senegal, a number of studies were produced by the Groupe d'Etudes et de Recherches sur la Marginalité et l'Exclusion au Sénégal (GERMES), which focus on various aspects of the colonial prison system, including the handling of juvenile delinquents, the imprisonment of women, and prison guards, to name just a few examples.[14]

Saint-Louis was the birthplace of, and launchpad for, the French colonial enterprise in West Africa. From 1815, the French gradually regained possession of a number of trading posts along the Atlantic coast and the Senegal River, which they had lost to the British in previous years. Recaptured in 1817, Saint-Louis exhibited a socioeconomic and political development that would profoundly influence French colonial expansion in Senegal, but also the future development of the penitentiary institution. The export trade in gum arabic in the city, dominated by French merchants, consistently expanded between 1817 and 1830, making 12 million francs a year in assets. It is believed that about 3,000 people, both French and African, partook in this booming activity in one way or another.[15] From Saint-Louis, the gum arabic business expanded gradually to the satellite trading posts along the Senegal River valley.[16] From barely 6,000 inhabitants in 1817, Saint-Louis's population grew to 13,000 inhabitants in less than twenty years. At the time, Gorée had only 2,500 inhabitants, and the military post of Dakar was not yet established. Obviously, Saint-Louis was already set to become the capital of a vast colonial domain, which is why the French worked to provide the city with the institutional and administrative infrastructure required of its status.[17]

Starting in the 1820s, the French began to construct a legal apparatus in the colony. There were a growing number of regulations dealing with trade, slavery, urban planning, and the like. The prison of Saint-Louis appears in the archives in the early 1830s. It consisted then of a row of small huts in the first floor of the Fort of Saint-Louis, until another detention facility was built in 1863. The prison held both civilian and military prisoners who were already convicted or had been indicted and were awaiting trial, a sizable population in the colonial capital. The new facility built in 1863 was both the largest and most secure of Senegal's prisons, which made it the destination for the most difficult prisoners from a large catchment area that reached beyond the capital. As a consequence of these factors, the prison at Saint-Louis had the lion's share of the country's prison population at any given time.

The most important primary sources for documenting the establishment and operation of the prison of Saint-Louis are the French colonial records, colonial newspapers, and other colonial publications. These primary sources give a wide range of perspectives on colonial society from different vantage points. There are abundant and largely untapped such resources in the Archives du Sénégal in Dakar, Senegal, especially the Sous-Série 3 F of the Fonds Sénégal Ancien. It contains all the archives related to the prisons in colonial Senegal.[18] These archives also include various administrative reports and correspondence between the prison manager and the colonial authorities, the governor of Senegal, or the governor-general of French West Africa. There are also many letters that prisoners wrote to their families that were intercepted by the administration. These research materials are crucial for understanding the evolution of the penitentiary system, the ways in which French administrators conceived of it, as well as the day-to-day operation of the prison of Saint-Louis. There are also resources in the Sous-Série 3 E: Conseil de Gouvernement et d'Administration, which contains the deliberations of the governor of Senegal's advisory board. This essay also draws material from the Centre des Archives d'Outre-mer, in Aix-en-Provence, France, especially the Série Sénégal et Dépendances, which was important for documenting the period before the 1860s. Woven together, these sources provide good insight into how the penitentiary institution evolved, from about 1834 to roughly 1895.

THE MÉTROPOLE, THE COLONY, AND PRISON REFORM

In the nineteenth century, as the French pushed more forcefully for territorial occupation, they inevitably clashed with a number of social, political, and economic forces opposed to the colonial enterprise. The heavy use of the military and the security apparatus as well as the establishment of a judiciary system were a direct consequence of the pressing need for control over the poorly understood environment that came with conquest. In this context, different types of punishments were used against Africans in the settlement of Saint-Louis and its satellite trading posts. Such punishments included flogging, banishment, deportation, and enslavement. As Saint-Louis attracted more and more people from the hinterland due to the trade boom, a number of security concerns arose, such as illegal slave trading, thefts, and fights.[19] In 1822, a royal ordinance established the Tribunal of First Instance of Saint-Louis. This was one of the first steps in the building of a penal system that could handle these emerging challenges.[20]

With their desire to transform Ndar[21] into Saint-Louis, a French city, the colonizers also came up with new urban planning policies, which a large majority of the population would not adopt willingly. In fact, many of the new regulations went against established cultural practices and beliefs that guided the daily lives of the African population of Saint-Louis. During Le Baron Roger's tenure as governor of Senegal, from 1821 to 1823, it was required that families clean up the surroundings of their houses on a weekly basis. If they did not do so, they would receive a fine of 2.55 francs and two to eight days of imprisonment.[22] It was also against the law to breed pigs in houses, have one's domestic animals in the streets, or slaughter animals by oneself. Some members of the Conseil de Gouvernement et d'Administration, the advisory board for the governor, had to lobby the administration for the repeal of these regulations, to allow Muslims to celebrate the annual holiday of the sacrifice without risking punishment.[23]

Also, Governor Roger put forth a set of guidelines for many African ceremonies, gatherings, and cultural practices in Saint-Louis. Any activity after eight o'clock in the evening involving drumming required special authorization from his office.[24] In the same vein, pounding millet on a mortar at night, between nine o'clock and three o'clock, and clapping or singing in the streets of Saint-Louis after eight o'clock, were unlawful in the city. The police were in charge of the enforcement of these regulations, and the punishment for those who broke them was imprisonment.[25]

Although a very delicate issue at the time, imprisonment began to play an important role in the handling of slavery. During the first half of the nineteenth century, many people in Saint-Louis and the other trading posts, including some colonial administrators, were still trading slaves, using servile labor for their personal needs, or renting slaves out for money. Governor Bouët Willaumez outlawed the trade in Saint-Louis in 1844, authorizing it only in a few places such as Galam and its immediate surroundings in the upper Senegal River valley. Among other things, this order mandated a punishment of up to five days in prison and a fine of fifteen francs for anyone caught selling or buying slaves. The large outcry over this decision and the strong opposition from people who continued to benefit from slavery made it difficult to enforce the governor's order.[26] Despite this opposition, slavery would eventually disappear in Saint-Louis. In the process, many slaves were freed, 65 percent of whom were children under fifteen years of age and women.[27]

Some of these freed slaves joined a diverse contingent of homeless people, beggars, prostitutes, and strangers who started to generate concerns for the administration about its security. Imprisonment primarily targeted these marginal people in the early years of the penitentiary institution. Beggars and homeless people caught in the streets of Saint-Louis were sentenced to three to six months in prison, employed by the colonial administration in special disciplinary workshops, or forced to perform various types of public works under police surveillance. From that time onward, putting people in jail to use them as free labor would become one of the main goals of imprisonment. An order issued in 1864 allowed the mayor of Saint-Louis to arrest and sentence to a maximum of fifteen days in prison prostitutes who were not in compliance with the laws and regulations guiding prostitution.[28] As for strangers, beginning in 1847, the administration devoted considerable efforts to monitoring their presence in Saint-Louis. Every stranger was given a registration number and was required to report to the colonial administration every day or to be punished by five days in prison and the obligation to work for the administration without pay for a certain time period.[29]

A report issued in November 1834 mentions various legislative instruments issued in the early nineteenth century relating to the very beginning of the prison system in Senegal.[30] Unfortunately, this report does not provide any substantial details about the role of these legislative acts in the organization and operation of the prison of Saint-Louis. However, the report gives us insight into the earliest history of the prison of the capital, which, at the time, consisted of a row of small huts on the first floor of the Fort of Saint-Louis.

When Louis Faidherbe became governor in 1854 and undertook the expansion of the colonial conquest, Saint-Louis was his base. Among other things, he moved the prison from the Fort to a new location, where it would emerge as the nodal center of and a model for the expansion of the penitentiary system. Starting with Faidherbe's tenure and for the rest of the nineteenth century, the prison system remained an important institution of colonization.[31]

The colonial enterprise came with a constant need for labor, which could be supplied only by the colonized populations.[32] The aggressive push undertaken by Governor Faidherbe and his successors, from Saint-Louis toward the south and the west, targeted the resources in a wide area stretching from the Senegal River valley on the border with Mauritania to the Casamance region south of the Gambia River. While vital for the colonial project, this expansion would be encroaching on independent kingdoms such as the Waalo, the Kajoor, the Bawol, the Siin, the Saalum, the Bundu, the Fuladu, and the Kaabu. As a consequence, this push would lead to vigorous resistance. This period was full of confrontations, with one of the most violent occurring during the French occupation of what is now Senegal. Eventually all these kingdoms were defeated by the superior military power of the French. However, maintaining the colonial order in the conquered land required a new set of policies and actions. The penitentiary institution played a crucial role in this endeavor.

Securing labor for the proper operation of the colonial enterprise was one of the most daunting preoccupations of the French in Senegal. There was an endemic budgetary insufficiency in the colonies, especially in the 1870s, to meet these needs. At the same time, the job market was not that attractive for independent job seekers, especially given the low monthly wages that the colonial government could pay. Often the administration resorted to radical solutions to overcome this formidable problem. For example, on June 9, 1877, the Saint-Louis police chief sent his officers out into the city to look for and capture the seasonal migrants who usually came to the capital from the hinterland, to force them to work for the administration.[33] On January 20, 1870, echoing the difficulties that the administration had in finding the workforce it needed, the director of roads and bridges wrote to the director of the interior that using the prison population was the only way the colony could get enough workers to handle the maintenance of its roads.[34]

The Judiciary Service was in charge of the application of penal law in the colony. As such, it had the responsibility to oversee the operation of the prison system. However, in this area, there was not a clear delimitation between the responsibilities of the chief of the judiciary and the governor. As a consequence, there was a permanent rivalry, sometimes punctuated with serious clashes, between these two branches of the colonial government. Until the 1870s, the judiciary, through regular interventions, was able to counter the governor's continuous attempts to design the penitentiary institution according solely to his own needs and in total disregard of the law and the well-being of the prisoners.[35] While the office of the governor pushed for an unregulated penitentiary and unrestricted use of prison labor, the Judiciary Service constantly advocated a more humane treatment of detainees.[36] However, toward the end of the 1870s, the Judiciary started to lose ground in this battle, making it easier for the governor's policies to prevail and dominate the administration of the prison system and the orientation of the penitentiary toward service of the colonial enterprise.[37]

There was not a clear description of the mission assigned to and mode of operation of the penitentiary institution. Most of the time, colonial administrators came up with haphazard regulations that primarily served their day-to-day needs and preoccupations. Even when they invoked in their official correspondence the penitentiary laws promulgated in France and the colonies, they never worked to enforce them in Senegal. Instead, they resorted to ad hoc practices based on the needs of the moment.[38] Up to the early 1900s, the French did not follow formal regulations in the operation of the prison system.[39] The Prison Commission did not have any real power as it was completely overshadowed by the director of the interior who, in the office of the governor of Senegal, was in charge of the prisons of Saint-Louis, Dakar, and Gorée, until 1898. Some officials, especially colonial inspectors, regularly complained that the *Consigne pour le Concierge,* which provided the guidelines for the operation of the detention facilities around the colony from the 1880s, was almost never applied.[40] A closer look at the prison of Saint-Louis gives a better idea of this situation.

THE PRISON OF SAINT-LOUIS: ORGANIZATION, OPERATION, AND EXPLOITATION OF PENAL LABOR

The handling of the colonial prison system showed the deeply held belief that imprisonment was not meant to be the exact replica of what was done in France at the time. In a letter addressed to the minister of the navy and the colonies in February 1886, the governor of Senegal wrote: "But I should right away let you know that it might be difficult to organize all these prisons using one uniform regulation, like in France. A number of dispositions necessary to handle certain details, in some colonies might not be applicable in others, which would result in difficulties that only specific regulations for each colony could help us avoid."[41] The management of the prison of Saint-Louis and the ways it impacted detention conditions and interactions within the prison space illustrate this conception of imprisonment. Over the years, the mission assigned to the penitentiary expanded widely and, along with it, the role that the prison of the capital played, as well as its footprint on the urban landscape of Saint-Louis. Since the huts in Fort Saint-Louis were deemed inadequate for the desired level of security, the administration decided to build a new prison, with "rocks and bricks," in 1863. The authorities also decided to implement a more structured penitentiary administration and a permanent prison staff. For this, it was decided to finally enforce a number of French laws and regulations that were theoretically applicable in Senegal. However, in the following decades, the evolution of the prison of

Saint-Louis took a completely different course from what was planned, because its operation did not follow any formal standards.[42]

The penitentiary was a very important institution for the colonial government in Senegal. The director of the interior, a senior member of the governor's cabinet, was in charge of the prisons of Saint-Louis, Dakar, and Gorée. Under his authority was the Prison Commission, which did not have much power. The director of the interior constantly intervened in the day-to-day operation of the prison. The prison director (*régisseur*) was responsible for the daily administration, with the assistance of the two *porte-clefs* and the prison guards. In many instances, the director of the prison appeared as a mere figurehead, and his position did not require any expertise in prison management.

As a consequence, for most of the nineteenth century the people who were appointed prison director came from different sectors of the colonial apparatus and brought different levels of competency to the job. When, in 1877, on a random visit, the director of the interior found out that the prison director, Michel, was "really old and clueless about his duties," he recommended his replacement by a younger man with the physical qualities necessary for the position. In the search for a replacement, the authorities considered replacing the *régisseur* with the security guard of the Saint-Louis cemetery. The authorities thought that Michel was good only for looking after dead people.[43] Part of the problem was that it was quite difficult to recruit the staff needed for the prison. Africans and Europeans in the colony abhorred these kinds of jobs due to the low salaries and the stigma attached to them.[44] Also, the army decided it would no longer provide the prison with guards. Colonial officials viewed this as diverting the troops from their most important duties.[45]

It is difficult to find substantial quantitative data for most of this period. If the information exists for some years, there is absolutely nothing available for other years. Without a doubt this gap has to do with the poor handling of the colonial penitentiary archives during the postcolonial era. Nonetheless, there is ample evidence showing that, at any given time, the prison of Saint-Louis had a population ranging from 70 to 120 detainees. During the nineteenth century the prison of Saint-Louis had more prisoners than Dakar and Gorée.[46] From the very beginning, the prison of Saint-Louis held both civilian and military prisoners, whether they were convicted or awaiting trial, with "no differentiation between people convicted for misdemeanor and those imprisoned for more serious crimes."[47] It was common practice to shackle prisoners in order to discipline and/or use them for "the most painful and most repulsive public works."[48] The situation was such that an administrative report from Paris criticized this mixing of prisoners, pointing out that the practice was against "the penal code promulgated in the colony," and "the Law of April 1833, on civil rights in the colonies," which granted the same rights to "all free people regardless of their skin color."[49]

Obviously, these conditions do not corroborate much official correspondence and reports that project the image of a clean environment, where detainees were held in separated categories.[50] In fact, reports from the colonial inspectors and the Judiciary Service, as well as letters and other writings from the prisoners themselves, offer a totally different picture of the situation. According to these sources, although the European detainees were mostly held in separate and individual cells, Africans, who represented the largest part of the carceral population, were mostly kept in one single quarter, regardless of their sex, age, or alleged crime. Also, these sources often highlighted the dilapidation of the prison facility to the extent that, in some instances, rain fell on the prisoners, resulting in a repulsive filthiness which was a potential cause for all sorts of diseases.[51]

The goal of imprisonment was to advance colonial interests and order, and this informed the way that incarceration was organized in Saint-Louis. The institution of a penal labor system provided the colonial enterprise with cheap workers, but also served as a tool for the eradication of any perceived or actual threat to the colonial order. Making the pain of punishment visible to the colonized populations, including those who were outside the prison, served to discourage attempts at challenging the colonial state.

In nineteenth-century France, penal labor was an integral part of the penitentiary regime. It was considered an important element of reform for the deviant.[52] To this end, workshops were built in most French prisons. This is clearly what inspired the guidelines that the Ministry for the Colonies issued in 1860 for the construction of workshops in the prisons in Senegal. By 1862, a local order inspired by this dispatch recommended that the prison of Saint-Louis should have workshops, but they were apparently not built until 1905.[53] Although at the time this kind of penal work was largely accepted in France and other Western countries as preparation for the convict's reintegration into society as a law-abiding member, its rehabilitative nature was not a priority for the colonial administration. The prison labor that the French focused all their energy on was exploitative, repressive, and very similar to slavery.

In the 1830s the colonial administration came up with new rules, including a range of sanctions aimed at prisoners who refused to work inside or outside the prison. Also, it was no longer against the law to shackle prisoners while they were working, or to punish them with up to eight days of solitary confinement if they refused to work.[54] From the early 1830s, many prisoners were put in leg irons and ankle straps while working. In the following decades, due to the drastic budget cuts that the colony was facing, the French continued to rely heavily on this exploitation of prison labor. The director of the interior, the highest official in charge of prisons in the governor's office, approved of this treatment of the detainees. For example, the roads in Saint-Louis and Dakar were regularly in "very bad shape," and fixing them was a pressing demand from the European population of these cities. To overcome this "serious situation," the administration resorted to using large numbers of detainees from the prison of Saint-Louis. The colonial authorities thought that using the carceral labor force was the only way to "get the job quickly done, at almost no cost." The prisoners who were selected would receive a small allowance.[55]

The colonial administration also benefited from prison labor indirectly. The authorities rented detainees to the city council of Saint-Louis, local administrators across the colony, and private individuals and business owners in need of labor.[56] In a report dated April 23, 1896, colonial inspector Espent wrote about this matter, pointing out the necessity to make it easier for private business owners to use prison labor. He thought that the cost of this labor force along with the responsibility for the surveillance of prisoners made it harder for private business owners to employ prisoners.[57] The colonial government made significant revenue by leasing prisoners. There is evidence that, over the years, this income amounted to a nonnegligible part of the budgetary resources of the colony.[58] Also, it was a very common practice for colonial officials to use prisoners for their own needs, although colonial inspectors criticized this practice in their reports. This was the case of Mr. Henriette, director of the prison of Saint-Louis in the late nineteenth century, who regularly used prisoners for work in his garden.[59]

The narrowly defined orientation for imprisonment shown in the use of prison labor did not allow for any significant rehabilitative action in the penitentiary institution's mission.[60] The *Consigne pour le Concierge,* which organized the daily operation of the prison, and the Surveillance Commission, which was in charge of its supervision, did not work properly. Colonial inspectors frequently emphasized these shortcomings in their reports. This use of prison work, while satisfying a daunting need for the colonial enterprise, also sent a clear message to the colonized populations. It helped create beyond the penitentiary walls what colonial authorities wanted to be "a salutary impression." For the colonizers, the brutal methods used at the prison of Saint-Louis and later throughout the colony, were more fitting than the "civilized French laws" to eradicate what they perceived as the innate laziness of Africans and their natural disposition to deviance. However, the French colonial project did not occur in a cultural vacuum. The colonized people responded to what was imposed on them, including this repressive penitentiary system.

From the very beginning, the colonized populations developed strong opposition to imprisonment. Ibrahima Thioub's thorough investigation of the responses to colonial imprisonment in Senegambia has revealed the host of meanings that Africans associated with incarceration. Besides the fact that it was frightening, incarceration was viewed not only as a sign of individual and/or collective decadence, but also as a dishonoring experience for the prisoner and their community. As a consequence, Africans sought actively to avoid jail, escape from it, and/or mitigate its repressive rigor. Besides confronting prison guards and the other colonial officials directly involved in the management of the prison, detainees resorted to different magico-religious practices informed by the general conception that the colonized populations had about imprisonment. There were also instances when prisoners used various strategies of negotiation and/or accommodation within the prison space to beat the system.[61]

Although imprisonment focused primarily on the detainees, in a way, it targeted almost every category of the colonized population. Foucault's concepts of "carceral continuum" and "carceral city" describe best the penitentiary institution and how it extended its tentacles far beyond the walls of the prison by connecting with other forms of punishment and control such as urban planning and education. Imprisonment was intended to make the detainees "feel their position [of inferiority]" and create fear among the people outside the prison who might be tempted to challenge the colonial state.[62] In fact, colonial authorities worried that the prisoners could "communicate easily with the outside" if surveillance weakened.[63]

As a consequence, whether they were from the land of the protectorate or were *originaires,* prisoners or not, the respective backgrounds and experiences that these people had with colonization informed their diverse responses to the system of social control. Mamadou Diouf writes about the ways in which the benefit attached to the acquisition of French citizenship in the Four Communes, discussed in Larissa Kopytoff's essay elsewhere in this volume, came hand in hand with a nonconformist if not rebellious culture toward the French *code civil.* This resistance materialized in the carceral space as one compenent of a more complex underground culture that the colonized could not apprehend, which is why it ultimately impacted the penitentiary institution profoundly.

CONCLUSION

When the French regained control of Saint-Louis in the early nineteenth century, they devoted themselves to making the city the launchpad for their expansion in West Africa. This work took place at a critical time for Senegal, marked by the emergence of many challenges for the colonial project. In response, the colonizers devised a system geared toward their vision of law and order, which relied heavily upon the penitentiary institution. Backed with deeply rooted ideologies such as a belief in the naturally wayward and uncivilized African, imprisonment had a clear utilitarian orientation, which made it a successful tool for the policing of the colonized space and the body. As such, the prison system gradually became an important institution of colonization. The fact that imprisonment targeted primarily the body of the detainee and cared less about reform was meant to send a clear message of intimidation beyond the prison walls. The organization and operation of the prison of Saint-Louis was a good illustration of this orientation of the penitentiary. But the penal policies conceived in Paris did not remain unchallenged and unchanged. The colonized people developed various responses that impacted the system profoundly. The history of imprisonment and social control in Saint-Louis shows how the first French prison in the colony set the stage for the politics of punishment for Senegal for decades to come. Saint-Louis remained the model for the expansion of the penitentiary system and its nodal center throughout the nineteenth century. The history of imprisonment, as it uncovers a facet that the scholarship in French colonialism has thus far neglected, opens up a new window into the history of the city and our understanding of the role played by the penitentiary in the larger colonial project.

NOTES

1. For example, see Babacar Diagne, "Saint-Louis du Sénégal et sa Population au XIXe Siècle: Les mutations politiques, economiques et sociales d'une ville coloniale," Thèse de 3e Cycle, Departement d'Histoire (Université Cheikh Anta Diop de Dakar, 2003); Kalala Ngalamulume, *Colonial Pathologies, Environment, and Western Medicine in Saint-Louis-du-Senegal, 1867–1920* (New York: Peter Lang Publishing, 2012); Hilary Jones, *The Métis of Senegal: Urban Life and Politics in French West Africa* (Bloomington: Indiana University Press, 2013); Alain Sinou, *Comptoirs et Villes Coloniales du Sénégal, Saint-Louis, Gorée, Dakar* (Paris: Karthala et Office de la recherche scientifique et technique outre-mer [hereafter ORSTOM]), 1993).

2. See contributions by Marieke Polfliet, Rebecca J. Scott, and Larissa Kopytoff in this volume.

3. Stephen Lukes and Andrew Scull, eds., *Durkheim and the Law* (Stanford, CA: Stanford University Press, 1995); Katayoun Baghai, "Punishment as Reason and Passion: Bentham, Kant, Nietzsche, Durkheim," unpublished paper presented at the annual meeting of the American Sociological Association, Montreal Convention Center, Montreal, Quebec, Canada, Aug. 10, 2006 *Online*. 2008-05-07, http://www.allacademic.com/meta/p101425_index.html.

4. See David Rothman, *The Discovery of the Asylum: Social Order and Disorder in the New Republic* (Boston: Little, Brown, 2002).

5. Michel Foucault, *Discipline and Punish: The Birth of the Prison* (New York: Vintage Books, 1979).

6. Marc Ferro, *Le Livre noir du colonialisme, XVIe–XXIe siècle: De l'extermination à la répentance* (Paris: Robert Laffont, 2003). In her book, *Les origines du totalitarisme: L'impérialisme* (Paris: Fayard, 1997), German American political theorist Hannah Arendt links colonial imperialism to communism and nazism. Anne Applebaum, "A History of Horror," A review of Joël Kotek and Pierre Rigoulot, *Le Siècle des Camps* (Paris: J. C. Lattès, 2000), *New York Review of Books,* October 18, 2001, 41.

7. Peter Zinoman, *The Colonial Bastille: A History of Imprisonment in Vietnam, 1862–1940* (Berkeley: University of California Press, 2001), 32.

8. Historians have extensively studied the panoply of colonial institutions of socialization that played a significant role in this area, which also included schools, youth organizations, and the military. However, this scholarship has almost completely neglected the penitentiary.

9. Lauren Benton, *Law and Colonial Cultures: Legal Regimes in World History, 1400–1900* (New York: Cambridge University Press, 2002), 2. See also Frank Dikötter and Ian Brown's coedited volume, *Cultures of Confinement: A History of the Prison in Africa, Asia, and Latin America* (Ithaca, NY: Cornell University Press, 2007). The contributors to this book portray the practice and ideology of incarceration in Africa, Asia, and Latin America as deeply influenced by the oppressive nature of the colonial state. This is why the carceral space appears in this volume as a contested one, where resistance and appropriation are the strategies simultaneously used to cope with imprisonment, which has contributed to reshaping profoundly the philosophy and politics of punishment.

10. Florence Bernault, ed., *A History of Prison and Confinement in Africa* (Portsmouth, NH: Heinemann, 2003).

11. Caroline Elkins, *Imperial Reckoning: The Untold Story of Britain's Gulag in Kenya* (New York: Henry Holt, 2005); David M. Anderson, *Histories of the Hanged: Britain's Dirty War in Kenya and the End of Empire* (London: Weidenfeld & Nicolson, 2005).

12. Donald Fyson, *Magistrats, police et société: La justice criminelle ordinaire au Québec et au Bas-Canada (1764–1837)* (Montréal: Hurtubise, 2010).

13. In June 2007, while attending the French Colonial Historical Society annual congress in La Rochelle, France, I visited the prison of Saint-Martin on the Island of Ré, where all the prisoners deported from French West Africa transited on their way to the penal colony of French Guyana. I was informed that the Archives Départementales de Charente-Maritime contains important resources on these prisoners and the Tirailleurs Sénégalais, who served as prison guards at Saint-Martin and/or aboard the ships that transported these detainees.

14. See Babacar Ba, "Histoire du personnel pénitentiaire colonial au Sénégal, 1863–1960," Mémoire de DEA, Université Cheikh Anta Diop, 1997; Dior Konate, "L'histoire des modes d'incarcération au Sénégal: Les femmes en prison 1925–1995," Mémoire de maîtrise, Université Cheikh Anta Diop, 1997–1998; Ibra Sene, "Contribution à l'histoire des établissements pénitentiaires au Sénégal: La prison de Saint-Louis de 1920 à 1944," Mémoire de maîtrise, Université Cheikh Anta Diop, 1998; Ibrahima Thioub, Babacar Ba, and Ibra Sene, "Sénégal: Un système pénitentiaire en crise. Acteurs et enjeux des débats en cours," *Revue française d'histoire d'Outre-mer* 86:324–25 (1999): 124–48; Ibra Sene, "Introduction à l'histoire de la main-d'oeuvre carcérale au Sénégal: De l'emploi des détenus des camps pénaux sur les chantiers des travaux routiers (1927–1940)," Mémoire de DEA, Université Cheikh Anta Diop, Dakar, 1999–2000; Ibra Sene, "Colonisation française et exploitation de la main-d'oeuvre carcérale au Sénégal: De l'emploi des détenus des camps pénaux sur les chantiers des travaux routiers (1927–1940)," *French Colonial History* 5 (2004): 153–71; Ibrahima Thioub, "La gestion de la marginalité juvénile dans la colonie du Sénégal: De l'abolition de l'esclavage aux écoles pénitentiaires, 1848–1906," *Les Cahiers Histoire et Civilisations* no. 1, 117–30.

15. Catherine Coquery-Vidrovitch, *L'Afrique et les Africains au XIXe siècle: Mutations, révolutions, crises* (Paris: Armand Colin, 1999), 252–53.

16. Diagne, "Saint-Louis du Sénégal et sa population au XIXe siècle," 203.

17. See ibid., 145. See also Sinou, *Comptoirs et villes coloniales du Sénégal*, 141.

18. Ngouda Kane, *Répertoire Série F: Sécurité Publique au Sénégal: Police, Gendarmerie, Prisons (1840–1956)* (Dakar: Direction des Archives du Sénégal, 1997).

19. Diagne, "Saint-Louis du Sénégal et sa population au XIXe siècle," 362.

20. This was part of a larger initiative devoted to providing the colony with the institutions it needed for its operation for the next century. See Sinou, *Comptoirs et villes coloniales du Sénégal*, 86–90.

21. Ndar is the Wolof name for Saint-Louis, still used today by most people in the city and around Senegal.

22. Archives Nationales du Sénégal (hereafter ANS) 3E 4, Conseil de gouvernement et d'administration, June 1, 1828.

23. ANS 3E 7, Conseil de gouvernement et d'administration, Order of interdiction of the slaughtering of animals in places other than the butchery of Saint-Louis, December 24, 1827.

24. ANS 3 E 8, Conseil de gouvernement et d'administration, Order of interdiction of drumming, July 4, 1829.

25. ANS 13/G 22. In the speech he gave in April 1839, at the inauguration of his successor, Governor Charmasson, Governor Soret voiced his disappointment that the police were not doing this job properly. He suspected that African police officers would not always report their fellow Africans who obviously broke the rule. See *Mémoire de remise de service à Monsieur le Gouverneur Charmasson par Monsieur le Gouverneur Soret*, April 14, 1839.

26. ANS 3E 17, Conseil d'administration, January 18, 1844. See James Searing, *West African Slavery and Atlantic Commerce: The Senegal River Valley, 1700–1860* (Cambridge: Cambridge University Press, 1993), 163–93; see also James L. A. Webb Jr., "The Trade in Gum Arabic: Prelude to French Conquest in Senegal," *Journal of African History* 26:2–3 (1985): 149–68.

27. Diagne, "Saint-Louis du Sénégal et sa population au XIXe siècle," 96.

28. Ibrahima Thioub, "Sénégal: La prison à l'époque coloniale: Significations, évitement et évasions," in Florence Bernault, ed., *Enfermement, prisons et châtiments en Afrique, du 19e siècle à nos jours* (Paris: Karthala, 1999), 289–91.

29. Diagne, "Saint-Louis du Sénégal et sa population au XIXe siècle," 120.

30. ANS 3F/00037, Letter of the warden of the prison of Saint-Louis to the Higher Commander of the Colonial Armies, June 2, 1894, regarding the organization of the prisons of the colony of Senegal.

31. On the role played by the penitentiary as an institution of colonization, see Ibra Sene, "Crime, Punishment, and Colonization: A History of the Prison of Saint-Louis and the Development of the Penitentiary System in Senegal, ca. 1860–ca. 1940," PhD diss., Michigan State University, 2008.

32. This is a well-documented aspect of colonialism. There were enormous labor needs for European colonizers in Africa. In their attempts to meet these needs, colonial officials ignored metropolitan labor laws and resorted to coercive labor policies such as the system of *travail forcé* (forced labor) and prison labor. The policies were critically important for French

colonialism, as they helped maximize profits through violent exploitation and brutalization of the colonized people. For more on this topic, see F. Cooper, *Decolonization and African Society: The Labor Question in French and British Africa* (Cambridge: Cambridge University Press, 1996); F. Cooper, "Conditions Analogous to Slavery: Imperialism and Free Labor Ideology in Africa," in F. Cooper, T. Holt, and R. Scott, eds., *Beyond Slavery: Explorations of Race, Labor, and Citizenship in Postemancipation Societies* (Chapel Hill: University of North Carolina Press, 2000), 107–49; B. Fall, *Le travail forcé en Afrique occidentale française, 1900–1946* (Paris: Karthala, 1993); Mamadou Diouf, "The Senegalese Murid Trade Diaspora and the Making of a Vernacular Cosmopolitanism," *Public Culture* 12:3 (September 1, 2001): 679–702.

33. ANS 3F/00038, Civil Prison of Saint-Louis, 1874–1875, Letter of Saint-Louis Police Chief Officer to the Chief of the Service of the Interior, June 9, 1877.

34. ANS 3F/00038, Civil Prison of Saint-Louis, 1874–1875, Letter of the Director *Ponts et Chaussées* of Senegal, to the Director of the Interior, January 20, 1870. Also see "Colonisation française et exploitation de la main-d'oeuvre carcérale au Sénégal: De l'emploi des détenus des camps pénaux sur les chantiers des travaux routiers (1927–1940)," *French Colonial History* 5 (2004): 153–71.

35. ANS 3F/00038, Civil Prison of Saint-Louis, 1874–1875, Letter of the Saint-Louis Police Chief Officer to the Head of the Service of the Interior, January 17, 1877. See also ANS 3F/00038, Civil Prison of Saint-Louis, 1874–1875, Letter of the manager of the prison of Saint-Louis to the Head of the Service of the Interior, April 9, 1877. In this letter, the prison manager writes about the Judiciary's influence on prisoners who no longer wanted to work outside the prison.

36. ANS 3F/00038, Civil Prison of Saint-Louis, 1874–1875, Letter of the *Juge d'instruction* to the Chief of the Judiciary Service, December 21, 1875.

37. ANS 3F/00038, Civil Prison of Saint-Louis, 1874–1875, Response of the Director of the Interior to the President of the Court of Appeal of Saint-Louis, August 26, 1875.

38. ANS 3F/00052, Civil Prison of Saint-Louis, 1903–1906, Incoming and Outgoing Correspondence of the Secretary General of Government (1903), Note of the Secretary General, November 20, 1903.

39. ANS 3F/00052, Civil Prison of Saint-Louis, 1903–1906, Monthly report on the operation of the prison of Saint-Louis, December 1905.

40. ANS 3F/00046, Civil Prison of Saint-Louis, 1892–1900, Case of Henriette, warden of the prisons of Saint-Louis (1892–93): Minute addressed to the Governor of Senegal, regarding warden Henriette, April 1893. ANS 3F/00037, *Nouvelle Consigne pour le Concierge* of the civil prison, signed by the Director of the Interior and the Chief of the Judiciary Service, and approved by the Governor of Senegal, May 15, 1872. See also Archives Nationales d'Outre-Mer (hereafter ANOM) Sénégal et Dépendances XI 21, 1816–1895 (Régime pénitentiaire; Saint-Louis; Dakar, Correspondance diverse). Note regarding the penitentiary regime in Senegal, Director of the Interior, December 10, 1885.

41. ANOM Sénégal et Dépendances XI, 21, 1816–1895 (Régime pénitentiaire; Saint-Louis; Dakar, Correspondance diverse). Letter of the Governor of Senegal and Dependences to the Minister of the Navy and the Colonies, Saint-Louis, February 14, 1886.

42. ANOM Sénégal et Dépendances XI, 21, 1816–1895 (Régime pénitentiaire; Saint-Louis; Dakar, Correspondance diverse), Excerpts from a report dated November 8, 1834, regarding the material situation and regime of the prisons in Senegal.

43. ANS 3F/00038, Civil Prison of Saint-Louis, 1874–1875, Note of the Chief of the Service of the Interior to the Governor du Senegal, 28 July 1877; Comments of the Governor of Senegal regarding the issue raised in the correspondence.

44. The correspondence between colonial officials shows that this was a concern for them. See ANOM Sénégal et Dépendances XI, 21, 1816–1895 (Regime pénitentiaire; Saint-Louis; Dakar, Correspondance): Letter of the Governor of Senegal et Dependances to the Minister of the Navy and the Colonies, August 9, 1884. In 1886 the director of the prison of Dakar wrote a letter to the governor of Senegal to complain about his working conditions and to request a salary raise. The governor of Senegal wrote a letter to the minister for the navy and the colonies to support the request. See CAOM: Senegal et Dependances XI: 21: 1816–1895 (Regime penitentiaire; Saint-Louis; Dakar, Correspondance): Letter of the Governor of Senegal et Dependances to the Minister for the Navy and the Colonies (the letter was not dated but reached the office of the Minister on June 25, 1886). Africans only served as prison guards or in lower-level clerical positions. Also, colonial officials preferred not to hire civilians as guards. Finally, working as a member of the prison staff was often viewed as being an accomplice of the colonial repressive politics. Prisoners often attacked guards and accused them of being sellouts.

45. ANS 3F/00037, The Senator and Minister of the Navy to the Commanders in Chief of the Armed Forces in the French colonies, Paris, January 8, 1892, about the application of the directive of the Minister of the War, dated October 27, 1891, regarding the reduction of the number of troops diverted from their military duties. See also ANS 3F/00037, Circular Letter, The Senator and Minister of the Navy to the Commanders in Chief of the Armed Forces in the French colonies, August 17, 1891; Letter of the Commander in Chief of the Armed Forces in Senegal to the Director of the Interior, March 8, 1892; Letter of the Commander in Chief of the Armed Forces in Senegal to the Governor of Sénégal et Dépendances, May 20, 1892.

46. ANOM Senegal et Dépendances XI, 21, 1816–1895 (Regime pénitentiaire; Saint-Louis; Dakar, Correspondance). In fact, the prison of the capital maintained this preeminence well into the twentieth century.

47. ANOM Sénégal et Dépendances XI, 21, 1816–1895 (Régime pénitentiaire; Saint-Louis; Dakar, Correspondance diverse), Excerpts from a report dated November 8, 1834, regarding the material situation and regime of the prisons in Senegal.

48. These public works included the maintenance of the streets of Saint-Louis, its wharf, but also other public buildings such as schools and government offices in the capital. Prisoners were also used for the building and maintenance of roads in different parts of the colony outside of Saint-Louis. See ANOM Sénégal et Dépendances XI, 21, 1816–1895 (Régime pénitentiaire; Saint-Louis; Dakar, Correspondance diverse), Excerpts from a report dated November 8, 1834, regarding the material situation and regime of the prisons in Senegal. For more details, see Ibra Sene, "Colonisation française et exploitation de la main-d'oeuvre carcérale au Sénégal: De l'emploi des détenus des camps pénaux sur les chantiers des travaux routiers (1927–1940)," *French Colonial History* 5 (2004): 153–71.

49. ANOM Sénégal et Dépendances XI, 21, 1816–1895, November 8, 1834.

50. ANOM Sénegal et Dépendances XI, 21, 1816–1895 (Régime pénitentiaire; Saint-Louis; Dakar, Correspondance): Notice about the penitentiary regime in Senegal, Director of the Interior, Saint-Louis, December 10, 1885.

51. ANOM Sénégal et Dépendances XI, 21, 1816–1895 (Régime pénitentiaire; Saint-Louis; Dakar, Correspondance): Report by Inspector General, Espent, to the Minister of the Colonies, April 13, 1888, regarding the operation of prisons of Senegal. See also ANS3F/00041, Civil Prison of Saint-Louis, 1886–89, Report on the Prison of Saint-Louis, General Clerk of the Direction of the Interior, July 23, 1888.

52. Patricia O'Brien, *The Promise of Punishment: Prisons in Nineteenth-Century France* (Princeton, NJ: Princeton University Press, 1982), 150–90. See also Jacques-Guy Petit, "Les travaux et les jours (1800–1875)," in Jacques-Guy Petit et al., eds., *Histoire des galères, bagnes et prisons, XVIIIe–XIXe siècles: Introduction à l'histoire pénale de la France* (Paris: Bibliothèque Historique Privat, 1991), 150–68.

53. ANS 3F/00038, Civil Prison of Saint-Louis, 1874–1875, Note on the prisons of Senegal. The note is not dated, but based on the events it mentions it must have been issued between 1872 and 1875; ANS 3F/00052, Prison civile de Saint-Louis, 1903–1906, Monthly Report on the Situation of the Prison of Saint-Louis, December 1905; ANS 3F/00038, Civil Prison of Saint-Louis, 1874–1875, Detainee Fatimata Ndiawar Diop to the Chief of Judiciary Service, September 18, 1871.

54. ANS 3F/00038, Civil Prison of Saint-Louis, 1874–1875, Response of the Head of the Service of the Interior to the Police Officer of Saint-Louis regarding the refusal of prisoners to work, April 7, 1877.

55. ANS 3F/00038, The Director of "Pont et Chaussées" to the Director of the Interior, January 20, 1870; see also ANS3F/00038, Note on the Prison System in Senegal, Director of the Interior, slnd [probably from the early 1870s].

56. ANOM Sénégal et Dépendances XI, 21, 1816–1895 (Régime pénitentiaire; Saint-Louis; Dakar, Correspondance diverse), Note regarding the penitentiary regime in Senegal, Director of the Interior, Saint-Louis, December 10, 1885.

57. ANOM Sénégal et Dépendances, XI, 21, 1816–1895 (Régime pénitentiaire; Saint-Louis; Dakar, Correspondance diverse), Letter of Inspector General Espent to the Minister of the Navy and Colonies, about the situation of the Prison of Saint-Louis, April 23, 1896.

58. ANS 3F/00105. See Art. 4 of the Decision of the Governor of Senegal, No. 75 GA, January 04, 1930.

59. ANS 3F/00046, Civil Prison of Saint-Louis, 1892–1900, Case of Henriette, warden of the prisons of Saint-Louis (1892–93), Minute addressed to the Governor of Senegal, regarding warden Henriette, April 1893.

60. ANS 3F/00038, Civil Prison of Saint-Louis, 1874–1875, Letter of the physician in charge of the health care of the prison, to the Chief Physician in Saint-Louis, February 26, 1870.

61. In the early twentieth century, a prisoner named Saliou Ndiaye had the habit of writing poems to praise the prison director and his wife. There is also the example of prisoner Ana

Faye, who obtained lots of favors for other detainees because she was having a sexual relationship with the prison director. Finally, there are many documented cases of physical confrontation between the prisoners and the guards. For more on this, see Thioub, "Sénégal: La Prison à l'époque coloniale"; Ibra Sene, "Crime, Punishment, and Colonization: A History of the Prison of Saint-Louis and the Development of the Penitentiary System in Senegal, ca. 1830–ca. 1940," PhD diss., Michigan State University, 2008, ch. 6: "*Sujets Francais, Originaires,* and Juvenile Delinquents: The Prison of Saint-Louis and the Colonial Society."

62. ANS 3F/00052: Civil Prison of Saint-Louis, 1903–1906, Warning to prisoner Mar Diop (1906), Acting prison manager, to the Secretary General of the Government, October 16, 1906.

63. ANS 3F/00038: Civil Prison of Saint-Louis, 1874–1875, Note on the prisons. This document is not dated but was probably issued in the early 1870s because it refers to the *Consigne du Concierge* of May 4, 1872, which was the text governing the organization of the penitentiary system in Senegal at that time.

CITIZENSHIP AND THE ABOLITION OF SLAVERY AFTER 1848

Conflicts of National Allegiance among the French in New Orleans

MARIEKE POLFLIET

> I have often been struck by the reverberations that our political passions had here, and by the analogy that still exists in this respect between the population of Louisiana and the population of France.
>
> —CONSUL GUILLEMIN to Alexis de Tocqueville, New Orleans, January 1, 1832

The year 1848 saw a series of events whose Atlantic dimension has recently been reasserted, affecting primarily the heart of the French colonial empire but also its peripheral areas.[1] Despite the length of time that by the mid-nineteenth century separated New Orleans from the French colonial period, the reverberations of events in France were still of major importance, because of links maintained with the former colonial power and with the colonies in the Antilles. The upheaval caused by the 1848 Revolution, both in the exercise of French citizenship and in race relations, highlighted the tensions and ambiguities that had arisen in the outer parts of the French Empire—which also included Saint-Louis du Sénégal—in defining the rights associated with nationality and practices of citizenship.

At the time, New Orleans was a major Atlantic hub—a commercial outlet for the production of the South and West of the United States, a major port for European immigration, and a former colonial capital that had maintained special links with the Antilles. A sea and river port of the first importance, backed up by a slave labor–based hinterland and economy, it was being transformed by swift economic and population growth.[2] Although no longer part of the French colonial empire following the Louisiana Purchase of 1803, it was a frontier area between the United States and the French Empire.[3] Interpersonal and legal links still connected it to the former colonial power. The Creoles of Louisiana, descended from French and Spanish colonists, along with members of the diaspora of refugees from Saint-Domingue, and more-recently established colonists from Martinique and Guadeloupe, formed coexisting generations of French colonial origin. There were also migrants from France, and thus a large number of French people in New Orleans continued to be governed by the French law of nationality and the authority of the French consuls. Under American law, the migrants also had the possibility of taking American nationality, but they were nevertheless in an ambiguous situation, as was revealed during periods of crisis and "civic wars" after 1848, because of the political upheavals that affected France and the United States at the time.[4]

Slavery was one of the major sources of tensions in the United States in the aftermath of the Mexican War, as a result of the debate about the status of the new territories acquired by the United States in the context of an upsurge in abolitionist movements. The abolition decree adopted by the provisional government of the French Republic, on April 27, 1848, following the February Revolution, was particularly important. The decision had a dual impact in New Orleans. First and foremost, it affected the colonies in the Antilles and was angrily received by the defenders of slavery in the South of the United States, who felt threatened by this new setback for the "peculiar institution," just as they had when the British abolished slavery.[5] Second, the abolition movement was striving for the universal propagation of emancipation, as advocated by Victor Schoelcher, and this directly affected the French population of Louisiana.

How did the provisions and effects of France's abolition of slavery challenge the frontiers of French nationality and citizenship in the Atlantic world? The case of the French of New Orleans raises questions that apply equally well to the trading station of Saint-Louis in Senegal. Although this peripheral territory of the French Empire had a population only one-tenth that of New Orleans, it was also a sea and river port, and an outlet for the production of a slavery-based system, illustrating the tensions generated at the outer edges of the empire by the universalist scope of the abolition decree.[6]

The effects of France's abolition of slavery on these peripheral territories—the main target being France's colonies in the Antilles—bear witness, despite the differences between the two cities, to the compromises and adaptations the French authorities had to concede in view of their specific circumstances.[7] In both cases, the clauses of the decree of April 27 that compelled French citizens living abroad to free their slaves or otherwise lose their nationality, turned out to be incompatible with local commercial and socioeconomic realities, and with the way the two port cities were integrated in their regional and continental territories. Conflicts of allegiance arose among the French living at the margins of the French colonial empire, facing a difficult choice between their motherland and their local socioeconomic status. This dilemma led French authorities to compromises and adaptations in the definition of the frontiers of citizenship and nationality.

The reverberations in New Orleans of France's abolition of slavery reveal that public life there became an Atlantic sounding board for the events of 1848. The peripheral position of the city in relation to the French Empire led to a negotiation of the frontiers of citizenship and nationality and to compromises on the part of the French authorities. As an American city of immigration, New Orleans also allowed some of its residents to take advantage of the two in-between nationalities—French and American—which each conveyed different assets but also obligations in political, commercial, or racial terms. Identification with a national allegiance and its interpretation could vary according to circumstances because of changing and conflicting meanings of the social and political pact and of race relations in the United States and in the Atlantic.

DEMONSTRATIONS OF OPPOSITION TO ABOLITION IN NEW ORLEANS'S PUBLIC SPACE

France's abolition of slavery had a truly Atlantic impact in that it affected not only the Antilles but also the continents of America and Africa.[8] The French population of New Orleans reacted robustly to events affecting the colonies in the Antilles, essentially because the port city had a special place in France's Atlantic migration after the loss of Saint-Domingue. The continuing immigration of French people to Louisiana after the end of the eighteenth century was largely based on a migration pattern determined by the resources of the economy of Louisiana, either through the establishment of plantations or through the commercial opportunities afforded by New Orleans. As François Weil has suggested, New Orleans at this time was at the heart of the "old" French Atlantic world, shaped by the colonial legacy, and distinct from the "new" Atlantic world springing from the beginnings of the industrial era.[9] For some French migrants, integration into a race-based society often involved the acquisition of slaves, who were seen as a symbol of status and enrichment. But the 1848 abolition decree affecting the French colonies dramatically changed this situation. The application of the decree in the colonies in the Antilles was fiercely criticized by part of the French population of New Orleans, and it revived the specter of slave revolt associated with the arrival of refugees from Saint-Domingue.

On April 27, 1848, the provisional government of the Second Republic enacted a decree abolishing slavery in the French colonies. The way this decision was received in New Orleans revealed the fragmentation in public opinion, both in the press and in public demonstrations. The predominant reaction among French-speaking whites was negative, and any supporters of abolition and racial equality were effectively reduced to silence.[10] All public expressions of support for abolition were prohibited in New Orleans and throughout the southern states,[11] reflecting the exacerbation of the "politics of slavery,"[12] with the whole of the political world considering abolition to be objectionable.[13] It is therefore no surprise to find that France's abolition decree was initially not reported in the French-language press. While the main French-language newspapers of New Orleans—*Le Courrier de la Louisiane* and *L'Abeille de La Nouvelle-Orléans*—had covered events affecting metropolitan France since February 1848 in great detail, they made no mention of the abolition decree.[14] Only one daily in New Orleans (*L'Orléanais*) published the decree of June 2, 1848, in full, without making any comment.[15] This limited press coverage may also have been the result of reluctance on the part of the French consular authorities called on to publish the decree by the provisional government. The New Orleans consul Aimé Roger claimed that he had fulfilled his duty of publication, but with no excessive zeal in view of the unpopularity of the text:

> The decree of April 27th was inserted in all American and Franco-American newspapers; it was very severely criticized in all the southern states of the Union and especially in Louisiana; it gave rise to the strongest complaints from the French who live in this state [. . .]. Being unable to increase in any way the degree of publicity, which was complete; and fearing the unnecessary reviving of controversies that are always counterproductive in view of the state of our relations with the American union [. . .], I will abstain from any further publication.[16]

However, the dim view of the decree taken by some of the French in the city was publicly expressed when news broke about the troubles—triggered by the precipitate announcement of abolition in Martinique and Guadeloupe—that led settlers there to leave and take refuge in New Orleans.[17] The French-speaking population of New Orleans that had maintained family or commercial links with the French colonies felt very closely concerned by the situation in the Antilles. The arrival of the French colonists in New Orleans revived the fears and rhetorical outbursts that had followed the arrival of the refugees from Saint-Domingue, and the long-running dispute about the way the former colonial power was managing the issue of compensation.[18] In July 1848, meetings of French colonists were held—the "refugees" together with some French people from the colonies who had settled in New Orleans since the 1830s—to plan for measures to be taken in the event of a bloodbath in the French colonies.[19] They directed their criticism at the new French authorities, and more specifically at the Commissioners of the Republic:

> The massacres that took place at Saint Pierre in May this year are widely disapproved, and have pained those who love justice, humanity and order [. . .] the unspeakable behavior of the first authority of Martinique in such tragic circumstances has attracted condemnation from everyone [. . .]. Freedom without order and without law means a continuous state of rioting, looting and murder.[20]

They accused the French state of having deceived the French people about the consequences of abolition, criticizing the "functionaries who, in moments of unrest, proclaim principles and adopt measures whose results they have not foreseen, without even taking the precautions dictated by an ordinary duty of care."[21] This clearly reflected the distance that so often separated the colonial population from the French metropolitan authorities, accused of failing to take local realities into account.

Furthermore, part of the white French-speaking population of New Orleans expressed their solidarity with the colonists, as their view that abolition was a source of ruin and disorder had been strengthened. France's abolition decree clearly set a new and unpleasant precedent for the defenders of slavery in the United States, after abolition by the British.[22] The multiple resolutions approved at public meetings thus exaggerated the dangers of abolition in order to strengthen the expression of sympathy and solidarity with the French colonists. The cruelty and savagery of the freed slaves were contrasted with the humanity and security of New Orleans, based on the paradoxical argument that slave-owning society was, according to its defenders, more "human" than a free society left in the hands of former slaves:

> The colonists compelled to leave their home towns so as not to fall victim there to the daggers of their former servants will find in New Orleans the humanity they come there to seek, and all the succor that their unfortunate position demands.[23]

> They will find in the land of America the freedom that the motherland promised them, and the security that it was unable to give them.[24]

Although no widespread revolt took place, these views clearly reflect the predominant perception of France's abolition of slavery in New Orleans, and show how this led to mistrust of the former colonial authorities. A second and even more direct issue stemmed from the militant dimension of abolition, which applied not only to the territories of the empire, but also to French populations beyond its frontiers, forbidding its nationals in foreign countries from owning slaves. Article 8 gave rise to a contradiction between the socioeconomic situation of some of the French in Louisiana and the legal obligations resulting from their nationality, and this triggered a crisis of national identification.

CONFLICTING ALLEGIANCES TO COMPROMISE: CHANGING FRONTIERS IN CITIZENSHIP AND NATIONALITY

French nationality law is laid down by the Civil Code of 1804 and is based on the legal concept of *jus sanguinis* (right of blood). It is distinct from the criterion of citizenship, which is governed by successive constitutions. The frontiers of nationality and citizenship are not therefore necessarily the same, particularly in the outer reaches of the colonial empire.[25] For the French of Louisiana, Article 8 is unacceptable because it calls into question their status in the society of the South of the United States. The allegiance conflict led the French authorities to make compromises relating to this principle and the ways it was applied, both in the context of the conservative change of direction of the empire, and in order to protect French commercial interests.

The unpopularity of France's abolition of slavery among the French of New Orleans resulted not only from the reasons given above, but also from the unprecedented perceived slight[26] it represented through Article 8, which was intended to spread abolition beyond French frontiers by its stipulation that "in the future, even in foreign countries, it is prohibited for any French person to own, purchase or sell slaves, and to participate either directly or indirectly in any trafficking or exploitation of such persons."[27] The prohibition was accompanied by a clause making it compulsory for French people who owned slaves to free them within three years, with failure to comply resulting in loss of nationality. According to the consul Aimé Roger, five to six thousand French people were affected by this measure in Louisiana—a figure that is hard to verify but substantial, bearing in mind that in 1850 there were more than 20,000 slave owners in Louisiana.[28]

This provision thus triggered a major crisis of allegiance for some of the French residents of Louisiana who had kept their original nationality. This was clearly demonstrated by the complaints made by Roger to the French Ministry of Foreign Affairs. The consul argued that the French of Louisiana remained attached to their motherland, and had "rejected the pressing demands of their families and disdained the advantages attached to American nationality, in order to die French."[29] Article 8, however, made their economic and social status incompatible with their national allegiance, and offered them no alternative to American naturalization: "If Article 8 is maintained, all the French who reside in Louisiana will, before the 3 years have elapsed, be naturalized as Americans, in order firstly to escape from the time-limit of this article, and secondly to lose their status as French nationals by an act of their will, rather than by the application of a stringent law."[30] Without their slaves, argued Roger, the French concerned would be reduced to "renouncing agriculture, the source of well-being and often wealth for many of them. They will be forced to abandon all the lucrative industries in which their intelligence and their activity guaranteed them an honorable rank; they will not even be able to struggle on with a host of small companies that are almost exclusively in their hands."[31] Their Americanization was presented by the consul as an outcome that would be tragic and counterproductive for France, putting an end to the Franco-Louisianan blend of economic opportunities, American republican culture, and the benefits of a potential return to France:

> They say, with a sense of very profound bitterness, that they have been condemned by the Republic to die American because they [. . .] obey [. . .] the conditions, necessities and laws of the country that has given them hospitality! Their children, raised in the great school of republican America, and their fortunes, painstakingly acquired in the hope of a return to their homeland, will be lost to France forever.[32]

This is why the consul called for the abrogation of Article 8: he was clearly convinced that the French would not obey the article, arguing that "not a single French person will follow the example of the wife of the consul of the Republic," who had chosen to comply with the decree, to free "a colored family that she [had] received from her grandfather.[33] In the end, his arguments were heard by the authorities in France who, although they did not repeal the provision, postponed its application.[34] The more conservative position adopted after the election of Louis-Napoléon Bonaparte in December 1848 led the government in 1851 to extend the grace period from three to ten years.[35]

Despite this initial compromise, the consul continued in the 1850s to deplore the contradictions between French law and Louisiana law. The more stringent legislation adopted in Louisiana compelled owners to pay for the passage of their freed slaves to Africa in 1852,[36] but then in 1857 manumission was purely and simply prohibited,[37] making Article 8 inapplicable. The imperial authorities then distanced themselves from the principle of propagating abolitionism and refused further involvement in the issue of slavery outside the French Empire.[38] The Act of May 28, 1858, excluded from the scope of the decree slaves owned in foreign countries before 1848 and those acquired subsequently by marriage, donation, or inheritance, thereby undermining the intention of the initial text.[39]

Lastly, the French authorities were aware of the risk of creating stateless people if the decree were strictly applied:

> What is [. . .] the nationality of French people who have broken the law on the ownership of slaves? While the full force of French law must be applied to them, they have in fact lost their status as French people: have they thereby become citizens of the United States?—No, since they have neither requested nor obtained letters of naturalization.[40]

Because of the still very inclusive definition of French nationality—based on the presumption that French people in foreign countries were driven by a "spirit of return" to the motherland, or the possibility of becoming French again (for those who had been naturalized)—such an exclusion seemed impossible, and no record has been found of any case of this type.[41] And so the lax application of the decree meant that, while its principle tended to discourage French people living in Louisiana from buying slaves, it remained unlikely that slave owners failing to comply would be punished.[42]

There were similar compromises between the principle and its application in Saint-Louis in Senegal. As far as Senegal was concerned, Article 7, stipulating that the presence of a slave on French territory resulted in that person's automatic emancipation, embodied a mission to spread freedom that was close to the heart of Schoelcher. This article too gave rise to local protests. The regional context of the French trading post, its commercial dependency on the slave economy and the need to preserve relations with nearby kingdoms, led in fact to substantial adaptations. The application of Article 7 was thus restricted, exposing fugitive slaves seeking refuge in Saint-Louis to the risk of expulsion.[43] Furthermore, the decision to establish inside the empire a distinction between nationality and citizenship meant that from 1855 it could be considered that, outside Saint-Louis and Gorée, populations that practiced slavery on territories that had been recently incorporated into the French Empire were "French subjects without being French citizens."[44] It was thus possible to extend the empire without calling into question either local slavery-based practices or French citizenship.

This situation bears out François Renault's observation that the French administration adopted a fluctuating and circumstantial attitude in applying the abolition decree, both in New Orleans and Saint-Louis. The preservation of diplomatic relations and French trade were given precedence over the application of a law that was intended to be humanitarian and universal.[45] These compromises led in New Orleans to a willingness on the part of the French authorities to tolerate the ownership of slaves by French people, and also by those who had become naturalized Americans but wished to regain their French nationality. But the issue of choice of nationality by the French population cannot only be seen in legal terms. Nationality-related practices should also be seen in the light of growing political tensions in the United States about race issues, in addition to those that were specific to the French situation.

THE USES OF CITIZENSHIP BY THE FRENCH OF NEW ORLEANS: RACIAL PREJUDICE AND POLITICAL DISSIDENCE

"Everywhere wrong causes place themselves under the shield of nationality. One must always beware of those who appeal to national sentiment."[46] These were the words of Jean-Charles Houzeau, a Belgian scientist with humanist and liberal values, who arrived in New Orleans in 1857. He witnessed the exacerbation of conflicts based on national allegiances in both Europe and the United States. His view was illustrated by the situation of the French in New Orleans, whose individual strategies were based on a multiplicity of allegiances. The 1850s saw an upsurge in native-born anti-immigrant movements, tensions about slavery, and movements of dissidence in relation to French and European politics following the failure of the 1848 Revolutions (referred to in France as the Printemps des Peuples, or Springtime of the Peoples). The result was a declension in the use of national allegiances for French people in the city as a way of dealing with these conflicts. The multiplicity of forms of national identification transcended merely legal considerations to reflect the growing diversity of this section of the population.

The choice of American nationality was based on a complex set of motives that could not be reduced to the question raised by Article 8 of the decree of April 27, 1848. The motivations behind a wish to switch nationality included a desire to migrate, together with factors linked to the political and economic context in both France and the United States. Although it remained difficult to determine how many naturalization applications were made, because of the dispersion and inadequacies of sources,[47] 953 naturalization applications by French people have been identified in New Orleans from 1848 to 1860,[48] and a total of 1,338 naturalizations of French people for Louisiana as a whole.[49] In other words, while French migrants did not systematically request American nationality, a significant proportion of such migrants did apply.

Naturalization could also be used as a way of justifying a position on political and racial issues. Some French migrants thus made use of their American nationality to defend the established slave-based order. Part of the city's French population, for whom the consul became the spokesman, consisted of slaveholders or others whose socioeconomic status was dependent on the slave economy. Even though slavery declined in the city, domestic slaves were still widely used among French of the middle and upper classes. The results of the 1850 census in New Orleans show that in the French Quarter, where most of the French-speaking population lived (both long-established Creole families and newcomers), 34 percent of the households of French natives owned slaves (with on average two to three slaves per household). Even in the less affluent 3rd Municipality, home to people of many nationalities and to free people of color, some 20 percent of the households of people born in France or its colonies owned slaves.[50] Unfortunately the census data do not distinguish between homeowners with French nationality and naturalized people. Although slave owners were a minority among the French of New Orleans—and indeed among the other residents of the city—they were nonetheless numerous and relatively influential, as they tended to belong to the political and economic elite.[51]

American nationality was also sometimes an instrument of opposition to the French imperial regime of the 1850s. This was the case for Republicans such as James Foulhouze, a former priest hailing from Auvergne, who became a lawyer and head of the Supreme Council of Louisiana in 1848, a body of French Republican freemasons. He made use of his American nationality to reject any subjection to the French government and to justify his racial prejudice. During quarrels in the late 1850s with the Grand Orient of France—headed at the time by Lucien Murat, a cousin of Napoleon III—he accused Murat of choosing as grand officer a representative who came originally from Haiti. Foulhouze dismissed the Haitian as a "representative of niggers" and took Lucien Murat to task in the following terms:

> Would you by any chance, as an ex-resident of New Jersey, be siding with the Abolitionists? [. . .] In Louisiana we continue to find your conduct in this matter—I will not use the term insulting—you are too innocent to insult anyone—but superbly misguided: and in truth, my Very Excellent Prince, it is painful for me to find you keeping such bizarre company, all the more because the strength of law and prejudice here is such that, despite the esteem in which many free people of color are held among us, we cannot however have dealings with them as Masons. [. . .] But what could you do? Excommunicate me! [. . .] Far be it from me to believe that such a preposterous idea could occur to you, and that you could have so little instruction in the law of people's rights as to summon before you an American citizen.[52]

Conversely, the French in the city did not all identify themselves with the slave-owning community. Claiming French identity could in fact go hand in hand with distancing oneself from, or even rejecting, the racial order of New Orleans. The new migrants, who tended to come from the middle and lower classes—particularly the large contingent from Alsace and Lorraine,[53] and the *proscrits* of the Second Empire (republicans, socialists, utopianists, and anarchists)[54]—differed from earlier generations in both their motives for migration and their insertion into the urban fabric of New Orleans. These new workers—"free men in a slavery-based society"[55]—formed part of the urban economy rather than the plantation economy. Some established themselves in ethnic groups and kept their distance from the white Creole or Creolized population. In 1856, the French of New Orleans, feeling threatened by violence against foreigners, harked back to their French origins, claiming that the consul Roger was in fact too Americanized:

> Having determined that [. . .] the present consul and the chancellor of the consulate have contracted in this country family alliances and own considerable interests there, and that as a result, finding themselves [. . .] continually divided between their affections and their interests on the one hand, and their duty [. . .] they are completely unable to take action and can provide no guarantee for the French population.[56]

These French nationals did not therefore necessarily support the proslavery cause: the newcomers' awareness had been raised by the contemporaneous debates in Europe about abolition, and also about slavery as a social issue. This is the case for example of Aimé Malespine, a French Republican who took refuge in the United States after the coup of December 2, 1851, moving to New Orleans where in 1856 he founded a new French-language newspaper, *L'Union,* which strove to promote social progress. *L'Union* stated that it was in favor of gradual emancipation, a widely held theory at the time, that was expressed by many American abolitionists and republicans, including Abraham Lincoln himself.[57] The expression of this proposed gradual process of emancipation was subject to many precautions.[58] It rejected certain solutions, ranging from "emancipation as carried out in the English and French colonies" to the hypothesis of importing Chinese workers. It laid greater emphasis on the industrialization of the South and the mechanization of agriculture, by dint of a "Work Company of the South, striving to establish agricultural working by the use of machines and the creation of manufacturing industry."[59]

Other French radicals, such as Élisée Reclus, Charles Testut, and Joseph Déjacque, were more outspoken in their denunciation of slavery.[60] Déjacque, a French anarchist worker who spent two years in New Orleans in the 1850s, proclaimed: "Ah! in Louisiana as indeed everywhere, morally and physically, 'slavery is murder!'"[61] Although the expression of abolitionist views was prohibited, he claimed to have taken the risk of expressing his support for racial equality at a public meeting in New Orleans:

> I was present, when working as a painter, at the opening banquet of a bar on Gravier street, [. . .] toasts were given; I also gave my own: "To the freeing of all men, BLACK or white. To the free and egalitarian communion of producers of all sexes and all races in the social banquet." I do not know if anyone felt furious inside at this; I only know that no-one was brave enough, or cowardly enough, to talk about having me flogged.[62]

In the troubled period of the 1850s, the identification of French people residing in the United States with their native country was thus affected by tensions that were exacerbated by local confrontations.[63] While New Orleans to some extent mirrored issues related to French colonialism, its position as part of America was increasingly coming to the fore. As Mary Ryan has suggested, the transition from local tensions to national conflict was linked to the undermining of the federal pact and to the emergence of regional or "sectional"[64] identities that reveal the fragmentation of national allegiances caused by the slavery issue.

*

France's abolition of slavery in 1848 reflected the complexity of changes in the status of citizenship and nationality in the Atlantic world, and the place occupied by New Orleans at the intersection of the political situation in France, America, and the colonies. For the French population of the city, the conflicts of allegiance triggered by the abolition decree bore witness to the contradictions between their local integration and their national identity. France's abolition of slavery opened up a breach in identification with a nation, highlighting the gap between attachment to one's roots and changes in the rights associated with French nationality. Furthermore, it illustrated the peripheral situation that New Orleans shared with Saint-Louis du Sénégal in relation to the French colonial empire, as the humanitarian approach advocated by the abolitionists in France clashed with the compromises made with slavery to preserve economic prosperity and the regional importance of these port cities. The adaptations reflected the malleability of practices related to nationality, whether in terms of the relative tolerance shown towards French or naturalized slave owners in the United States, or of the creation of territories and individual statuses that were alternatives to full and complete citizenship in Senegal.

These solutions, however, turned out to be relatively short-lived. In New Orleans, the strong influence of American political tensions, at a local and then nationwide level, gave rise to multiple uses of nationality and naturalization that transcended colonial issues and became caught up in the American slavery debate. The Civil War, which split the American union into two opposing factions, led to radical changes in the sense of belonging of the French in New Orleans. Sentimental and patriotic attachment to France on the one hand, and the defense of a socioeconomic status based on slavery on the other, gave rise to opposite trajectories, while also revealing the coexistence of contradictory allegiances. Charles Hémard, who hailed from Lorraine and became a cotton broker in New Orleans, thus stated in 1863: "Although an American citizen first and today a Confederate (I am nonetheless still French above all), I am a Confederate not because of patriotism but because in fact my personal interests totally depend on it."[65]

NOTES

Note to epigraph: Discussion between De Tocqueville and the consul of France Guillemin, New Orleans, January 1, 1832, Alexis de Tocqueville, *Oeuvres complètes: Voyages en Sicile et aux États-Unis,* Tome 5-1 (Paris: Gallimard, 1957), 136.

1. Jean-Luc Mayaud, ed., *1848: actes du colloque international du cent cinquantenaire, tenu à l'Assemblée nationale à Paris, les 23–25 février 1998* (Paris: Créaphis, 2002); Guy P. C. Thomson, ed., *The European Revolutions of 1848 and the Americas* (London: Institute of Latin American Studies, 2002); Kay Boardman and Christine Kinealy, eds., *1848, the Year the World Turned?* (Newcastle, UK: Cambridge Scholars Pub., 2007); Timothy Mason Roberts, *Distant Revolutions: 1848 and the Challenge to American Exceptionalism* (Charlottesville: University of Virginia Press, 2009).

2. Joseph Logsdon, "Immigration through the Port of New Orleans," in Mark Stolarik, ed., *Forgotten Doors: The Other Ports of Entry to the United States* (Philadelphia: Balch Institute Press,

1988), 105–24; Frederick Marcel Spletstoser, "Back Door to the Land of Plenty: New Orleans as an Immigrant Port, 1820–1860," PhD diss., Louisiana State University, 1978. In 1850, there were 48,601 inhabitants, or roughly half of the population, who had been born in foreign countries: 20,200 in Ireland, 11,425 in German states, and 7,522 in France. In addition to this ethnic composition, the city was itself a melting pot, with 10,300 free people of color and 19,697 slaves (in New Orleans, Algiers, and Lafayette). In 1860, the city's population was 168,675, of whom 64,621 were born in foreign countries, including 10,564 French; there were 10,680 free people of color and 13,385 slaves. J. D. B. De Bow, *Statistical View of the United States . . . Being a Compendium of the Seventh Census to Which are Added the Results of Every Previous Census, Beginning with 1790* (Washington: Beverley Tucker, Senate Printer, 1854), 247–48, 397–99; Joseph C. G. Kennedy, *Population of the United States in 1860; Compiled from the Original Returns of the Eighth Census* (Washington, DC: Government Printing Office, 1864), 195, 615.

3. Mark L. Thompson, "Locating the Isle of Orleans: Atlantic and American Historiographical Perspectives," *Atlantic Studies* 5:3 (2008): 305–33.

4. Gerald Neuman, *Strangers to the Constitution: Immigrants, Borders and Fundamental Law* (Princeton, NJ: Princeton University Press, 1996); Mary P. Ryan, *Civic Wars: Democracy and Public Life in the American City during the Nineteenth Century* (Berkeley: University of California Press, 1997).

5. Edward Bartlett Rugemer, *The Problem of Emancipation: The Caribbean Roots of the American Civil War* (Baton Rouge: Louisiana State University Press, 2008); Seymour Drescher, *Abolition: History of Slavery and Antislavery* (Cambridge: Cambridge University Press, 2009).

6. Saint-Louis had a population of 12,000–13,000 at the time, including some 6,000 slaves. The 1845 census indicates that there were 166 European residents, 5,346 free inhabitants, 618 indentured inhabitants, and 6,008 slaves, making a total of 12,138 inhabitants: Martin Klein, *Slavery and Colonial Rule in French West Africa* (Cambridge: Cambridge University Press, 1999), 23. The slaveholders in Saint-Louis were primarily indigenous inhabitants: Roger Pasquier, "À propos de l'émancipation des esclaves au Sénégal en 1848," *Revue française d'histoire d'outre-mer* 54:194–97 (1967): 188–208, 193.

7. François Renault, *L'abolition de l'esclavage au Sénégal: L'attitude de l'administration française* (Paris: Société française d'histoire d'outre-mer, 1972), 7; Lawrence C. Jennings, "L'abolition de l'esclavage par la IIe République et ses effets en Louisiane, 1848–1858," *Revue française d'histoire d'outre-mer* 56:205 (1969): 375–76.

8. Nelly Schmidt, *L'engrenage de la liberté: Caraïbes-XIXe siècle* (Aix-en-Provence: Université de Provence, 1995).

9. François Weil, "The Purchase and the Making of French Louisiana," in Peter J. Kastor and François Weil, eds., *Empires of the Imagination: Transatlantic Histories of the Louisiana Purchase* (Charlottesville: University of Virginia Press, 2009), 301–26.

10. In her essay in this book entitled "Asserting Citizenship and Refusing Stigma: New Orleans Equal-Rights Activists Interpret 1803 and 1848," Rebecca J. Scott focuses on the restrictions of public expression imposed on free people of color; in 1862 freedom of speech became possible when the city was occupied by Union troops.

11. Since 1830, the publication and dissemination of abolitionist views had been prohibited in Louisiana. Although the term *abolition* is not explicitly used, the Act of Legislature of March 16, 1830, severely punishes "any thing having a tendency to produce discontent among the free colored population of the state, or insubordination among the slaves therein," Act passed March 16, 1830, *Acts Passed at the Tenth Legislature of the State of Louisiana* (New Orleans: John Gibson, 1831), 96–97. I am grateful to Rebecca Scott for sharing this document.

12. The expression "politics of slavery" refers to the way in which slavery, from the 1830s onwards, suddenly became a major issue in all American party political and electoral battles, and led candidates in the southern states to adopt increasingly extreme positions as they claimed to be the strongest defenders of the "peculiar institution": William J. Cooper, *The South and the Politics of Slavery, 1828–1856* (Baton Rouge: Louisiana State University Press, 1978), xii–xv; John M. Sacher, *A Perfect War of Politics: Parties, Politicians, and Democracy in Louisiana, 1824–1861* (Baton Rouge: Louisiana State University Press, 2003), 80–81.

13. This was demonstrated by the opposition expressed in New Orleans between newspapers linked to a political party. The Democratic newspaper *Le Courrier de la Louisiane* and the pro-Whig *L'Abeille* accused each other of abolitionism. The French consul noted that "in Louisiana, there is only one way to success, and that is to be clearly in favor of slavery," French Ministry of Foreign Affairs (*Ministère des Affaires étrangères,* hereafter MAE), Political Correspondence of Consuls (*Correspondances Politiques des Consuls,* hereafter CPC), United States, 2, Dispatch from Aimé Roger, Consul of France in New Orleans, to the Minister of Foreign Affairs, October 29, 1848.

14. For a discussion of the significance of this silence, see also Rebecca Scott's essay in this book.

15. *L'Orléanais,* June 2, 1848.

16. Centre des Archives Diplomatiques de Nantes (hereafter CADN), Consular Archives, New Orleans, A, 5, Dispatch from the consul of France in New Orleans to the Minister of Foreign Affairs, New Orleans, September 10, 1848.

17. The abolition decree of April 27 stipulated that abolition would not come into force until August 10. Myriam Cottias has shown that this delay gave rise to rumors in the French colonies, and to growing impatience. This uncertainty had a decisive effect on the slave uprisings that took place on May 22, 1848, in Martinique. The troubles led local authorities to proclaim immediate abolition from May 23 to May 26, without awaiting the official orders from the French authorities: Myriam Cottias, "Ces 'hommes dangereux' de 1848: L'amnistie à l'épreuve de l'abolition de l'esclavage," *Genèses* 66:1 (2007): 30–50.

18. Ashli White, "The Limits of Fear: The Saint Dominguan Challenge to Slave Trade Abolition in the United States," *Early American Studies* 2:2 (2004): 362–97; Frédérique Beauvois, "L'indemnité de Saint-Domingue: 'Dette d'indépendance' ou 'rançon de l'esclavage'?," *French Colonial History* 10 (2009): 109–24.

19. Among the organizers of the meeting of July 1 were French people hailing from the Antilles who had moved to New Orleans from the 1830s onwards: *Le Courrier de la Louisiane,* July 3, 1848. The Assembly of July 8 brought together the population of New Orleans, and included

representatives of the three municipalities, Creoles, descendants of Saint Dominguan refugees, and Americans: *L'Abeille de La Nouvelle-Orléans,* July 9, 1848.

20. *Courrier de la Louisiane,* July 3, 1848.

21. *L'Abeille de La Nouvelle-Orléans,* July 9, 1848.

22. Rugemer, *The Problem of Emancipation,* 123–24.

23. *Courrier de la Louisiane,* July 3, 1848.

24. *L'Abeille de La Nouvelle-Orléans,* July 9, 1848.

25. Patrick Weil, *Qu'est-ce qu'un Français? Histoire de la nationalité française depuis la Révolution* (Paris: Grasset, 2004), 37–38, 286.

26. Great Britain had adopted a law in 1843 that prohibited the ownership of slaves by British people in foreign countries, but certain exceptions were tolerated, and infringements were punished only by a fine: Jennings, "L'abolition de l'esclavage," 380.

27. Decree of April 27, 1848, published in *L'Orléanais,* June 2, 1848.

28. "Duty compels me to say that if the government does not intend to denationalize 5,000 to 6,000 French people living in Louisiana, or if it wishes to avoid this outcome, it must repeal Article 8 of the abolition decree," MAE, CPC, United States, 2, Dispatch from Aimé Roger, consul of France in New Orleans to the Minister of Foreign Affairs, New Orleans, July 6, 1848. In 1850, the federal census indicated that there were 255,491 white residents in Louisiana, of whom 20,670 were slaveholders. The place of birth of the slaveholders is not indicated. It is known, however, that the number of native-born French at this time was 11,552. If the consul's estimates are accurate, the French would account for one-quarter of slave owners in Louisiana, which seems a considerable number: De Bow, *Statistical View of the United States,* 95, 118, 135.

29. MAE, CPC, United States, 2, Dispatch from Aimé Roger, consul of France in New Orleans to the Minister of Foreign Affairs, New Orleans, July 6, 1848.

30. Ibid.

31. Ibid.

32. MAE, CPC, United States, 2, Dispatch from Aimé Roger, consul of France in New Orleans, to the Minister of Foreign Affairs, New Orleans, October 29, 1848.

33. Ibid.

34. Édouard Drouin de Lhuys, Minister of Foreign Affairs, stated in a dispatch to the French consul in 1849 that he had noted the observations submitted by the consul "in the interest of our nationals residing in Louisiana, concerning Article 8 of the decree of April 27 [. . .]." He added that he reserved the right to "examine subsequently what should be done in this respect," MAE, CPC, United States, 1, Dispatch from the Minister of Foreign Affairs to the consul of France in New Orleans, Paris, February 23, 1849.

35. Law of February 11, 1851, quoted in Jennings, "L'abolition de l'esclavage," 389–90.

36. "The law I am passing on to you results in a completely new situation for the French of Louisiana," MAE, CPC, United States, 3, Dispatch from Aimé Roger, consul of France in New Orleans, to the Minister of Foreign Affairs, New Orleans, June 18, 1852. "An Act concerning the emancipation of slaves in this State," March 18, 1852, in Judith Kelleher Schafer, *Becoming Free, Remaining Free: Manumission and Enslavement in New Orleans, 1846–1862* (Baton Rouge: Louisiana State University Press, 2003), 182–83.

37. "An Act to prohibit the emancipation of slaves," March 6, 1857, in Judith Kelleher Schafer, *Slavery, the Civil Law, and the Supreme Court of Louisiana* (Baton Rouge: Louisiana State University Press, 1997), 183–84.

38. Jennings, "L'abolition de l'esclavage," 382, 392–95.

39. Law of May 28, 1858, quoted in Augustin Cochin, *L'Abolition de l'esclavage* (Paris: J. Lecoffre, 1861); Patrick Weil, "Politique de la mémoire: L'interdit et la commémoration," *Esprit* 2 (2007): 124–42.

40. CADN, Washington, 1217, Memorandum to the Minister of Foreign Affairs, Consulate of New Orleans, 1858.

41. As early as 1834, Louis Sérurier, minister of France in Washington, stated that French people who had been naturalized American "are French by origin and can again become so. This is more than enough to give them a respectable entitlement to my undivided interest [. . .]. They are part of the big family, they are foreign *France*," CADN, Consular Archives, New York, 474PO/1/92, Dispatch from Sérurier, Legation of France in Washington, to the New York general consul De la Forest, Washington, April 14, 1834.

42. In the discussion of the Law of May 28, 1858, French legislators mentioned that "the dispositions of this article were unprecedented and we must add that to this day they remained unexecuted due to their imperative and absolute character," *Collection complète des lois, décrets, ordonnances, règlemens et avis du Conseil d'État,* 58 (Paris: Pommeret et Moreau, 1858), 186.

43. M'Baye Guèye, "La fin de l'esclavage à Saint-Louis et à Gorée en 1848," *Bulletin de l'Institut fondamental d'Afrique noire, Série B* 28:3–4 (1966): 637–56, 647–49; Klein, *Slavery and Colonial Rule,* 26–27; Mamadou Badji, "L'abolition de l'esclavage au Sénégal: Entre plasticité du droit colonial et respect de l'État de droit," *Droit et cultures* 52:2 (2006), accessed November 1, 2015, http://droitcultures.revues.org/729.

44. Report by Carrère, Head of the Judicial Department of the Board of Directors of the colony of Senegal, April 10, 1855, quoted in Renault, *L'abolition de l'esclavage,* 86–88.

45. Renault, *L'abolition de l'esclavage,* 75.

46. Letter from Jean-Charles Houzeau to his parents, New Orleans, November 7, 1857, Jean-Charles Houzeau, Hossam Elkhadem, Annette Felix & Liliane Wellens-De Donder, *Lettres adressées des États-Unis à sa famille, 1857–1868* (Brussels: Centre National d'Histoire des Sciences, 1994), 80.

47. Many data are missing, all the more as the naturalization process could take place anywhere in the United States. The federal law of April 14, 1802, stipulated that naturalization could take place after a period of five years of residence in the United States and two years after filling in a declaration of intention to adopt American nationality and renounce any other national allegiance. Each judicial echelon in the states and the federal courts of the United States was empowered to carry out these procedures: Neuman, *Strangers to the Constitution,* 42. Certain French people naturalized on the eastern coast of the United States before traveling to Louisiana have been identified: James Foulhouze, the influential New Orleans lawyer and freemason, arrived in Philadelphia in 1835, filled in a declaration of intention there on April 27, 1835, and pledged an oath of allegiance on October 1, 1839, at the Court of Common Pleas; data gathered via Ancestry.com on April 17, 2012, after P. William Filby, *Philadelphia Natural-*

ization Records: An Index to Records of Aliens' Declarations of Intention and/or Oaths of Allegiance, 1789–1880 (Philadelphia: Gale Research Company, 1982).

48. For the period 1817 to 1860, 1,650 naturalization applications (Declarations of Intention and Certificates) by French people have been identified in New Orleans. The data were obtained from Naturalization Records on microfilm at the New Orleans Public Library: U.S. District Court for the Eastern District of Louisiana, New Orleans, Certificates and Declarations of Intention (1813–1932); Orleans Parish Court, Certificates (1836–1846), Declarations of Intention (1827–1844); 2nd District Court of New Orleans, Certificates (1850–1884), Declarations of Intention (1849–1853); 3rd District Court of New Orleans, Certificates (1846–1856); 4th District Court of New Orleans, Certificates (1854–1979); 5th District Court of New Orleans, Certificates (1854–1877), Declarations of Intention (1847–1855); 6th District Court, Certificates (1853–1864), Declarations of Intention (1850–1856); Criminal Court, Orleans Parish, Certificates (1845–1846; 1853–1855).

49. From 1820 to 1860, 2,029 French were naturalized in Louisiana: Card index to naturalizations in Louisiana (P2087), National Archives and Records Administration (hereafter NARA), Washington, DC; data gathered via Ancestry.com on April 17, 2012.

50. Figures collated for the 1st Ward of the 1st Municipality (Vieux Carré), which had 278 households (1,097 free people and 270 slaves) that included at least one person born in France (metropolitan France and colonies), of which 95 households owned slaves; and for the 1st Ward of the 3rd Municipality (Faubourg Marigny) which had 387 households (1,681 free people and 205 slaves) that included at least one person born in France, of which 77 households owned slaves: New Orleans Public Library (hereafter NOPL), US Census and US Slave schedules, Louisiana, Orleans Parish, 1850.

51. In 1850, the city of New Orleans (including the suburbs of Algiers and Lafayette) had a total of 133,650 inhabitants, including only 10,300 free people of color (7.7% of the population) and 19,697 slaves (14.7%): De Bow, *Statistical View of the United States,* 397–99. Among the residents of the French Quarter, Pierre Soulé, senator of the United States in 1846–1847 and 1849–1853, owned nine slaves in 1850; the Musson family, headed by Germain Musson, who was born in Saint-Domingue and was a cotton broker, also owned nine slaves: NOPL, US Slave Schedules, Louisiana, Orleans Parish, 1850.

52. Lucien Murat, a nephew of Napoleon Bonaparte, settled in the United States in 1825 and joined other exiled members of his family in New Jersey during the Bourbon Restoration. James Foulhouze, *Mémoire à consulter sur l'origine du rite Écossais Ancien et Accepté* (New Orleans: L. Marchand, 1858), 88–96.

53. Camille Maire, "L'émigration des Lorrains en Amérique, 1815–1870," PhD diss., Université de Metz, 1980, 125–41; Nicole Fouché, *L'émigration alsacienne aux États-Unis, 1815–1870* (Paris: Publications de la Sorbonne, 1992), 119.

54. Carl A. Brasseaux, *The "Foreign French": Nineteenth-Century French Immigration into Louisiana, Vol. 3 (1849–1852)* (Lafayette: Center for Louisiana Studies, University of Southwestern Louisiana, 1990).

55. Michel Cordillot, *Des hommes libres dans une société esclavagiste: Les ouvriers du Sud des États-Unis, 1830–1861* (Paris: Les Belles Lettres, 1990); Ira Berlin and Herbert G. Gutman, "Na-

tives and Immigrants, Free Men and Slaves: Urban Workingmen in the Antebellum American South," *American Historical Review* 88:5 (1983): 1175–1200.

56. *Le National,* June 13, 1856.

57. Eric Foner, *The Fiery Trial: Abraham Lincoln and American Slavery* (New York: W. W. Norton, 2010), 182.

58. *L'Union,* April 21, 1857.

59. *L'Union,* April 26, 1857.

60. Elisée Reclus, *Correspondance, Tome I, Décembre 1850–Mai 1870* (Paris: Schleicher Frères, 1911); Marie-Louise Lagarde, "Charles Testut: Critic, Journalist, and Literary Socialist," PhD diss., Tulane University, 1948.

61. "La Nouvelle-Orléans," *Le Libertaire, Journal du Mouvement Social,* July 16, 1858.

62. "Le Socle de Pasquin," *Le Libertaire, Journal du Mouvement Social,* August 31, 1858.

63. The debate on the significance of national allegiance also affected people of color in New Orleans: Rebecca Scott has shown how in the 1860s the native-born Frenchman Edouard Tinchant applied for American nationality in order to defend the idea of racial equality, in opposition to the conceptions of Armand Lanusse. Rebecca J. Scott and Jean M. Hébrard, *Freedom Papers: An Atlantic Odyssey in the Age of Emancipation* (Cambridge, MA: Harvard University Press, 2012), 118–24.

64. Ryan, *Civic Wars,* 157–60.

65. Howard Tilton Memorial Library, Tulane University, Hémard Family Papers, MSS 686, Letter from Charles Hémard to his cousin Ernest Venderscher, New Orleans, September 18, 1863.

ASSERTING CITIZENSHIP AND REFUSING STIGMA

New Orleans Equal-Rights Activists Interpret 1803 and 1848

REBECCA J. SCOTT

In the nineteenth-century Atlantic world, the idea of citizenship was a concept under development, one with neither stable criteria nor stable implications. It might rest on an ancient reciprocity between allegiance of the subject and protection by the sovereign, but it could also encompass shifting constructs of nationality, emergent claims to specific rights, or even radical assertions of equality. When the Union occupation of New Orleans in 1862 opened up public space for the discussion of topics that had long been taboo in slaveholding societies, members of the city's population of African descent added their voices to debates on citizenship, rights, and stigma. Many of these men and women spoke and sometimes read both English and French. Residents of a port city through which flowed a stream of people, newspapers, and books, they could draw upon recently arrived allies and find encouragement among overseas interlocutors.

Out of this tumult emerged several strains of radical assertion, drawing on multiple languages of rights. Some of these reflected features of antislavery debate particular to the United States, given great urgency by the circumstances of war. Others incorporated ideas of a real or imagined France, its empire, and its former colony of Saint-Domingue/Haiti into a panorama of precedents, heroes, and principles that seemed closely connected to the future in Louisiana. Activists could reach for inspiration back to the French Revolution of 1789, to the Treaty of Cession through which Louisiana joined the United States in 1803, and to the Revolution and abolition of 1848.

Enthusiasts of France's languages of rights were nonetheless obliged to confront the evident imperial ambitions of Napoleon III in neighboring

Mexico. The emergence of a new regime there could be read favorably in the light of Mexico's early abolition of slavery and formal absence of discriminatory practices, which contrasted with the continuance of slavery in the United States. But it could also be denounced by those who recalled Napoleon III's repression of partisans of the 1848 Revolution and his attacks on workers in the streets of Paris. With federal citizenship in the United States now a potential source of rights, moreover, the Monroe Doctrine itself took on new appeal, reinforcing republican denunciations of empire and monarchy. These tasks of interpretation and transformation of memories associated with France constituted an indirect linkage between New Orleans and Saint-Louis, Senegal. Each of the two port cities had developed a lively and often vocal free population characterized as of African or mixed African and European ancestry. Events emanating from France, moreover, repeatedly framed the terms in which public debate would be carried out, both within the imperial fold in Saint-Louis and outside the imperial fold but within the francophone cultural orbit in postcolonial Louisiana.[1]

The status designation "free person of color," of course, did not by itself necessarily represent a class or a caste, much less a group with a clear shared identity. Although law, labeling, and census takers could provide an appearance of commonality each time they wrote the phrase *gens de couleur libres,* as a practical matter the individuals designated in this way occupied various and sometimes overlapping social niches—freedperson, slaveholder, artisan, workman, merchant, trader, and so forth. No single consciousness should be attributed to the members of such a heterogeneous group. What this largely bilingual class of persons in New Orleans did share, however, was a privileged access to news and understandings that reached them through paths other than Anglo-American ones. At key moments, some of the most visible activists among these men and women drew upon ideas and evidence associated with France as they configured their own claims to rights.[2]

Two emblematic episodes stand out in this evocation of precedents: 1803, with the Treaty of Cession of Louisiana to the United States, and its ambiguous language concerning citizenship; and 1848, with its complex example of popular mobilization and the abolition of slavery. The present essay does not attempt a full analysis of the many dimensions along which bilingual and francophone activists of color engaged with things French and Caribbean.

Instead, it aims to signal some of the ideas in play and the modes of their transmission, while pointing to additional sources that may enable us to explore the underpinnings of what would prove to be an extraordinarily robust rights-consciousness.

1803: "THE ENJOYMENT OF ALL THESE RIGHTS"

In the midst of the struggles of Reconstruction in Louisiana, the state's supreme court in 1873 heard an appeal to a small case concerning landownership, and in the process made a large statement about the long history of citizenship in Louisiana. The court declared, "By the treaty whereby Louisiana was acquired, the free colored inhabitants of Louisiana were admitted to citizenship of the United States." In the case at hand, this meant reversing the action of a Louisiana official who in 1860 had declined to grant the patent that would perfect the title to land of Charles Lallande. The clerk had refused on the grounds that Lallande was "a free negro," hence not a citizen, and thus ineligible for title to public land by preemption under state and federal law. The 1873 court concluded: "We think the facts of this case justify us in saying that Lallande was a citizen of Louisiana at the time he acquired the land in question; that he had the capacity to acquire it, and he has the better right to the land."[3]

In constitutional terms, the invocation of the 1803 treaty was an ingenious maneuver around Chief Justice Taney's declarations in *Dred Scott v. Sandford* that denied the possibility of federal citizenship for persons of African descent. Even after the ratification of the Fourteenth Amendment, a man of color in recognized possession of national citizenship might under the logic of *Dred Scott v. Sandford* be dispossessed from property he had acquired earlier, on the grounds that he had not been qualified to acquire it at the time of his purchase. On that reading, the citizenship conferred after the Civil War was a new acquisition, and could not be said to have existed prior to 1868 (or 1866, perhaps, with the Civil Rights Act of that year.)[4]

Like the Republicans in Congress who had faced similar questions about the qualifications for office of Senator Hiram Revels (which depended on discerning a starting date for counting the years during which Revels had been a citizen), Louisiana's supreme court in *Walsh v. Lallande* sought to sustain a claim to citizenship and to date it back well before the Civil War. In order to seat Hiram Revels in 1870, the Senate had to address the requirement that any member have been a citizen for at least nine years. In order to protect the validity of the prewar federal grant of land to Charles Lallande, the Louisiana Supreme Court needed for Lallande's citizenship to extend back to the time of the 1844 grant.[5]

Aside from meeting the pragmatic need for an argument to validate the land claim, the court's reasoning in *Walsh v. Lallande* is suggestive as evidence of a memory of the implications of the 1803 treaty, one accessible enough that the members of the state's highest court could locate it as they looked for a basis on which to rebuke the clerk who had canceled Lallande's preemption claim. Indeed, for some within Louisiana's population, the 1803 document may long have been seen as implying a smooth transition between a French *citoyenneté* (however fleeting) and citizenship in the United States.

The actual text of the relevant clause in the treaty had nonetheless been considerably less categorical than the court in *Walsh v. Lallande* chose to acknowledge:

> The inhabitants of the ceded territory shall be incorporated in the Union of the United States and admitted as soon as possible according to the principles of the federal Constitution to the enjoyment of all these rights, advantages and immunities of citizens of the United States, and in the mean time they shall be maintained and protected in the free enjoyment of their liberty, property and the Religion which they profess.[6]

On the question of citizenship, then, the treaty was not, in lawyer's terms, "self- executing." The language "shall be . . . admitted" and "as soon as possible" implied that some action would need to be taken at a future time to confer citizenship on those who were promised it. Moreover, if one parsed the text suspiciously, the word "inhabitants"—*habitants* in the French—carried its own indeterminacy. "Inhabitants" in its broadest sense meant "those who live in a place." But the drafters of the treaty were not likely to have had resident slaves in mind when they spoke of "the free enjoyment of their liberty." Was the term "inhabitants" in the treaty implicitly limited, then, to those with free status, or perhaps limited by color or by property-holding?[7]

The word *habitants* was used in some contexts to refer specifically to property holders, but not necessarily as a reference to color or ancestry. In Saint-Louis, Senegal, it designated long-settled residents of perceived mixed African and European descent. For more conservative thinkers in 1803 Louisiana, by contrast, it could be limited to "le *propriétaire,* le colon, le vrai Louisianais," in the words of the intendant Laussat.[8] The 1798 Dictionary of the Académie Française, however, simply defined it as "Qui fait sa demeure en quelque lieu," which drew it close to the broadest sense of the English term "inhabitants."[9]

Ominously for the prospects of those who were categorized as "free persons of color," however, the phrase "according to the principles of the federal Constitution" could signal a further narrowing of the category of potential citizens if admission followed the 1790 statutory requirement that any candidate for naturalization be a "free white person."[10] That is, even if formal naturalization were not required, the restrictions on eligibility for naturalization might be thought to apply as well to the new entrants into US citizenship by territorial acquisition. Perhaps the admission to citizenship for the residents of the previously French territory should not be seen as parallel to naturalization, and the lack of reference to color in the treaty should prevail. But as a matter of law and policy the interpretation was open to dispute.

Interpreting the ambiguous text of the treaty as an immediate grant of citizenship was nonetheless something more than just the ingenious rereading put forward by the state supreme court seventy years later. Louisiana militiamen of color who feared a loss of privilege with the cession had been quick to claim at the time that the promise of rights and privileges *did* apply to them. The very first lines of a petition from the militia members in 1804 anchored their claim in their long residency in the "province," and with it their identity as "free Citizens of Louisiana." Rejoicing at the transfer of Louisiana to the sovereignty of the American republic, they reported themselves "duly sensible that our personal and political freedom is thereby assured to us for ever." Although they were writing to confirm that their standing as militiamen would be respected, they took the fundamental guarantees of "personal and political freedom," as well as citizenship, to be already in place. In effect, from their point of view, the 1803 treaty negotiated by France should be viewed as self-executing, with its key rights conferred by declaration.[11]

Less well known than the explicit demands of the militiamen are the simple bureaucratic procedures that reinforced the legitimacy of a general claim to citizenship independent of color. When heading onto the high seas, ordinary sailors—black and white—could request "seamen's protection certificates" in order to document their claim to US citizenship, in hopes among other things of avoiding impressment if accosted by the British. The archived files of applications for such certificates from Louisiana show local notaries and Territorial Governor William C. C. Claiborne signing off on the citizenship claims of men of color, and invoking their residence in the territory prior to 1803 by way of justification.[12]

One example provides the flavor: On January 4, 1811, Étienne Augustin, a free man of color, born in Môle Saint-Nicolas in Saint-Domingue (Haiti), certified before a New Orleans notary that "he was a citizen of this place previous to the 30th April 1803 and is still a resident in said territory," hence a citizen of the United States. Two other free men of color swore out the usual statement that they were "well acquainted" with the claimant and believed the deposition to be "true and correct."[13] This young sailor, who had been a child and then a teenager at the time of the Haitian Revolution, had evidently made his way to Louisiana before 1803 (or could credibly claim to have done so). As a French national presumably residing in Louisiana at the time of the cession, he and his neighbors, and the notary, now took it for granted that he had automatically become a citizen of the United States, without any need of further naturalization.

The year before, in 1810, Governor Claiborne had himself overseen the oath of allegiance of one Philip Aquino, who said "that he was an Inhabitant of the Territory of Orleans previous to the 30th of April 1803 and still resides therein." The governor was concerned to make sure that Aquino, "a colored man," was not a slave, and he noted that the two men who vouched for him "have bound themselves to answer any Claims against his freedom." But once Aquino's status was established to be that of a free man, Claiborne seemed to assume that his citizenship would not be in question.[14]

Well before Louisiana's admission as a state, then, the authorities of the Orleans Territory, as part of their routine tasks of certification, were treating at least some free men of color as citizens for the purpose of acquisition of these certificates. It is not difficult to see why: the United States had a strong interest in blocking the impressment of sailors by the British, and in asserting protective authority over those who served in the new nation's merchant marine. These procedures were designed to advance that larger interest, transforming local knowledge and documentation into a standardized certificate that might avert impressment or help a sailor extract himself from foreign custody.[15]

The certificates, however, could have an additional meaning for those who carried them, reinforcing their conviction that as Louisiana residents they had been recognized as citizens, hence as carriers of those "rights and privileges" invoked in the Treaty of Cession of 1803. Equally pragmatically, a man in possession of such a certificate might thereby gain a degree of mobility and a presumption of freedom. (It was, famously, a borrowed seaman's protection certificate that Frederick Douglass would use in 1838 to travel safely as he fled by train from the place where he had been held as a slave.)[16]

For long-standing residents of the Orleans and Louisiana territories, the text of the 1803 treaty provided a thread of direct connection to France and to its (episodically) expansive definitions of citizenship. When free persons of color invoked the treaty in order to claim rights, however, they stepped away from identification with France and asserted loyalty to the United States, while at the same time trying to enforce provisions negotiated for Louisiana's inhabitants by France. An imagined citizenship implied by their fleeting moment as residents of a French colony might thus be transformed by the act of cession into a forward-looking claim to citizenship in the United States.

FRANCE'S REVOLUTIONS: 1830 AND 1848

While Governor Claiborne acknowledged the citizenship of mariners who were men of color, the long-term prospects for an explicit recognition of state or national citizenship for free persons of color were not encouraging. As Louisiana law and custom rapidly fell in line with that of the other slaveholding states, stigmatizing free persons of color and mandating their continued deference to the state's white residents, some men and women looked toward France itself to see how comparable rights were faring there. With the installation of a constitutional monarchy in France in 1830, a more expansive set of "civil, political, and public" rights became available to French citizens, and debate on whether there should be any restrictions on the basis of color moved into the open. In 1833, the French parliament passed a statute to be applied to the colonies of the Caribbean and the Indian Ocean, abrogating "all restrictions and exclusions that have been declared in reference to the exercise of civil and political rights on behalf of men of color and freedpeople."[17]

Although documents favorable to abolition and equal rights could not safely be published in New Orleans, given the legal prohibition on speech or action designed to elicit discontent among the populations of color, word of the widening debate in France could reach the city through personal communications. For some New Orleans families who had ties to France, enabling them to receive correspondence and detailed information about their prospects there, this was a moment to explore the possibility of migration, or at least of sending their children to Europe for schooling. For others, the news could reinforce the sense of legitimacy of earlier claims to equal citizenship, however stifled the expression of such claims might continue to be.[18]

News could also arrive directly, carried by radicals among the French immigrants to New Orleans—although their attempts to organize in Louisiana were promptly repressed.[19] Continued commercial and migratory movement between France and Louisiana nonetheless accelerated the transmission of news, making it more difficult to suppress what was happening on the other side of the Atlantic. To take one family as an example: When the carpenter and *homme de couleur libre* Jacques Tinchant and his wife Elisabeth Vincent decided to leave New Orleans for the Basses-Pyrénées in southern France in 1840, they were following in the footsteps of Jacques's mother Marie Françoise Bayot, who had done the same a decade earlier (in part to legalize her cross-racial marriage and legitimate her younger children). Jacques and Elisabeth's eldest son Louis remained in New Orleans after his parents' departure, and Jacques recrossed the Atlantic at least once in the 1840s to follow up on the family's business affairs in the city. Letters went back and forth, and notarized powers of attorney were sent along to facilitate transactions. The family was well on its way to crafting an itinerant commercial citizenship, one that could under certain circumstances push them toward new claims in the political domain as well. Meanwhile, the younger Tinchant sons were in school in the town of Pau as the crisis of the French monarchy accelerated, culminating in the events of February 1848.[20]

By 1848, any old-timers in New Orleans who had acquired seaman's protection certificates by virtue of having resided in the territory prior to France's cession of Louisiana to the United States, or who imagined their citizenship to have been confirmed by their earlier militia service, were now getting well on in years. A spate of repressive statutes from the Louisiana legislature had further constrained the rights and privileges of all persons of color, stigmatizing them as a perpetual menace to public order. To the extent that such men and women still held themselves to be full citizens of the United States, they could only do so on the basis of a vernacular conviction that they possessed such rights, even as many of the benefits of those rights were denied them.[21]

As the situation in New Orleans became more difficult, however, the news arriving from France became even more tantalizing. At first, it was easy to learn about the revolution that began in Paris in February 1848. The official newspaper of the state was *The Courier/ Le Courrier,* a bilingual publication sympathetic to the Democratic Party whose French-language pages paid close attention to events in Europe. Their first reports on 1848 were breathless and enthusiastic: France was once again a Republic! The Monarchy was gone! The sister Republics of the United States and France were destined to be drawn yet further together! An article on April 6 transcribed a speech of congratulation given by M. Goodrich, addressed to the Provisional Government in the name of Americans in France, and delivered in front of the Hôtel de Ville in Paris. It was received graciously by minister François Arago, and followed by shouts of "Vive la République."[22]

Throughout the month of April, the editors of *Le Courrier* waited impatiently for further news, but were thwarted when the usual newspapers and letters from France via Boston did not arrive promptly. The paper was therefore reduced to reporting the news secondhand, translating what it referred to with some disdain as "des feuilles du Nord" that had arrived in port on board the *Caledonia.* But no matter: A grand meeting in front of the Bourse Saint Louis in New Orleans was convoked for April 11, "en l'honneur de la France," and *Le Courrier* published a statement titled "Frères de Paris," signed by five hundred French residents of New Orleans. Banquets, the classic 1848 mode of displaying political support, were planned for the following week.[23]

On through early May, reports on the revolution in France continued to appear in both the French- and English-language pages of the paper, enabling the residents of New Orleans to follow events as they unfolded, albeit with a certain lag time. The editors shared their exasperation at the delays in the arrival of trunks of French newspapers, but they conveyed the news as it arrived from the North via telegraph. By early May, the long-awaited packets of papers from Europe finally reached the city, and *Le Courrier* was able to print detailed reports of the meetings of the Assemblée Nationale in Paris. By this point, however, the editors were presumably beginning to learn that the Provisional Government had formed a commission charged with resolving the issue of slavery, and that it was to be headed by the abolitionist Victor Schoelcher. On this, their reporting initially remained silent.[24]

In Paris, on April 27, 1848, the Provisional Government signed the anticipated proclamation abolishing slavery in the French Empire. Less than two weeks later, minister François Arago issued the decrees of implementation for the colonies, and barred the passage of any local legal measures that would pose obstacles to "social equality."[25] From the point of view of the editors of *Le Courrier*, here was news that was truly not fit to print. Oblique indications of impending action on slavery in the French colonies had already been filtering into the paper via reports sent from Guadeloupe in late March: "Bientôt sans doute nous aurons la république et l'abolition de l'esclavage moyennant indemnité" ("Soon we will doubtless have a republic and the abolition of slavery through compensation"), wrote a correspondent from Basse-Terre. A report from Martinique was even more explicit, worrying about how those still held in slavery would react to a decision to postpone the implementation of abolition until after the harvest. One way or another, the definitive news of the April signing of the official decree of abolition must have reached New Orleans by late May.[26]

At this point *Le Courrier* fell nearly silent on the subject of the revolution's policy on slavery, concentrating instead on the struggle for power between different groups in Paris, on the Mexican war, and on the upcoming elections in the United States. The French consul reported back to Paris in September that he had arranged as instructed for the decree of abolition to be published in "tous les journaux américains et franco-américains" ("all the

American and Franco- American papers")—a claim that the surviving issues of *Le Courrier* do not seem to support. The consul then explained that he would cease further publicity, given the strength of local opposition to the measure. Over the course of the next years the consul himself would show relentless hostility to the decree of abolition; he was not the man to count on for the radical 1848ers' project of using French abolition as a wedge with which to undercut slavery elsewhere.[27]

Any news of abolition by the French government was triply alarming for New Orleans slaveholders. First, there was the obvious problem of speaking about a topic that represented a slaveholder's nightmare, and whose open discussion was politically dangerous. Second, the early enthusiasts within Louisiana's Democratic Party would have to try to understand how the leaders of the much-heralded republican revolution had turned out to share the views of what the English-language pages of *The Courier* characteristically referred to as "scoundrel abolitionists." Third, the framing of the 1848 decree put direct pressure on French citizens abroad to divest themselves of their slaves or risk losing their nationality. This could affect a substantial group of slaveholders in New Orleans.[28]

At the same time that they avoided direct discussion of the abolitionist policies of the Provisional Government, the French pages of the paper conveyed selective news and rumor from Haiti, Martinique, and Guadeloupe. It is difficult to discern the precise intentions behind the choice of information from the Antilles that the editors of *Le Courrier* published, but most of the items reiterated the familiar themes of the risks of emancipation and a corresponding danger to the white population. As might have been expected, many of those held in slavery in the Antilles found the news of a promised abolition more compelling than the call to respect the delay in its implementation. Published rumors of violence and plantations in flames soon swirled in advance of and out of proportion to the actual scope of rebellious action.[29] Writing on the neighboring country of Haiti, *Le Courrier* reported with particular zeal on conflict between those they characterized as *noirs* and those labeled *de couleur.*[30] Constructing and reinforcing such a distinction in Louisiana, of course, was one strategy for trying to conjure away the risks of alliances among those situated at varying degrees of distance from the experience of slavery.[31]

For free men and women of color in New Orleans, the search for further information about the decrees of abolition and promises of equal citizenship required some ingenuity. In this they were aided by their access to French-language materials, which might be less closely policed for abolitionist tendencies than the more proximate English-language northern papers.[32] Some papers within the bundles of the French press that arrived on transatlantic boats, or transshipped from New York and Boston, were presumably destined for subscribers among the *gens de couleur*. Under the circumstances, even one copy of a newspaper from Paris could transmit information to an entire network of friends and acquaintances.

The local bookstores, moreover, carried a variety of journals. Some years earlier, the *Revue des Deux Mondes* from Paris had published a detailed report of the activities of the French abolitionist societies. Issues of the *Revue* were available in New Orleans in 1848 at the bookstore of M. Lavie, 56 Chartres Street. Since earlier issues of the *Revue* had already introduced the abolitionist dramatis personae and their views to any attentive reader, later references to the role of these figures in the Provisional Government might encourage the inference that abolition was on their agenda.[33]

One New Orleans publication did indeed publish the entire text of the April 1848 decree of abolition: *L'Orléanais,* a paper that printed official notices from the city's Third Municipality.[34] That issue could presumably pass from hand to hand, both among slaveholders still holding French nationality who were uneasy about the implications for themselves, and among persons of color who saw that a sister republic had seized the time, ending slavery and redefining the boundaries of citizenship.

News arriving via the press was supplemented by direct communication with persons arriving from France. The eldest of the Tinchant sons in France, Joseph, had by the late 1840s finished his studies at the lycée in Pau and moved to Paris. He was there during the Revolution of February 1848 and the fierce repression of the "June Days." Soon thereafter, he took his leave, booking passage for New Orleans out of Bordeaux on the ship *Mount Washington.* He joined his brother Louis, who ran a grocery store in the city. New Orleans might offer greater economic opportunity than his parents' farm, but Joseph now found himself placed into the social and legal categories "mulatto" and *homme de couleur libre*.[35]

If trusted patrons of Louis's grocery store, or other friends of the family, sought news of Paris—and in particular of the declaration of "social equality" independent of color—they could presumably ask the recently arrived Joseph. In these years of increasing apprehension among slaveholding whites, topics that were off-limits in the press had to be channeled into face-to-face conversations, or into belles lettres whose ambiguous meanings and more limited readership put them out of the line of fire. Fortunately for people like Joseph Tinchant (albeit unfortunately for the historian seeking traces of such conversations), the apparatus of repression in antebellum New Orleans seems to have been less keenly attuned to the words uttered in bars and on street corners than were its French Ancien régime counterparts. Further digging into lower-level court cases and correspondence may nonetheless eventually yield some additional clues.[36]

Although the young Joseph Tinchant seems initially to have been a bit at loose ends, he soon settled into work in the city. He and Louis developed a small-scale cigar manufactory, and Joseph became active in the group of men and women who supported the private school for children of color, the Institution Catholique. Even in that social setting, it was of course necessary to be discreet about one's political beliefs. Joseph was a well-educated, well-read man of considerable ambition, with a vivid experience of civil equality back in France. He could bide his time if necessary. Like many others, he would not yet speak publicly about the ideals of 1848. But he did not forget. The example of 1848 would surge back into view when, fourteen years later, the political structures keeping men of color silent were abruptly overturned.[37]

EPILOGUE: 1862–1868

Union forces occupied New Orleans in April of 1862, transforming the public sphere of the city. Advocacy of the abolition of slavery and the hope for a full and cross-racial citizenship could now be expressed openly. An exceptionally lively newspaper began publication, channeling that discussion and sharing it with a wide French-speaking population of color in the city and beyond. Across the pages of *L'Union,* and its successor the bilingual *Tribune,* one can see the detailed information about 1848 and its aftermath that had been accumulated over the previous years by the paper's editors, correspondents, letter writers, and readers.

One crucial link between *L'Union* and the European experience of 1848 was Jean-Charles Houzeau, a Belgian who had come to the Americas in the 1850s. The cosmopolitan and sophisticated scientist Houzeau served as a direct conduit from the culture of radical republican banquets in 1848 to the expansive political debate reflected in the pages of the wartime newspapers. Working with the Louisiana activist and editor Paul Trévigne, and with the publisher Louis Charles Roudanez (himself a veteran of the events in Paris in 1848), Houzeau helped to shape the news-gathering, prose style, frame of reference, and editorial policy of the publication.[38] Houzeau's private letters, and the surviving issues of *L'Union* and *La Tribune,* provide further glimpses into that remarkable experiment in journalism.[39]

The evocation of 1848 in the pages of this Civil War and Reconstruction era newspaper extends far beyond what one would expect from the presence of a single certified 1848er on the staff.[40] The paper is suffused with references to France's revolution, and with language that traces closely to the rhetoric associated with those events.[41] To take just one example: an essay titled "La Liberté" quotes the poet and republican politician Alphonse de Lamartine on liberty. Echoing the 1848ers' linking of slavery to the loss of free will, and tying abolition to human dignity, the author writes that to deny liberty was to deny all grandeur and dignity to man.[42]

In early April of 1863, *L'Union* printed multiple excerpts from an essay by Eugène Pelletan, a charismatic French journalist and 1848er who had directly addressed the question of slavery. These selections from Pelletan's pamphlet *Adresse au roi Coton* ("Address to King Cotton") provided Francophone readers in New Orleans with a brief history that contrasted the continuance of slavery in the United States with a stirring account of the abolition of slavery by the French republicans in 1848. In that summary, Pelletan emphasized the French Republic's "tendresse pour la dignité humaine"—its careful concern for human dignity—in order to explain the context of abolition.[43]

This line of thinking, nourished by references to France's long revolutionary tradition, was fused with observations drawn directly from the ongoing breakdown of slavery initiated by the Civil War, and from evidence that an expansion of claims to citizenship would soon follow. During the days between President Lincoln's issuance of the preliminary Emancipation Proclamation and the promulgation of the definitive text, Avocat Gen. Edward Bates had been at work on a formal opinion concerning citizenship. The resulting official communication to Secretary of the Treasury Salmon Chase, dated November 29, 1862, held that free men of color, if born in the country, were indeed citizens of the United States. The executive branch of the federal government was thus formally disowning the reasoning that had been insisted upon by Justice Taney in *Dred Scott v. Sandford.* The government printing office in Washington promptly published copies under the title *Opinion of Attorney General Bates on Citizenship.*[44]

Within weeks the editors of *L'Union* were reporting on the opinion, which in their hands expanded from a matter of formal interpretation into a question of rights. They promptly serialized a French translation of the *Opinion de l'Avocat-Gen: Bates sur le droit de citoyenneté* ("on the right of citizenship") and offered the translation in pamphlet form, at ten cents a copy. Linguistic pluralism had come full circle. Ideas that had filtered into the city from France and the French-speaking Caribbean were now to be complemented by ideas from Washington that the carriers of those French revolutionary memories would translate and transmit back into the world of French-speakers.[45]

Joseph Tinchant, the witness to 1848 in Paris who was now a cigar-maker in New Orleans, addressed a mass meeting in Economy Hall in late June 1863, joining in the call for men of color to volunteer to serve in the Union army. Soon he would be commissioned a lieutenant in the Union Sixth Louisiana Volunteers.[46] Within a year, his brother Edouard would also begin to make himself known in the pages of the *Tribune* as an advocate of citizenship, equality, and universal manhood suffrage. Too young to have been an 1848er himself, Edouard nonetheless used a language drawn from those struggles, anathemizing Napoleon III as the "assassin of the 4th of December" and denouncing the imperial French invasion of Mexico. In the atmosphere of Civil War New Orleans, however, he also invoked the Monroe Doctrine to reinforce his critique of the intrusion of a European power into the Americas. When challenged by a more conservative man of color who doubted whether the Union would really offer full citizenship, and who counseled emigration to Maximilian's Mexico instead, Tinchant quickly reached for the opinion of Attorney General Edward Bates.[47]

The familiar distinctions between "Gallic" cultures and "American" innovations seem, in this context, to lose much of their meaning.[48] A minor figure in a major city at a moment of transformation, Edouard Tinchant had been born in France of parents born in Saint-Domingue and Baltimore who had married in New Orleans. A self-described "son of Africa," and a veteran of service in the Union army, Tinchant was moving rapidly toward a thoroughgoing eclecticism. What mattered was to find a language in which to claim a full array of "civil, political, and public rights" and to assert dignity.[49] France's Revolution of 1848 could offer one set of touchstones. But France was now ruled by Napoléon III, an enemy of that revolution. The United States, by contrast, was governed by a president whose official policy seemed to imply the extension of rights of citizenship independent of color, and the Union army in the field was making possible an end to slavery. Edouard Tinchant chose to declare allegiance to the United States.

The fusion went in both directions, as a major figure in the Anglo-American world of abolitionism repaid the compliment to France's Revolution of February 1848. Frederick Douglass wrote in 1865 that Victor Hugo, Alphonse de Lamartine, Victor Schoelcher, Louis Blanc, Edgar Quinet, and other ministers of the Provisional Government "were names that men of color everywhere should cherish and honor."[50]

With the federal Military Reconstruction Acts of 1867 came sweeping electoral rights in the building of a "reconstructed" postwar state. During the ensuing struggle to draft and enforce the radical state constitution of 1868, men and women of color in Louisiana sought to give their state and national citizenship substantial meaning. When after some years of relative success they were turned back, they began another wait—this time even longer than the one separating 1803 from 1862.

Nearly two decades after the formal end of Reconstruction, and in the face of a statute mandating separation by color in railway cars, the New Orleans Committee of Citizens sought to win their claim of equal public rights by taking the case of Homer Plessy to the US Supreme Court. As the legal obstacles mounted, committee member Rodolphe Desdunes, like the members of the generations before him, tried to help shape the memory that they would now carry forward in defeat: "'It is well for a people to know their rights even if denied them,' and we will add that it is proper and wise for people to exercise those rights as intelligently as possible, even if robbed of their benefits."[51]

By the time the case of *Plessy v. Ferguson* was joined, it was not likely that anyone would deny the formal citizenship of the members of the committee defending Homer Plessy and challenging the constitutionality of Louisiana's Separate Car Act. Instead, it was the rights and privileges associated with such citizenship that had become the battleground. White supremacists sought to persuade the courts to continue evacuating much of the content of federal citizenship, allocating any protection of rights to the states instead. State laws could then impose stigma as a means of denying public respect to a segment of the state's citizens, facilitating the practical denial of one after another right. By the end of the century, it was clear that the process of constructing the concept of citizenship was going to last far longer than the grassroots optimists of wartime New Orleans had ever imagined.

NOTES

I would like to thank David Blight, Emily Clark, Jean Hébrard, Jennifer Heuer, Martha S. Jones, William Novak, Vernon Palmer, Richard Pildes, Marieke Polfliet, Lawrence Powell, Richard Primus, Peter Railton, Edward Rugemer, Scott Shapiro, Cécile Vidal, and John Witt for discussions of these topics, and Sandra Zeff, Bryan LaPointe, and Barbara Brown for assistance in locating research materials.

1. For a discussion of the shifting terms of debate on 1848 in Saint-Louis, see Ibrahima Thioub, "Stigmas and Memory of Slavery in West Africa: Skin Color and Blood as Social Fracture Lines," *New Global Studies* 6:3 (2012).

2. Two monographs discuss these ideological developments: Caryn Cossé Bell, *Revolution, Romanticism, and the Afro-Creole Protest Tradition in Louisiana, 1718–1868* (Baton Rouge: Louisiana State University Press, 1997); and Shirley Elizabeth Thompson, *Exiles at Home: The Struggle to Become American in Creole New Orleans* (Cambridge, MA: Harvard University Press, 2009).

3. Walsh v. Lallande 25 La. Ann. 188, 189 (1873). Charles Lallande, a freeborn man of mixed ancestry, had in 1844 purchased a 160-acre tract of public land in Pointe Coupée Parish. He lived on and cultivated the land, as required by the rules for preemption, and filed for the patent that would perfect his title. After that patent was denied in 1860, the land was conveyed to William Walsh, a white man from New Orleans. After the Civil War, however, Lallande

reclaimed the land and resumed planting on it. Walsh then sued to try to expel him. The manuscript record is Docket #4526, now held in the Historical Archives of the Supreme Court of Louisiana, in Special Collections, Earl Long Library, University of New Orleans.

4. For an examination of the components of citizenship that free people of color *did* claim and exercise before the Civil War, see the work of Martha S. Jones, including "*Hughes v. Jackson:* Race and Rights beyond Dred Scott," *North Carolina Law Review* 91 (2013): 1757–83, and *Birthright Citizens: A History of Race and Rights in Antebellum America* (New York: Cambridge University Press, 2018).

5. For an examination of the argument in the Senate, see Richard Primus, "The Riddle of Hiram Revels," *Harvard Law Review* 119 (2006): 1680–1734.

6. Article III, Treaty between the United States of America and the French Republic, Paris, 30 April 1803, as transcribed on the website of the US National Archives: http://www.archives.gov/exhibits/american_originals/louistxt.html.

7. The French text reads "Les habitants des territoires cédés seront incorporés dans l'Union des États, aussi prochainement qu'il sera possible et admis, suivant les principes de la Constitution fédérale, à la jouissance de tous leurs droits, aux avantages et immunités des citoyens des États-Unis, et en attendant seront maintenus et protégés dans la jouissance de leurs libertés, propriétés et dans l'exercice des religions qu'ils professent." In French colonies, "habitant" could also refer to someone who had taken root and settled for good, owning or renting a piece of land and heading a household. See Sylvie Dépatie, "El ser más independiente del mundo? La construcción del 'habitant' canadiense," in *Discurso colonial: La construcción de una diferencia americana,* ed. Catherine Poupeney Hart, Albino Chacón Gutiérrez (Heredia [Costa Rica]/Montréal: Editorial Universidad National [EUNA]/Presses de l'Université de Montréal, 2002), 189–221.

8. Letter from Laussat to Barbé Marbois, French Minister of the Public Treasury, 17 Vendémiaire an XII/10 October 1803, in the Laussat Papers, MSS 125.282, Historic New Orleans Collection. I thank Marieke Polfliet for this citation.

9. See the entry "habitant" in the *Dictionnaire de l'Académie française,* 5th edition (1798), as accessed through artfl-project.uchicago.edu.

10. An Act to establish a Uniform Rule of Naturalization, 1 Stat. 103 1789–1799.

11. "Address from the Free People of Color, January 1804," Clarence Edwin Carter et al., comp., *Territorial Papers of the United States* (Washington, DC: Government Printing Office, 1934–1975), 9:174. See also Bell's discussion in *Revolution,* 9–40.

12. Proofs of Citizenship Used to Apply for Seamen's Protection Certificates for the Port of New Orleans, Louisiana, Record Group 36, Records of the U.S. Customs Service, U.S. National Archives, Microfilm publication M1826, accessed through ancestry.com (hereafter Proofs of Citizenship).

13. See the application of Etienne Augustin, 4 January 1811, in Proofs of Citizenship.

14. See the application of Philip Aquino, 1 March 1810, in Proofs of Citizenship.

15. See Ruth Priest Dixon, "Genealogical Fallout from the War of 1812," *Prologue* 24 (1992); and Nathan Perl-Rosenthal, *Citizen Sailors: Becoming American in the Age of Revolution* (Cambridge, MA: Harvard University Press, 2013), especially 208–43.

16. "Seeing that I did not readily produce my free papers, as the other colored persons in the car had done, he said to me in a friendly contrast with that observed towards the others: 'I suppose you have your free papers?' To which I answered: 'No, sir; I never carry my free papers to sea with me.' 'But you have something to show that you are a free man, have you not?' 'Yes, sir,' I answered; 'I have a paper with the American eagle on it, that will carry me round the world.' With this I drew from my deep sailor's pocket my seaman's protection, as before described. The merest glance at the paper satisfied him, and he took my fare and went on about his business." Frederick Douglass, *Life and Times of Frederick Douglass* (Boston: De Wolfe and Fiske, 1892), 247.

17. See the lectures delivered in Paris in the 1830s and 1840s by the jurist Pellegrino Rossi in P. Rossi, *Oeuvres complètes* (Paris: Librairie de Guillaumin, 1866). For the 1833 statute, see Jean Baptiste Joseph Pailliet, *Manuel de droit français,* pt. 2 (Paris: Le Normant, 1837), 1915.

18. On perceptions of France from the vantage point of New Orleans in the 1830s, see Rebecca J. Scott and Jean M. Hébrard, *Freedom Papers: An Atlantic Odyssey in the Age of Emancipation* (Cambridge, MA: Harvard University Press, 2012), 65–99. On the prohibition of publications that might elicit discontent, see "An Act to punish the crimes therein mentioned, and for other purposes," approved March 16, 1830, and published in *Acts at the Second Session of the Ninth Legislature of the State of Louisiana,* 96–97.

19. Marieke Polfliet has turned up evidence of a short-lived radical newspaper published in French in New Orleans in 1831, and quickly suppressed. Marieke Polfliet, personal communication, 2013.

20. On these steps in the Tinchant itinerary, see Scott and Hébrard, *Freedom Papers,* 83–99.

21. The 16 March 1830 statute called for imprisonment at hard labor or death to those who communicated information that could produce "discontent among the free coloured population." "An Act to punish the crimes therein mentioned, and for other purposes," approved 16 March 1830.

22. "Les Américains à Paris: Grande démonstration faite par des citoyens américains," *Le Courrier* (New Orleans), 6 April 1848. On the reception of the news of 1848 in New Orleans, see Marieke Polfliet, "Citoyenneté et abolition de l'esclavage après 1848: Les Français de La Nouvelle-Orléans au coeur des conflits d'allégeances nationales" (unpublished, courtesy of the author), and her doctoral dissertation, "Émigration et politisation: Les Français de New York et La Nouvelle Orléans dans la première moitié du XIXe siècle (1803–1860)," PhD diss., Université Nice Sophia Antipolis, 2013.

23. See *Le Courrier,* 2 April, 6 April, 10 April, and 11 April 1848.

24. See *Le Courrier,* April and May 1848. On the commission, see Maurizio Gribaudi and Michèle Riot-Sarcey, *1848: La Révolution oubliée* (Paris: La Découverte, 2009), 139.

25. See Myriam Cottias, *D'une Abolition, l'autre: Anthologie raisonnée de textes consacrés à la second abolition de l'esclavage dans les colonies françaises* (Marseille: Agone Editeurs, 1998); and the decree of implementation issued by Arago for Martinique, published as Circulaire ministérielle No. 358, 7 May 1848, *Bulletin officiel de la Martinique,* 594.

26. These brief reports from Martinique and Guadeloupe, dated in late March and early

April, appear under the heading "Effets de la Revolution Française dans les Antilles," in *Le Courrier,* 10 May 1848.

27. On the consul's statements, see Polfliet, "Citoyenneté et abolition"; and Lawrence Jennings, "L'abolition de l'esclavage par la IIe République et ses effets en Louisiane, 1848–1858," *Revue Française d'Histoire d'Outre-Mer* 56:205 (1969): 375–97.

28. The phrase "scoundrel abolitionists" appears in the article "Practical Abolition," *The Courier* (English-language pages), April 1848. See also Polfliet, "Citoyenneté et abolition"; Jennings, "L'abolition de l'esclavage."

29. See, for example, "Effets de la Révolution Française dans les Antilles," 10 May; partially retracted in "Nouvelles de la Martinique" on 13 May; followed by "Nouvelles de la Guadeloupe," 31 May; and then an oblique discussion of the harm done by the Provisional Government to planters in the islands, under the title "Assemblée en faveur des colons de la Martinique et de la Guadeloupe," 5 July; all in *Le Courrier,* 1848. Edward Rugemer sees a similar pattern in the reporting in the United States on events in the British Caribbean. See Edward Bartlett Rugemer, *The Problem of Emancipation: The Caribbean Roots of the American Civil War* (Baton Rouge: Louisiana State University Press, 2008).

30. See "Nouvelles d'Hayti," 9 June 1848; and "Progrès de la Guerre Civile à Haiti," 2 June, both in *Le Courrier,* 1848.

31. On the concept of "genealogical distance from slavery," see Adriana Chira, "Uneasy Intimacies: Race, Family, and Property in Santiago de Cuba, 1803–1868," PhD diss., University of Michigan, 2016.

32. Detailed information about the abolitionist Cyrille Bissette, for example, appeared in Frederick Douglass's *The North Star,* 5 October 1849. But it would be worth one's life to be caught reading Frederick Douglass's paper in New Orleans.

33. "Société Française pour l'Abolition de l'Esclavage," in the *Revue des Deux Mondes* dated April–May 1837. See the reference to the bookstore in the notice titled "Revue des Deux Mondes," *Le Courrier,* 5 July 1848.

34. Many thanks to Marieke Polfliet, who identified, located, and graciously shared a copy of *L'Orléanais* for 2 June 1848. Internal evidence suggests that there may have been some tension between the editors of *Le Courrier* and those of the *Orléanais.* See the squib titled "À l'Orléanais," in the issue of *Le Courrier,* 11 May 1848.

35. On Joseph Tinchant, see Scott and Hébrard, *Freedom Papers,* 93–99, 217n48. On the events of June in Paris, see Gribaudi and Riot-Sarcey, *1848,* 209–35.

36. See Scott and Hébrard, *Freedom Papers,* 100–120. I have not located a vein of archival material from New Orleans for this period comparable to the reports of police informers in Paris used by the historian Arlette Farge in *The Allure of the Archives,* trans. Thomas Scott-Railton (New Haven, CT: Yale University Press, 2013). See, however, the PhD dissertation in progress by John K. Bardes, Tulane University, provisionally titled "Mass Incarceration in the Age of Slavery and Emancipation: Fugitive Slaves, Poor Whites, and Prison Development in Louisiana, 1805–1898."

37. Scott and Hébrard, *Freedom Papers,* 100–120.

38. The first part of Houzeau's retrospective appeared as "Le journal noir, aux États-Unis, de 1863 à 1870 (1)," *Revue de Belgique* 11 (1872): 5–28. A translation of the series, edited with an introduction by David C. Rankin, is Jean-Charles Houzeau, *My Passage at the New Orleans Tribune* (Baton Rouge: Louisiana State University Press, 1984). Mark Charles Roudané's privately printed volume, *The New Orleans Tribune: An Introduction to America's First Black Daily Newspaper,* draws on an obituary written by Paul Trévigne, the editor of *L'Union,* in documenting Roudanez's direct connection with Paris in 1848. See also Nathalie Dessens, "Louis Charles Roudanez, A Creole of Color of Saint-Domingue Descent: Atlantic Reinterpretations of Nineteenth-Century New Orleans," *South Atlantic Review* 73 (2008): 26–38; and Kristi Richard Melancon, "An African American Discourse Community in Black & White: The *New Orleans Tribune,*" PhD diss., Louisiana State University, 2011.

39. Jean-Charles Houzeau, *Lettres adressées des États-Unis à sa famille, 1857–1868,* edited by Hossam Elkhadem, Annette Félix, and Liliane Wellens-De Donder (Brussels: Centre National d'Histoire des Sciences, 1994). The digital images of the *Union* and the *Tribune* are available on the subscription database America's Historical Newspapers.

40. See Houzeau's 6 May 1866 letter to his parents, in *Lettres,* 391.

41. There are many references to the date 1848 itself, some drawing analogies with events in the United States. See, for example, the article published on 20 July 1865 in *La Tribune* under the title "John Brown: Le Christ des Noirs," by P. Vesinier. The author draws a parallel between John Brown and those executed in Paris during the June days of 1848.

42. See "La Liberté," signed F. B******, *L'Union* (New Orleans), 18 October 1862, 1. It seems likely that the author was the Creole activist of color François Boisdoré, who is discussed in Bell, *Revolution,* 225, 227.

43. On Pelletan, see Sudhir Hazareesingh, *Intellectual Founders of the Republic: Five Studies in Nineteenth-Century French Republican Political Thought* (Oxford: Oxford University Press, 2001), 167–225. The "Adresse au Roi Coton," including the quoted phrase, appears in *L'Union* on 11 April 1863. On the continuing importance of the term *dignity* in political thought in Louisiana, see also Rebecca J. Scott, "Discerning a Dignitary Offense: The Concept of Equal 'Public Rights' during Reconstruction," forthcoming in the *Law and History Review.*

44. *Opinion of Attorney General Bates on Citizenship* (Washington, DC: Government Printing Office, 1862).

45. See, for example, the segment of the opinion published in French in *L'Union* on 29 January 1863, and the advertisement for the pamphlet in the 7 April 1863, issue.

46. *L'Union,* 30 June 1863. On Joseph Tinchant's service, see Scott and Hébrard, *Freedom Papers,* 115–16.

47. See Scott and Hébrard, *Freedom Papers,* 121–38.

48. Scholarly critiques of the "Americanization" framework for understanding New Orleans include, most recently, Eberhard L. Faber, *Building the Land of Dreams: New Orleans and the Transformation of Early America* (Princeton, NJ: Princeton University Press, 2016).

49. Edouard Tinchant's role in inserting the phrase "public rights" into the 1868 state constitution is described (and mocked) in the hostile *New Orleans Times,* 28 December 1867, and

confirmed in the *Official Journal of the Proceedings of the Convention for Framing a Constitution for the State of Louisiana* (New Orleans: J. B. Roudanez, 1867–1868), 115–17.

50. Letter of Frederick Douglass to M. Melvil-Bloncourt, 18 August 1865, published in *La Tribune,* 16 December 1865.

51. This quotation from Desdunes is cited as translated in Rebecca J. Scott, *Degrees of Freedom: Louisiana and Cuba after Slavery* (Cambridge, MA: Harvard University Press: 2005), 269.

FRENCH CITIZENSHIP AND COLONIAL RULE IN SAINT-LOUIS, SENEGAL

LARISSA KOPYTOFF

In the early twentieth century, the inhabitants of Saint-Louis, Senegal, saw their legal protections, political fortunes, and official status under French colonial rule shift rapidly and dramatically. Over the course of just a few years, they confronted court rulings and decrees that threatened to abrogate long-claimed rights, participated in an election that fundamentally reshaped politics in the colony of Senegal, and wrestled with the implications of a law that declared the residents of Saint-Louis and three other coastal towns, Gorée, Dakar, and Rufisque, to be full French citizens.

Saint-Louis had long been a cultural, political, and economic center for the expanding French Empire in West Africa. In the early twentieth century, the city found itself at the center of a debate about the rights and obligations of subjects and citizens in that empire. This essay explores the changing political landscape in Saint-Louis at this time through the lens of French citizenship, examining how citizenship became such a complex and contentious issue in Senegal, how attempts to resolve that issue prompted new questions and legal dilemmas, and how the administration of citizenship called attention to the weaknesses of French colonial bureaucracy in West Africa.[1]

SAINT-LOUIS, THE FOUR COMMUNES, AND THE *ORIGINAIRES*

As military campaigns extended France's reach throughout West Africa in the second half of the nineteenth century, Saint-Louis and other French settlements in coastal Senegal appeared increasingly out of place within the rapidly expanding empire. The inhabitants of Saint-Louis and Gorée—island trading posts with a French presence dating to the seventeenth century—had long histories of engagement with Europeans and were often described as being more fully "assimilated" to French culture and traditions than Africans elsewhere in the region. In Saint-Louis, the *métis* (mixed-race) community, linked to French metropolitan merchants and political elites through personal and professional ties, was heavily involved in French trade and other commercial activity and dominated politics in the colony.[2] Dakar and Rufisque, though settled by the French much more recently than Saint-Louis and Gorée, were emerging administrative and economic centers with fast-growing populations. And, as *communes de plein exercice* (full-fledged French municipalities with elected councils and designated budgets) since the 1870s and 1880s, these four towns held a legal and administrative status distinct from the rest of Senegal and French West Africa.[3] At the turn of the century, Saint-Louis was still the intellectual and cultural hub of Senegal, as well as the colony's capital, but it was soon overshadowed by other urban centers in West Africa. Its economic strength, largely based on trade along the Senegal River, diminished with the construction of railroads and bigger ports in the region, and its political importance declined after Dakar became the capital of the newly created Federation of French West Africa in 1902.

By the early twentieth century, the African inhabitants of the "four communes," referred to as *originaires,* claimed and exercised political and legal rights not available to most colonial subjects under French rule.[4] They could elect a deputy to the National Assembly in Paris, had access to a state-established Muslim tribunal in Saint-Louis, and were generally considered exempt from the *indigénat,* the repressive and often arbitrary legal code applied to colonial subjects.[5] The originaires' close proximity to the colonial administrative centers of Saint-Louis and Dakar also brought with it social and economic opportunities, as well as greater familiarity with and access to the workings of the colonial bureaucracy. To many, the originaires appeared to be anomalies within a French Empire that consisted primarily of French colonial subjects lacking their political and legal rights and privileges. Yet it remained unclear whether, or to what extent, their legal status under French colonial rule truly differed from the status of those subjects. French government documents sometimes referred to the originaires as citizens, and at times they referred to themselves as such. Yet there was no consensus built around this definition of their status and, in the first years of the twentieth century, debates about the originaires' status and rights became increasingly contentious. It was not until September 29, 1916, when the French National Assembly passed a law stating that "the originaires of the communes de plein exercice of Senegal and their descendants are and shall remain French citizens,"[6] that it appeared that their ambiguous status had been definitively resolved.

Despite the many questions about the originaires' status, which continued through much of the colonial era in Senegal, their status as French citizens often appears in historical scholarship as a foregone conclusion, and as *the* defining characteristic of the four communes. Furthermore, historians have often grouped the four communes together, glossing over the differences among them while presenting them as a single "exceptional" space characterized by laws, political systems, and populations that did not represent (and therefore cannot explain) the history of French colonialism or of West Africa outside of that space. Hilary Jones has offered a compelling argument against this, and an appeal for the history of Saint-Louis to be examined on its own terms, writing: "Approaching the history of Senegal's colonial towns through the lens of this arbitrary administrative designation reinforces the separation of town and country created by colonial administrators. . . . [and] obscures the particular characteristics of each place and the pattern of interaction that existed between commune residents and the inhabitants of the interior."[7]

Yet it remains that these arbitrary designations—however incompletely and inconsistently enforced—were nevertheless significant, as the boundaries that colonial administrators sought to create could have very real effects on the lives of those within and outside those boundaries, and on their claims to rights or a particular legal status. People regularly moved into, out of, and through these towns; those living within them maintained close ties with family members and others living elsewhere; and the official boundaries of the communes did not reflect long-established trade networks and migration patterns. It is precisely *because* these administrative designations so often did *not* accommodate how people lived that they serve as such a useful lens through which to explore how both colonial officials and originaires themselves thought about the communes and their inhabitants.

FRENCH CITIZENSHIP IN COLONIAL SENEGAL

The early twentieth-century debates about the citizenship rights of the originaires were not new. Ever since the French Revolution had introduced new ways of thinking about citizenship, the French Empire had been a site of discussions about who was to be considered French and what that meant for one's political and legal rights and obligations.[8] Senegal was no exception. Moments that might have brought clarity to the issue had, throughout the nineteenth century, instead only raised more questions, leaving colonial officials, politicians, jurists, and those living within and outside of the four communes with varied interpretations of administrative and legislative language, and conflicting assumptions about what it meant to be French within the French Empire.

In the spring of 1789, months before the French Revolution began, free and property-owning residents of Saint-Louis engaged with this question, framed in the context of economic rights and privileges. Upon hearing that the Estates-General would be meeting for the first time since 1614, notables in Saint-Louis prepared a letter to be sent to France, voicing their grievances against the Compagnie du Sénégal's monopoly on the gum and slave trade in the region. The *cahier de doléances* (register of grievances) included a direct engagement with the role of race and descent in determining who was French: "Negroes or Mulattoes, we are all French since it is the blood of Frenchmen that runs in our veins. . . ."[9] These residents of Saint-Louis called attention to the notion that there were rights due those who identified themselves as French, at a moment when what it meant to be French was about to be fundamentally reimagined. Five years later, the 1794 decree abolishing slavery would echo this sentiment with its statement that "men, without distinction of color, living in the colonies, are French citizens. . . ."[10] (The practical impact of emancipation was short-lived in much of the French Empire, however, as Napoléon Bonaparte suspended the decree and reinstated slavery in French colonies in 1802.)

Until the mid-nineteenth century, the French presence in Senegal was largely limited to Saint-Louis, Gorée, and a few small trading posts on the coast and the Senegal River. During the first half of the century, these areas saw the halting and often haphazard introduction of French political, administrative, and judicial principles, processes, and institutions to Senegal, many directed primarily at the European and métis communities of Saint-Louis and Gorée.[11] With respect to citizenship, the most significant among these was the extension of the French civil code to Senegal. An 1830 decree stated that all freeborn men in Senegal would enjoy the rights granted to French citizens by the civil code. Three years later, a law was passed declaring that all freeborn men and legally freed slaves in French colonies would enjoy French civil and political rights. That freed slaves, and not only those who were born free, were explicitly included made clear that this act was not intended to apply only to those of metropolitan origin, but how exactly those living in French colonies would exercise their civil and political rights—and what formal, legal status was implied by the exercise of those rights—remained unclear.[12]

The introduction of the French civil code to Senegal also launched a debate about the compatibility of French and Muslim law and, by extension, about granting French citizenship rights to Muslim individuals or communities. Adherence to French civil law was considered a defining characteristic of the French citizen, and with the extension of the civil code, as Richard Roberts has written, colonial officials "confronted the fact that the majority of the Senegalese inhabitants of these towns were Muslim. For them, marriage and the organization of the family were founded in . . . religiously sanctioned law" rather than French civil law.[13] This tension would be at the heart of future debates about whether the originaires were, or could ever be considered, full French citizens.[14]

In the early twentieth-century debates about the citizenship status of the originaires, the long history of the French civil code in Senegal was presented by some as a sign of just how long they had been considered French; others argued that the civil code had merely extended to the inhabitants of Saint-Louis and Gorée the *rights of* French citizens but *not* citizenship itself. Framing these arguments was the question of the relevance of decisions made by previous administrations under radically different circumstances, given the rapid expansion and dramatic changes in French colonial rule in the region since the 1830s.

In 1848, another revolution brought further upheaval to France, and a fundamental shift in the framework of political and legal rights took place in

Senegal. On March 5 of that year, France's provisional government issued a decree stating that "suffrage shall be universal and direct." Voting instructions were issued the following month, clarifying and confirming this extension of political rights and establishing guidelines for elections in Senegal, and an election that year sent Durand Valentin, a métis merchant from Saint-Louis, to Paris as Senegal's deputy to the National Assembly.[15] The voting guidelines left questions about whether eligibility to vote in the election necessarily implied full French citizenship or simply locally bound electoral rights. This would become a point of contention decades later as administration officials took issue with the notion that those registered on the electoral lists in the four communes were necessarily citizens. An investigation into voting "irregularities" in the communes in 1905 found that no clear resolution on the issue had ever emerged and that this confusion—a blurring of the line between voter and citizen, between the political rights of citizens and citizenship itself—had, in essence, become the rule.[16]

On April 27, 1848, the provisional government issued a decree abolishing slavery (again) in French colonies, as newly freed slaves throughout the empire were made citizens, with representation in the French legislature. Included in the emancipation decree was an article extending the principle of "free soil"—the notion that slaves who reached French soil were free—throughout France's colonies.[17] Although written primarily with the plantation colonies of Guadeloupe, Martinique, Guyana, and Réunion in mind, the decree also included Senegal by name, as well as the other French possessions in Africa and India.[18] Almost immediately, the universal rhetoric of the decree freeing slaves "in all French colonies and possessions" would be tested by local authorities in Senegal, who saw the ideals of the decree as being at odds with the particular circumstances they faced. Emancipation had a significant impact on the economic and political power structures and dynamics within Saint-Louis, in ways that scholars continue to debate.[19] Yet it was in the proximity and close relationship of Saint-Louis to the towns and trade along and beyond the Senegal River—to soil that was not, yet, French—that the application of the decree appeared to be particularly problematic. French officials under Governor Louis Faidherbe raised concerns that emancipation might have a destabilizing effect on neighboring, slave-holding territories and their leaders, and on the expansion of French rule beyond the coast and riverbanks. As those officials sought to balance support for emancipation with a desire not to alienate local leaders who relied upon slave labor—leaders upon whom the French themselves relied—they argued for a restrictive interpretation of the law, offering reluctant adherence to its letter, but not its spirit.

One argument put forth by Faidherbe's administration following the emancipation decree was that the decree was only applicable in the areas that had been considered French *in 1848.* In 1857, Faidherbe—following the logic put forth by Frédéric Carrère, the chief of the judicial service, who had argued for the expansion of French rule without further emancipation—wrote: "The emancipation decree of 27 April 1848 does not apply to the villages and territories annexed after the time the decree was implemented. . . . [where] the natives became *French subjects, but not French citizens,* with the right to keep their slaves, to sell and to buy them."[20] As Richard Roberts has described, Faidherbe discovered that he "could minimize the consequences of the abolition decree by limiting the physical space where French law prevailed."[21] Somewhat paradoxically, *limiting* where French law was applicable in this case would help France to successfully *expand* its reach into areas that would, in time, become French. As the cultural and political center of the growing French colony, Saint-Louis was the space from which the French administered their expanding territories in the region; in the wake of the emancipation decree, it also became a space that would remain administratively and legally distinct from those territories.

The colonial administration's creation of a Muslim tribunal in Saint-Louis in 1857, after years of petitions from the town's Muslim inhabitants, made the status of the originaires still harder to discern.[22] The tribunal was established and supported by the state; Ghislaine Lydon has described it as "an important element of France's 'Muslim policy' in West Africa, and arguably its centerpiece."[23] Yet it also renewed questions about whether Muslim law was compatible with French civil law (and, by extension, French citizenship). By the early twentieth century, the tribunal's existence was cited as justification for why the originaires of Saint-Louis should not be considered French citizens, regardless of any statements to the contrary in the decrees of the 1830s and 1840s. When they chose to "revert" to Muslim law and accept the rulings of the tribunal rather than taking their civil affairs to French magistrates, the argument went, they had given up the rights of French citizenship.

Whether or not they had truly been citizens before, the originaires had become colonial subjects again by virtue of their adherence to Muslim, rather than French, law.[24]

By the turn of the century, as France consolidated its control throughout West Africa—and with Saint-Louis, Gorée, Dakar, and Rufisque firmly established as full-fledged French communes—colonial officials began to question the rights of the originaires, and the special status of the communes, more directly. They presented Saint-Louis in particular—with its influential métis community, history of exceptional legal rights, and politically engaged population—as an outlier and a cautionary tale for the future of French rule in the region. A series of court rulings and administrative decrees between 1907 and 1911 chipped away at the originaires' long-claimed rights, as French officials argued that the originaires had never been truly French. Instead, according to these rulings and decrees, they had been granted limited and locally bound electoral rights which did not in any way imply or confer portable, comprehensive French citizenship.[25] In 1912, a particularly controversial decree limited the originaires' legal rights when they traveled or lived outside of the boundaries of the communes—potentially subjecting them to the indigénat—and required that all individual naturalization applications include a renunciation of Muslim law, something that had not previously been required of the originaires.[26] This prompted outrage among originaires who saw it as yet another challenge to their long-held (if ill-defined) rights, and they responded at the ballot box.[27]

In the spring of 1914, the voters of Saint-Louis, Gorée, Dakar, and Rufisque elected Blaise Diagne as Senegal's deputy to the National Assembly. Diagne was himself an originaire of Gorée, and the first black African deputy elected to the chamber; he had spent years outside of Senegal working as a customs officer in other French colonies, far from the metropolitan French and métis who had long dominated the colony's political scene from Saint-Louis.[28] His unexpected victory signaled to the colonial administration, as well as to the political elites of Saint-Louis, that, with originaires throughout the four communes exercising their right to vote, the foundations of political power in the colony had shifted.

Diagne's victory certainly reflected the electoral strength of the communes' voters, but were those voters French citizens? That question remained unanswered for the time being, though the election provoked further debate about the originaires' citizenship status.[29] Diagne's opponents questioned whether he was in fact eligible to run for the office, arguing (as the 1912 decree had stated) that "the exercise of the voting rights of the inhabitants of Senegal is a limited one. . . . Outside of the colony, they must be considered to be merely French subjects" and, therefore, were likely ineligible to serve in the National Assembly.[30] The final report on Diagne's eligibility sidestepped the issue, concluding that the Assembly's Chamber of Deputies "was the sole judge of the ineligibility of its members" while acknowledging that "the question raised by Blaise Diagne's opponents" regarding his citizenship status "is of the most sensitive nature" for the governance of Senegal.[31]

Less than three months after the election, war broke out in Europe, and France soon looked to its empire to recruit troops. Wartime recruitment needs would transform the fortunes of the originaires by presenting an opportunity for Diagne to fulfill a central promise of his campaign: to gain formal recognition of their citizenship status.[32]

CITIZENSHIP AND THE FAILURES OF PAPERWORK[33]

On October 19, 1915, the French National Assembly passed a law—introduced by Diagne—that placed originaires serving in West African military regiments (known as the *tirailleurs sénégalais*) within French metropolitan forces. The law did not address citizenship explicitly, but it effectively minimized the distinction between citizen and subject for originaires in the armed forces. Furthermore, by recognizing and rewarding the originaires' military service to France in a time of war, it posed a challenge to those who sought to dismiss their claims to French citizenship.[34]

Less than a year later came the 1916 citizenship law, also introduced by Diagne, with its direct statement that "the originaires of the communes de plein exercice of Senegal and their descendants are and shall remain French citizens subject to the military obligations" of the previous year's law. After decades of uncertainty about the meaning and scope of the originaires' political and legal rights, this law appeared to resolve the issue: the originaires and their descendants were French citizens. Yet the law brought with it little agreement about what full French citizenship *meant* for the originaires, and whether the ambiguities in their status had, in fact, been laid to rest once and for all. Questions of both principle and practice remained unanswered, and new ones emerged.

One such question was whether the originaires' status had in fact *changed.* Had the 1916 law *created* new French citizens, or had it provided formal recognition of a preexisting status held by the originaires? For many originaires, the law was an official acknowledgment of a position in society that they believed they had acquired decades earlier. The law's single article, stating that the originaires "are and shall remain" citizens, was of little help; its simplicity and brevity left no doubt that the originaires were to be considered citizens from that point forward, but did not weigh in on whether they had been previously. This uncertainty is visible in the reports that circulated within the colonial administration at the time. One draft of a political report sent from the governor of Senegal to the governor-general of French West Africa in late 1916 stated that, with the law's passage, "French citizenship has been granted . . . to the originaires and their descendants." The word *granted* is underlined by hand, with *recognized* handwritten above it; a later draft of the report shows *granted* to have been replaced with *recognized.* Yet other reports and memoranda after this date continued to use *granted.*[35]

The ambiguities that remained regarding the originaires' status were of particular concern to Muslim originaires, who constituted the vast majority of the communes' inhabitants. They had, up to that point and almost alone in the French Empire, retained their *statut personnel* (personal, or religious, status, including adherence to Muslim law) even while exercising political rights usually reserved for French citizens.[36] Whether Muslim originaires would continue to hold this exceptional position once their status as French citizens was formally secured was not a foregone conclusion at the time. The matter was not addressed explicitly in the text of the 1916 law, and it prompted considerable debate.[37] It depended, in part, on whether that status (and, therefore, the coexistence of Muslim statut personnel and full-fledged French citizenship) was something new (and, therefore, untested) or whether Muslim originaires had already been, legally, fully French and Muslim.[38]

One of the most significant issues left unresolved with the law's passage was how the originaires' new, or newly recognized, citizenship status would actually be administered. Separating the population of the communes into citizens and subjects proved much more difficult in practice than it was on paper, as attempts to apply the laws generated confusion and exposed bureaucratic loopholes within which French officials, citizens, and subjects could maneuver. Given the relative paucity of reliable birth and other civil status records, how were colonial officials to distinguish an originaire from an African colonial subject? Answering this question depended, in part, on knowing who, exactly, counted as "originaires of the communes de plein exercice of Senegal and their descendants."

The connections that so many inhabitants of Saint-Louis maintained with family members living along the Senegal River or elsewhere in the region made this a practical, as well as theoretical, concern. How many generations removed from birth or residence in Saint-Louis could one be while claiming originaire—and now French citizen—status? The descendants of Muslim originaires from Saint-Louis living in Kayes, in neighboring French Soudan, had in 1905 lobbied successfully for the establishment of a Muslim tribunal akin to that of Saint-Louis, arguing that as originaires living outside of the communes, they were entitled to the legal protections held by those originaires who had remained in Saint-Louis.[39] How such cases would be addressed in the future, and how official decisions would be enforced, prompted concern and confusion in the wake of the law's passage. Furthermore, the communes were urban spaces into, out of, and through which people moved on a daily basis, and the boundaries of the communes themselves were not fixed. Debates intensified about where the precise limits of Saint-Louis were, and how its fast-growing *banlieues* (outskirts) fit into the picture, as officials considered that the definition of originaire—or the utility of the term—might change over time as the boundaries of the communes themselves changed.

Determining and documenting who was now a French citizen required the maintenance of accurate *état-civil* (civil registry) records of births, marriages, and deaths, as well as the existence of courts that could effectively handle the cases in which records were unavailable, untrustworthy, or inconclusive. And those cases were many, as civil registry records simply did not exist for many inhabitants of the communes.[40] Though the 1916 law recognized the citizenship of the descendants of originaires, comprehensive records from before the 1870s were especially rare; as a result, the birthplace of the parents of many originaires, including those now potentially subject to military service as French citizens, remained undocumented. Those records that did exist were often deemed unreliable for a range of reasons, including local naming traditions that French officials found confusing, the inadvertent or deliberate falsification of birth records by African civil servants, and individuals who used gaps in the paperwork or confusion over the law's application to their advantage.[41]

Colonial officials confronted with insufficient or unreliable records regularly cited the challenges of managing what were seen as all-too-casual naming practices that made it difficult, if not impossible, to keep track of individual originaires. A letter to the governor of Senegal, regarding the enforcement of the 1915 military service law, noted that "if it is easy to find birth records for natives of the communes, it becomes difficult or even impossible to find death certificates, as the native is born under one name, lives under another, and dies under a third."[42] In Saint-Louis, the attempt by Amadou Niang (or, perhaps, Amadou Gnang) to enlist in the military as an originaire prompted a lengthy investigation into his identity and birthplace. Only after a flurry of paperwork passed among officials in three cities was the conclusion reached that, "based on the information gathered . . . Amadou Niang and Amadou Gnang are one and the same, born in this commune [Saint-Louis] in 1871" and therefore eligible to enlist in the military among French citizens.[43]

At times, French officials blamed African civil servants for mishandling the production and maintenance of records. In October 1916, a French colonial administrator expressed dismay over irregularities in the birth records of the residents of Saint-Louis, complaining that the originaires had always shown "indifference" to the importance of the official civil registry of births, marriages, and deaths. He criticized local officials for relying on unsupported statements from individuals "claiming to be originaires" when drawing up lists of residents, voters, and would-be military recruits—and, as a result, for being unable to properly distinguish between those Africans in Saint-Louis who were colonial subjects and those who were French citizens.[44]

In some cases, officials believed that individuals were deliberately committing fraud so as to register as French citizens individuals who were really colonial subjects. In December 1916, an administrator remarked upon the suspicious case of a man who had recently registered his newborn daughter's birth in Saint-Louis without the daughter herself being present. He went on to voice his concern that some children born "in the bush" were later declared by their parents to have been born in Saint-Louis so that they could benefit from the rights accorded to citizens.[45] Suspicions about the abundance of false birth records and an investigation of bribes accepted by Muslim magistrates in Saint-Louis to produce such records prompted various proposals for bureaucratic reforms, but the few reforms enacted did little to address the problem at hand: the limited ability of the government to control the information passing through the hands of its subjects and citizens.[46]

Such failures of the colonial bureaucracy were not uncommon, or unexpected, throughout much of the region, but they were particularly worrisome in the four communes, and in Saint-Louis especially. Long the center of French power in the region, Saint-Louis was home to well-established political and legal institutions and a population touted for its successful assimilation to French society, culture, and bureaucratic practices. If "the colonial state" was present and visible anywhere in France's African colonies, it would be here. Yet the French in Saint-Louis could not tell their own subjects from their citizens. That those officials worked so hard and found it so difficult to apply their own legal categories—even in those spaces that constituted "nodal points of colonial authority"[47]—reflects the fragility of the daily operations of empire in French West Africa.

ASSIMILATION AND THE ACCIDENT OF BIRTH

Much of the paperwork that circulated among administrators in Senegal and France focused on practical matters, such as the challenges of administering the new citizenship regime of the four communes on a daily basis. Yet questions of legal principle were raised as well. The only path to French citizenship throughout much of the empire was the selective and rare naturalization of sufficiently "assimilated" individuals, and the creation (or, perhaps, recognition) of African citizens en masse based on the "accident of birth" in one of the four communes prompted widespread consternation among administration officials and jurists alike.[48]

This particular criticism both reinforced and undermined a central element of the historical narrative of colonial Saint-Louis. Assimilation to

French culture, and successful navigation of French political and legal institutions, were among the defining characteristics of the city. The 1916 law drew upon that narrative of assimilation—a narrative that helped to explain how the originaires had come to be considered French in the first place—even as it solidified the political power of the originaires of all four communes at the expense of the smaller (and, many argued, more assimilated) métis community of Saint-Louis.

Some argued that the law was unfair to those born just outside the limits of the communes or in the coastal urban areas of Dahomey and Côte d'Ivoire, whose inhabitants, colonial officials in those areas argued, could justifiably claim a similar degree of assimilation to French culture as the originaires of Saint-Louis. Politicians in France worried that the law would cause unrest among colonial subjects throughout the region.[49] Governors of other colonies in French West Africa voiced concern both at the preferential treatment of the originaires at the expense of their "constituents" and at the possibility that their own colonial subjects might demand similar treatment, arguing that the law should be repealed because of the arbitrary nature of its application to one group of individuals and not to others who might be as worthy (or unworthy).[50]

The other side of this argument—that it would be illogical to extend citizenship to anyone born within one of the communes, regardless of their background—was also a frequent refrain. Taking the notion of "the accident of birth" to its logical extreme, François Clozel, governor-general of French West Africa, had raised the prospect that a woman from elsewhere in the region brought to Dakar to stand trial for a serious crime might give birth within the boundaries of the commune to a child who would automatically be granted French citizenship.[51] Similarly, Gabriel Angoulvant, then governor of Côte d'Ivoire and later governor-general of French West Africa, criticized the law by comparing Senegal's communes to metropolitan France, writing: "What would we say in France about a law that granted a civil and political privilege to those born in Paris, for instance, and refused it to their neighbors in the suburbs, to their parents born in the provinces?"[52]

The notion that citizens within metropolitan France might be subject to different citizenship regimes in different cities may have sounded nonsensical to Angoulvant—as he clearly hoped it would to others—but it was not at all out of place within the jurisdictional patchwork of colonial French West Africa.[53] Furthermore, what made one French within France was not necessarily clear or intuitive. Rather, Patrick Weil has argued, "What distinguishes France from other countries is that . . . it has experimented with many ways of defining who is 'French by birth,' and has tried virtually all possible rules for attributing or withdrawing nationality. . . . and policies governing French nationality have been the subject of continual political and legal confrontation."[54]

In this light, the originaires' "exceptional" status appears *not* as an exception, but rather as one among many possibilities for the structuring of the French Empire. The debates about citizenship in Saint-Louis and the other communes remind us that that what it means to be "French"—and how that status has been defined, granted, or claimed—has long been reinterpreted and reimagined, both in the metropole in the colonies.

CONCLUSION

The 1916 citizenship law was not repealed, despite periodic pleas from French legal scholars, politicians, and colonial administrators who argued that it was politically and legally untenable. (The perceived incompatibility of French and Muslim law, the political implications of extending citizenship based on birthplace, the practical challenges of administration: critics of the law would raise these issues repeatedly for years to come.[55]) Neither was the law extended beyond the boundaries of the four communes. It was not until after World War II that France's relationship with its African colonies and colonial subjects was renegotiated in ways that significantly changed how citizenship functioned throughout its empire. Then, Frederick Cooper has shown, "it was the Senegalese system of citizenship that became the basis of French constitutional law."[56] As Cooper makes clear, this was not the only available option at the time. Nor was it the only option when it became "the Senegalese system of citizenship" decades earlier, in Saint-Louis and the other communes. The extension of French citizenship in Senegal was not a foregone conclusion but was instead the product of legal ambiguities, contentious political battles, and complex historical contingencies. Even as the originaires' citizenship status came to be regarded as a defining characteristic of the four communes, the principles and practices of citizenship in the communes continued to be debated, by jurists and politicians and administrators, and by subjects and citizens, from Saint-Louis to Paris.

NOTES

The author would like to thank Emily Clark, Ibrahima Thioub, and Cécile Vidal, as well as the anonymous reviewers, for their feedback and suggestions. Thanks also go to Alexandre Dubé, Lindsey Gish, Hilary Jones, Martin A. Klein, Rebecca J. Scott, and Sarah Zimmerman for conversations that helped me to think more clearly about this project, and to Edward Berenson, Frederick Cooper, Michael A. Gomez, and Adrian O'Connor for their feedback on the larger project from which this material is drawn.

1. On the debates over French citizenship in Senegal during the nineteenth and early twentieth centuries, see Larissa Kopytoff, "The Boundaries of Citizenship: Political Imagination and French Colonial Administration in Senegal's Quatre Communes," PhD diss., New York University, 2018.

2. On the métis community of Saint-Louis, see Hilary Jones, *The Métis of Senegal: Urban Life and Politics in French West Africa* (Bloomington: Indiana University Press, 2013).

3. On the establishment of the communes and accompanying municipal institutions, see H. O. Idowu, "The Establishment of Elective Institutions in Senegal, 1869–1880," *Journal of African History* 9:2 (1968): 270.

4. The word *originaires,* referring to "natives of" or "those from" a particular place, is often used as shorthand for *originaires des quatre communes* or *originaires des communes de plein exercice* in contemporary sources as well as in the historical scholarship. The classic work on politics in the four communes during the colonial period remains G. Wesley Johnson, *The Emergence of Black Politics in Senegal: The Struggle for Power in the Four Communes, 1900–1920* (Stanford, CA: Stanford University Press, 1971). On the evolution of the originaires' rights and Muslim identity, see Mamadou Diouf, "Assimilation coloniale et identités religieuses de la civilité des originaires des Quatre Communes," *Canadian Journal of African Studies/Revue Canadienne des Etudes Africaines* 34:3 (2000): 565–87.

5. On the indigénat, see Gregory Mann, "What Was the Indigénat? The 'Empire of Law' in French West Africa," *Journal of African History* 50:3 (2009), 331–53.

6. *Journal Officiel de la République Française: Lois et Décrets,* October 1, 1916, 8667–68.

7. Jones, *The Métis of Senegal,* 17.

8. On the emergence of a language of citizenship and rights in the French Empire during the Revolution, see Laurent Dubois, *A Colony of Citizens: Revolution and Slave Emancipation in the French Caribbean, 1787–1804* (Chapel Hill: University of North Carolina Press, 2004), and Carolyn E. Fick, "The Haitian Revolution and the Limits of Freedom: Defining Citizenship in the Revolutionary Era," *Social History* 32:4 (2007): 394–414.

9. "Doléances des habitants du Sénégal, Saint-Louis du Sénégal, 15 avril 1789," in Monique Poulquien, *Doléances des peuples coloniaux à l'assemblée nationale constituante (1789–1790)* (Paris: Archives nationales, 1989), 99. The document was originally published in Dominique Lamiral, *L'Affrique et le peuple affriquain considérés sous tous leurs rapports avec notre commerce et nos colonies* (Paris: Dessenne, 1789). Also see Guillaume Aubert, "'Nègres ou mulâtres nous sommes tous Français': Race, genre et nation à Gorée et à Saint-Louis du Sénégal, fin XVIIe–fin XVIIIe siècle," in Cécile Vidal, ed., *Français? La nation en débat entre colonies et métropole, XVIe–XIXe siècle* (Paris: Éditions de l'École des hautes études en sciences sociales, 2014), 125–47.

10. Collection genérale des décrets rendus par l'Assemblée Nationale avec la mention des sanctions et mandats d'execution donnés par le Roi, vol. 46, January 20–February 18, 1794 (Baudouin: Paris, 1794).

11. See Diouf, "Assimilation coloniale et identités religieuses," and H. O. Idowu, "Assimilation in 19th Century Senegal," *Cahiers d'études africaines* 9:34 (1969): 194–218.

12. During the early twentieth-century debates about citizenship in Senegal, legal scholars as well as colonial administrators in France and Senegal frequently referred back to the extension of the civil code; see Pierre Dareste, "Le droit électoral des indigènes du Sénégal," *Recueil de législation de doctrine et de jurisprudence coloniales* 2 (1910): 1–16. Diouf, Idowu, and Johnson, among others, have discussed the civil code's introduction to Senegal.

13. Dominique Sarr and Richard Roberts, "The Jurisdiction of Muslim Tribunals in Colonial Senegal, 1857–1932," in Kristin Mann and Richard Roberts, eds., *Law in Colonial Africa* (Portsmouth, NH: Heinemann, 1991), 133.

14. Patrick Weil has noted that it was not Muslim *religious* belief in and of itself that French officials found incompatible with French civil law. They argued that French citizenship "did not oblige . . . Muslims to renounce their religion—they could retain it as a moral code and a collection of religious prescriptions—but it did oblige them to respect the French Civil Code, that is, to refrain henceforth from practicing . . . customs that were incompatible with that code," including, and discussed most often by colonial officials in Senegal, polygamy. See Patrick Weil, *How to Be French: Nationality in the Making since 1789* (Durham, NC: Duke University Press, 2008), 216.

15. The electoral rights of Saint-Louis's inhabitants were soon suspended under Napoleon III, to be reinstated in the 1870s under France's Third Republic.

16. Archives Nationales du Sénégal, Dakar, Senegal (hereafter ANS), 20G17(17), Report of Inspector-General Verrier on the Senegalese election lists (June 25, 1905).

17. For more on the antislavery context of the decree, see Lawrence C. Jennings, *French Anti-Slavery: The Movement for the Abolition of Slavery in France, 1802–1848* (Cambridge: Cambridge University Press, 2000).

18. The law's strongest advocate, abolitionist Victor Schoelcher, spent time in Senegal in early 1848 on a fact-finding mission for the abolitionist cause, and later wrote of the influence of his experiences there. On Schoelcher, see Nelly Schmidt, *Abolitionnistes de l'esclavage et réformateurs des colonies: Analyse et documents* (Paris: Karthala, 2000).

19. See Martin A. Klein, *Slavery and Colonial Rule in French West Africa* (Cambridge: Cam-

bridge University Press, 1998), especially ch. 2; Mohammed Mbodj, "The Abolition of Slavery in Senegal, 1820–1890: Crisis or the Rise of a New Entrepreneurial Class?" in Martin A. Klein, ed., *Breaking the Chains: Slavery, Bondage, and Emancipation in Modern Africa and Asia* (Madison: University of Wisconsin Press, 1993).

20. ANS K11, letter from Governor Faidherbe (November 14, 1857). Underlining in original. On the 1855 report from Carrère, see Klein, *Slavery and Colonial Rule,* 28.

21. Richard Roberts, *Litigants and Households: African Disputes and Colonial Courts in the French Soudan, 1895–1912* (Portsmouth, NH: Heinemann, 2005), 42.

22. See, among other references, Archives Nationales d'Outre-Mer, Aix-en-Provence, France (hereafter ANOM), Sénégal-VII-23bis, "Aux termes de l'article 2 du décret du 20 Mai 1857" (February 8, 1884). On the Muslim tribunal of Saint-Louis, see Sarr and Roberts, "The Jurisdiction of Muslim Tribunals," and Bernard Schnapper, "Les Tribunaux musulmans et la politique coloniale au Sénégal (1830–1914)," *Revue historique du droit français et étranger* 39 (1961): 90–128.

23. Ghislaine Lydon, "Obtaining Freedom at the Muslims' Court of Ndar: Colonial Kadijustiz and Women's Divorce Litigation in Senegal," in Shamil Jeppie, Ebrahim Moosa, and Richard Roberts, eds., *Muslim Family Law in Sub-Saharan Africa: Colonial Legacies and Post-Colonial Challenges* (Amsterdam: Amsterdam University Press, 2010), 136–37.

24. Weil, *How to Be French,* 356n147. One example of this argument can be found in ANOM Sénégal-VII-8, Rapport no. 46.

25. These court rulings and administrative decrees addressed the importance of birthplace in determining one's legal status, the distinction between political rights and comprehensive citizenship, the portability of the originaires' political and legal rights, and the rights of originaires' descendants; see "Cour de Cassation, Chambre civile: Audience du 24 juillet 1907," *Recueil de législation, de doctrine et de jurisprudence coloniales* (Paris: Marchal & Billard, 1907), 281–84; "Cour de Cassation, Chambre civile: Audience du 22 juillet 1908," *Recueil de législation, de doctrine et de jurisprudence coloniales* (Paris: Marchal & Billard, 1908), 278–85; "Cour de Cassation, Chambre civile: Audience de 26 avril 1909," *Recueil de législation, de doctrine et de jurisprudence coloniales* (Paris: Marchal & Billard, 1909), 145–46; "Cour de Cassation, Chambre civile: Audience de 8 avril 1910," *Recueil de législation, de doctrine et de jurisprudence coloniales* (Paris: Marchal & Billard, 1910), 130–31; and "Cour de Cassation, Chambre civile: Audience de 17 mai 1911," *Recueil de législation, de doctrine et de jurisprudence coloniales* (Paris: Marchal & Billard, 1911), 198–201.

26. On the debates about the 1912 law and its impact on politics in the four communes, see Alice Conklin, *A Mission to Civilize: The Republican Idea of Empire in France and West Africa, 1895–1930* (Stanford, CA: Stanford University Press, 1997), and Johnson, *The Emergence of Black Politics.* On how the law affected originaires living outside of the communes, see Rebecca Shereikis, "From Law to Custom: The Shifting Legal Status of Muslim *Originaires* in Kayes and Medine, 1903–13," *Journal of African History* 42:2 (2001): 261–83.

27. Johnson writes that, for one living in the communes, "the most odious part of the decree made him subject to the hated *indigénat* . . . whenever he ventured outside of the Com-

munes. Thus he could be summarily tried like any other French subject . . . and imprisoned . . . without benefit of a hearing . . ." G. Wesley Johnson, "The Ascendancy of Blaise Diagne and the Beginning of African Politics in Senegal," *Africa: Journal of the International African Institute* 36:3 (1966): 245.

28. For a brief assessment of Diagne's life, see Hilary Jones, "Blaise Diagne (1872–1934): Senegal's First Black African Deputy to the French National Assembly," in Beatriz Mamigonian and Karen Racine, eds., *The Human Tradition in the Black Atlantic, 1500–2000* (Lanham, MD: Rowman & Littlefield, 2010), 89–102. On the 1914 election, see Iba Der Thiam, *La Révolution de 1914 au Sénégal, ou L'élection au Palais Bourbon du député Blaise Diagne (de son vrai nom Galaye Mbaye Diagne)* (Dakar: Harmattan Sénégal, 2014). For a recent reinterpretation of the 1914 election that examines how colonial schooling contributed to a reconfiguration of African politics in the preceding decades, see Kelly M. Duke Bryant, *Education as Politics: Colonial Schooling and Political Debate in Senegal, 1850s–1914* (Madison: University of Wisconsin Press, 2015).

29. For debates about Diagne's eligibility, see ANS 17G234(108) and ANOM Sénégal-VII-81.

30. ANOM Sénégal-VII-81, Note sur la formation des listes électorales au Sénégal (June 17, 1914).

31. "Rapport de M. Leredu sur l'élection de M. Diagne en 1914," *Journal Officiel du 8 juillet 1914, Séance du mardi 7 juillet*, 2735.

32. On French colonial subjects in the war, see Richard S. Fogarty, *Race and War in France: Colonial Subjects in the French Army, 1914–1918* (Baltimore: Johns Hopkins University Press, 2008).

33. The phrase "failures of paperwork" comes from the title of Ben Kafka's book *The Demon of Writing: Powers and Failures of Paperwork* (Cambridge, MA: MIT Press, 2012).

34. On the originaires and military service during the war, see Sarah Zimmerman, "Citizenship, Military Service, and Managing Exceptionalism: *Originaires* in World War I," in *Empires in World War I: Shifting Frontiers and Imperial Dynamics in a Global Conflict,* ed. Andrew Tait Jarboe and Richard S. Fogarty (London: I. B. Tauris, 2014).

35. These drafts can be found in ANOM Affaires Politiques 597, Rapport politique (3rd trimester, 1916).

36. This position was exceptional but not unique within the French Empire; citizenship in the *cinq comptoirs* (five trading posts) of French India functioned similarly. See Damien Deschamps, "Une citoyenneté différée: Sens civique et assimilation des indigènes dans les Établissements français de l'Inde," *Revue Française de Science Politique* 47:1 (1997): 49–69.

37. See, for instance, Fernand Hauser, "Des citoyens français, peuvent-ils être polygames?" *Le Journal,* June 1, 1922, and Maurice Delafosse, "Vers la fin d'une anomalie," *La Dépêche Coloniale,* June 7, 1922.

38. Richard Roberts has noted that "even the celebrated 1916 citizenship law, which formally recognized the originaires as French citizens, maintained the ambiguities surrounding French civil and Muslim personal status." Richard Roberts, "Text and Testimony in the *Tribu-*

nal de Première Instance, Dakar, during the Early Twentieth Century," *Journal of African History* 31:3 (1990): 451n10. On the tensions between French citizenship and adherence to Muslim law in the debates about the 1916 citizenship law, see Larissa Kopytoff, "French Citizens and Muslim Law: The Tensions of Citizenship in Early Twentieth-Century Senegal," in Richard Marback and Marc W. Kruman, eds., *The Meaning of Citizenship* (Detroit: Wayne State University Press, 2015), 320–37.

39. See Shereikis, "From Law to Custom."

40. A 1917 government report on the issue states directly: "A large number of the originaires of Senegal's communes . . . do not appear in the civil registry." ANS 2G16/27: Rapport annuel sur la situation générale pendant l'année (January 29, 1917).

41. This section has benefited from conversations with Sarah Zimmerman and from her work on the bureaucracy of originaire status for soldiers and veterans; see Zimmerman, "Citizenship, Military Service, and Managing Exceptionalism."

42. ANS 4D20, letter to the governor of Senegal (November 2, 1915).

43. ANS 4D24, dossier 3, document 21.

44. ANOM Affaires Politiques 534: 20ème rapport sur le fonctionnement du Service Judiciaire (October 1916).

45. ANS 5M584(184): Mayor of the commune mixte de Thiès to Monsieur le Procureur de la République (December 9, 1916).

46. ANS 4D27: letter from Angoulvant (October 1916); ANS 4D26: letter from the lieutenant-governor of Saint-Louis (1915).

47. Frederick Cooper, *Colonialism in Question: Theory, Knowledge, History* (Oakland: University of California Press, 2005), 48–49.

48. See Pierre Dareste, "Les nouveaux citoyens français," *Recueil de législation, doctrine, et jurisprudence coloniales* (Paris: Challamel; Marchal & Billard, 1916), 1–16. On individual naturalizations in French West Africa, see Catherine Coquery-Vidrovitch, "Nationalité et citoyenneté en Afrique occidentale français: Originaires et citoyens dans le Sénégal colonial," *Journal of African History* 42:2 (2001): 285–305, and Ruth H. L. Dickens, "Defining French Citizenship Policy in West Africa, 1895–1956," PhD diss., Emory University, 2001.

49. Maurice Viollette, "La Proposition Diagne," *Les Annales coloniales,* July 8, 1916.

50. ANS M83 includes comments from governors and other administrators throughout French West Africa regarding the "preferential" treatment of originaires.

51. ANS 4D23: governor-general of French West Africa to Minister of the Colonies (December 9, 1915).

52. ANOM Affaires Politiques 539: A.s. de la proposition de loi tendant à faire accorder la qualité de citoyen français aux natifs des communes de plein exercice du Sénégal, Dakar (September 3, 1916), 9.

53. For a discussion of citizenship and nationality in France, see Weil, *How to Be French.* On the jurisdictional patchwork of colonial legal regimes, see Lauren Benton, *Law and Colonial Cultures: Legal Regimes in World History, 1400–1900* (Cambridge: Cambridge University Press, 2002).

54. Weil, *How to Be French,* 3.

55. For some examples, see Maurice Viollette, "La Proposition Diagne," *Les Annales coloniales,* June 8, 1916; Delafosse, "Vers la fin d'une anomalie"; and Francis Mury, "Les citoyens français les plus favorisés se trouvent au Sénégal," *Le Courrier colonial,* February 3, 1922.

56. Frederick Cooper, *Citizenship between Empire and Nation: Remaking France and French Africa, 1945–1960* (Princeton, NJ: Princeton University Press, 2014), 8.

III
MYTHIC PERSISTENCE

TRANSATLANTIC CURRENTS OF ORIENTALISM

New Orleans Quadroons and Saint-Louis Signares

EMILY CLARK AND HILARY JONES

Orientalism emerged as a widespread discourse just as Atlantic world sites began to grapple with the place of mixed-race people where Europeans sought to reserve the rights and status of citizenship to themselves. This essay explores the circulation of the trope of the exoticized mixed-race woman as a transatlantic phenomenon that touched both New Orleans and Saint-Louis. Characterizations of American quadroons and the signares of Senegal share strikingly similar content. Each figure emerged and was deployed when European claims to cultural and political superiority were threatened by a shift in historical circumstances. During the first half of the nineteenth century in New Orleans, the threat of black power embodied in the Haitian Revolution produced the stereotype of the sexualized mixed-race woman who lived to pleasure white men. The submissive New Orleans quadroon served as a counterweight to the prospect of black male rebellion. The signares likewise functioned in the second half of the nineteenth century to mitigate apprehension about the ways that mixed-race Senegalese might challenge the French colonial project. The Christianized, economically powerful métisses of Saint-Louis were recast as women whose preoccupations with sexual seduction and exotic sartorial display vitiated any threat they might pose to the French projection of cultural superiority.

The figurative versions of the New Orleans quadroon and the signare of Saint-Louis are both indebted to Orientalist themes and tropes. Orientalist portraits of Ottoman women produced in the eighteenth century were mined to produce an index of the exotic that was applied to mixed-race women in the French Atlantic, first in Saint-Domingue and New Orleans and later in Senegal. The shared French language and the circulation and exchange of immigrants, merchants, and government personnel that connected Saint-Domingue, New Orleans, and Saint-Louis provided vectors for the migration of the figure of the Orientalized woman from one side of the Atlantic to the other.

THE NEW ORLEANS CASE

The trope of the New Orleans quadroon was discursively developed in English during the first half of the nineteenth century, drawing substantially upon the prototype of *la mulâtresse* developed in Saint-Domingue in the late eighteenth century. Two widely circulated works published in the 1790s by François Alexandre Stanislas, Baron de Wimpffen, and Médéric Louis Élie Moreau de Saint-Méry sketched detailed and influential portraits of the free women of color of the French sugar colony.[1] Wimpffen and Moreau de Saint-Méry were in turn indebted to the emergent Orientalist discourse launched by Lady Mary Wortley Montagu's 1763 *Turkish Letters.* Her account of a visit to the seraglio that housed the harem of the grand vizier of Adrianople is a foundational text that established the defining characteristics of the Orientalized woman as incomparably beautiful, extravagantly dressed in exotic attire, bejeweled, languid, sensual, and skilled in the arts of seduction.[2]

Montagu met the sequestered wives and concubines of the grand vizier in a seraglio under the guard of eunuchs, the women's sexual favors preserved for the exclusive pleasure of the Ottoman official. Montagu establishes in detail their extraordinary beauty and luxurious dress. Along the corridor through which she was escorted by the eunuch guards she passed between "two ranks of beautiful young girls, with their hair finely plaited, almost hanging to their feet, all dressed in fine light damasks, brocaded with silver." The principal wife's attire was even more splendid, though decidedly not in the style of Europe. "She was dressed in a *caftan* of gold brocade, flowered with silver, very well fitted to her shape, and showing to advantage the beauty of her bosom, only shaded by the thin gauze of her shift." Instead of a skirt or petticoat, she wore trousers of "pale pink, green and silver" from which peeped "her slippers, white, finely embroidered." Her jewelry was abundant and conspicuously expensive, "her lovely arms adorned with bracelets of diamonds, and her broad girdle set round with diamonds." Her opulent ensemble was completed with a headdress made of a "rich Turkish handkerchief of pink and silver," with "her own fine black hair hanging a great length in various tresses," set off by "some bodkins of jewels" on one side.[3]

The private chamber of the grand vizier's wife was as luxurious, sensuous, and exotic as was her attire, a "pavilion, built round with gilded sashes, which were most of them thrown up, and the trees planted near them gave an agreeable shade, which hindered the sun from being troublesome." All of the senses were indulged in the lady's quarters, from the "jessamines and honeysuckles that twisted round" the trunks of the shade trees "shedding a soft perfume," to the "white marble fountain playing sweet water in the lower part of the room, which fell into three or four basins with a pleasing sound." At one end of this remarkable chamber stood a platform covered with Persian carpets bearing the satin-cushioned sofa upon which the grand vizier's wife lounged, accompanied by two young daughters, "lovely as angels, dressed perfectly rich, and almost covered with jewels." The lady was attended by no fewer than twenty maidservants.[4]

The beauty of Montagu's hostess was equally extraordinary. "I have seen all that has been called lovely either in England or Germany, and must own that I never saw any thing so gloriously beautiful, nor can I recollect a face that would have been taken notice of near hers," Montagu reported. The English visitor was literally struck dumb by the "surprising harmony of features! that charming result of the whole! that exact proportion of body! that lovely bloom of complexion unsullied by art! the unutterable enchantment of her smile! But her eyes! large and black with all the soft languishment of the bine!" Montagu found herself at "every turn of her face discovering some new charm."[5]

The grand vizier's wife instructed her servants to entertain Lady Montagu, and several "began to play some soft airs on instruments between a lute and a guitar, which they accompanied with their voices, while the others danced by turns." Montagu is discreet but unambiguous as she describes a performance designed for sexual arousal. "Nothing could be more artful, or more proper to raise certain ideas. The tunes so soft!—the motion so languishing!—accompanied with pauses and dying eyes! half-falling back, and then recovering themselves in so artful a manner, that I am very positive the coldest and most rigid prude upon earth could not have looked upon them without thinking of something not to be spoken of."[6]

Montagu's seminal description of an Ottoman seraglio, and the women of the harem who inhabited it, introduced elements that became standard in subsequent reports on Ottoman society. The Barbary Wars that took place between 1785 and 1815 generated a spate of Orientalized accounts that fed the European imaginary first inspired by Montagu. Combining the voyeuristic with the didactic, the seraglio and the women of the harem confined to it delineated the ideals of European womanhood by describing its corrupt Eastern opposite.[7]

In the fabulously wealthy French sugar colony of Saint-Domingue, free women of color bearing the generic label *mulâtresse* threatened social and political order by embodying the antithesis of European womanhood. French men took them as their partners, and those partnerships produced divided loyalties among the colony's whites. French men who were ensnared by the beauty and sensuality of free women of color were at odds with the principles of white supremacy and racial hierarchy that anchored Saint-Domingue's slave society. The mulâtresse was cast as the culprit in the corruption of French men, a state of affairs that insured France's defeat in the slave rebellion that became the Haitian Revolution. When Moreau de Saint-Méry and Wimpffen crafted their late eighteenth-century portraits of these dangerously seductive women, Montagu and her successors provided them with a ready index of exotic beauty and sexuality to use.[8]

The Saint-Domingue mulâtresse presented by Moreau de Saint-Méry and Wimpffen was given to sartorial luxury and excess reminiscent of the seraglio at Adrianople. She wore "the most beautiful things that India produces, the most precious muslins, handkerchiefs, cloths and linens," embellished with "rich lace, jewels, valuable in their multiplicity rather than their type." Arrayed in their glittering finery, these women evoke the bejeweled ladies of the seraglio, while their seductive eyes and languid walk with "swaying hips and nodding head" are reminiscent of the dancing servants of the grand vizier's wife.[9]

The sexual charm of the women of the harem is likewise replicated by the mixed-race women of Saint-Domingue, though Moreau de Saint-Méry and Wimpffen are more direct than Lady Montagu when they describe the erotic virtuosity of the mulâtresse. Moreau de Saint-Méry exclaims, "The whole being of a Mûlatresse is a book given to pleasure, and the fire of this Goddess burns in her heart until she dies." Wimpffen likewise attested that these women "have reduced voluptuousness to a kind of mechanical art, which they have carried to the highest point of perfection." The rather discreet sensuality of the harem observed by Lady Montagu is amplified exponentially in Moreau de Saint-Méry's mulâtresse. "The imagination cannot conceive of anything more inflamed that she has not felt, guessed, accomplished. To charm all the senses, to raise them to the most delicious ecstacies, to suspend them by the most seductive raptures: this is her only object of study," he declares.[10]

The Saint-Domingue temptresses described by Moreau de Saint-Méry and Wimpffen disappeared with the Haitian Revolution only to resurface in New Orleans. Their migration was, in part, a literal one. Thousands of free black women from Saint-Domingue sought refuge in New Orleans in the early nineteenth century, many of them arriving in a massive influx in 1809.[11] They more than doubled the number of free women of color in the city and became a literary obsession of Anglophone authors, who merged the romanticism of Montagu's account with the salacious characterizations of Wimpffen and Moreau de Saint-Méry to create an enduring stereotype that came to function as a synecdoche for New Orleans.[12]

Irishman Thomas Ashe published a description of New Orleans free women of color in 1808 that recapitulates Montagu's descriptive details with startling fidelity. The Turkish lady "was dressed in a *caftan* of gold brocade, flowered with silver," and on her feet were "slippers white, finely embroidered." Her New Orleans counterpart, according to Ashe, wore petticoats "ornamented at the bottom with gold lace or fringe richly tasseled," and slippers "composed of gold embroidery." In the Turkish seraglio, the golden kaftan of the grand vizier's lady, "very well fitted to her shape, and showing to advantage the beauty of her bosom," made a good model for Ashe's "jacket made of velvet, fitted tight to the shape." The New Orleans women's headdress, "either a handkerchief of gold-gauze braided with diamonds, or else chains of gold and pearls twisted in and out through a profusion of fine black hair," echoes Montagu's details of her hostess's "rich Turkish handkerchief" and "bodkins of jewels."[13] According to Ashe, these fabulously dressed women of New Orleans, like the mulâtresse of Saint-Domingue, sought to seduce white men.[14]

Antebellum fiction is unabashedly explicit in its Orientalizing of the New Orleans quadroon, and Joseph Holt Ingraham's writing exemplifies the practice. His 1839 short story, "The Quadroon of Orleans," tells of a young aristocrat, the Baron Championet, who comes to New Orleans in 1793 to flee the French Revolution. At St. Louis Cathedral the baron notices a beautiful young woman, Emelie, at prayer, and falls instantly in love with her.[15] Ingraham sketches Emelie and her native city of New Orleans with hyperbolic Orientalism. Upon entering the cathedral, Baron Championet immediately singles out the beautiful quadroon, "and although he passed a score of houris, that opened their large black eyes, and were ready to fall in love with him, he took not his eyes from her he sought till he came where she stood." Improbably, St. Louis Cathedral was filled not with angels, but with houris, the beautiful virginal beings believed to welcome faithful Muslim men to Paradise.[16] The young woman who stood out among all others in the cathedral conjured the Orient in still other ways. "Her raven hair was gathered behind, and fell in rich tresses about her finely shaped head. She wore no bonnet, but instead, a black veil, that fell from a gold comb set with precious stones, down to her feet." Upon noticing the stares of the baron, the quadroon blushed and exited the church with gestures that are reminiscent of the dancing maidservants that Lady Montagu described. "Hastily wrapping her veil about her head, she passed him with a stately, undulating motion, and by a side door, hitherto concealed by a curtain, left the Cathedral, though not without glancing over her shoulder ere she disappeared." The young baron discreetly follows the quadroon to her home, a place "adorned with verandahs, half buried in orange and lemon trees, with glass doors and windows to the ground; the whole thrown open, displaying within apartments furnished with oriental magnificence." Ingraham's readers were thus granted, like Baron Championet, a glimpse into an American harem, one liberally based upon the Turkish pavilion shaded by exotic plants and furnished with luxurious carpets and cushions that Lady Montagu described.[17]

Ingraham's lavish deployment of Orientalizing tropes is unmatched in degree, but not in kind, by other authors who retained for their quadroon heroines the dark, mesmerizing eyes that served as an indicator of exotic origins. The appearance of Aurore, the quadroon heroine of Mayne Reid's best-selling

1856 novel, *The Quadroon; or, A Lover's Adventures in Louisiana,* upholds the conventions deployed by Ingraham, as does that of the quadroon mother in James Peacocke's *Creole Orphan.*[18] Along with their exotic beauty, sartorial opulence, and chambers decorated with Persian carpets and cushions, the New Orleans quadroons mimicked the women of the harem in one other, important way. The conventions and privileges of European Christian marriage were denied the New Orleans quadroon, who was prohibited by law from wedding her white lover. Like so many of the occupants of the seraglio, they were concubines, not wives.

Literary critics have noted Orientalist elements in the discursive production of the novels featuring the New Orleans quadroon, but have not systematically investigated Orientalism as a theme in this genre and explored its implications for historical interpretation.[19] Historians, for their part, have generally accepted the Orientalizing fiction and nonfiction antebellum quadroon discourse as a reliable reflection of actual practice in New Orleans.[20] Recent work has elaborated a more complex history of New Orleans free women of color that reveals that the quadroon concubine delineated in travel accounts and fiction was more imagined than real. In fact, early nineteenth-century free women of color with roots in colonial New Orleans were as likely to marry as were white women, and were stalwarts of the Catholic Church.[21]

The notion that New Orleans free women of color were universally exotic temptresses dedicated to the sexual satisfaction of white men did important cultural and political work in antebellum America.[22] The married, devoutly Catholic free women of color of New Orleans challenged the presumed incapacity of African-descended women to achieve the sexually chaste contours of ideal American (white) womanhood at the same time that they contested white male fantasies about the natural lasciviousness of black women. Free women of color married to free black men were an inconvenient truth that disproved assumptions about white mastery and superiority. The exotic quadroon found in literature was a more convenient representation of black womanhood than the flesh-and-blood free black wives and mothers who inhabited antebellum New Orleans.[23]

* * *

THE SENEGAL CASE

The signare of Senegal has received less attention from historians and literary scholars than the New Orleans quadroon.[24] Some historical scholarship does acknowledge the role that signares played in shaping French and African relations before the colonial era, but this work pays little attention to the deliberate construction of the signare as a type, the deployment of her image at particular moments, and its relationship to a transnational discourse about free women of mixed race in the Atlantic world. The portrayal of the Senegalese signare in travel accounts, fiction, and sketches does not make the kind of explicit reference to the Turkish harem that marks the portraits penned by Wimpffen, Saint-Méry, and Ingraham. Nonetheless, by the late nineteenth century, literary representations of the signare did correspond in numerous ways to the West Atlantic's trope of the Orientalized exotic woman of mixed race who existed for the pleasure of white men.

Like the quadroon of New Orleans, the signare of Senegal served as a way to explain and respond to the reality of intimate encounters between Europeans and Africans, in this case on the West African coast. In mid- to late nineteenth-century West Africa, the image of the signare and her métisse daughter as described by European travelers and illustrators took on new meaning as a means of policing social boundaries as the port city of Saint-Louis became the cultural capital of the Senegal colony. In an unlikely coincidence, the image of the signare as exotic, decadent, and seductive proliferated around the same time that Third Republic France launched wars of conquest in the Senegalese countryside and sought to consolidate its control within the territory of French West Africa. The deficient character ascribed to the signare signaled and symbolized the shortcomings that the French claimed rendered all Senegalese fit for the subordination of colonial rule.

The term *signare* comes from the Portuguese *senhora.* Portuguese merchants who established trade relations on the Senegambian coast in the fifteenth century used the term to describe African women who owned property and served as hosts for European strangers. By the seventeenth century, when the French gained control of trade posts on Gorée and Saint-Louis, the term came to refer to women of high social standing who owned property and entered into temporary marital unions with European merchants or officials. These domestic arrangements, known as *mariage à la mode du pays* (marriage in the style of the country), conformed to marital norms among the Wolof societies of the mainland, with the exception that the unions dissolved upon the death of the male spouse or his permanent departure from the region.[25]

Before the nineteenth-century French colonization campaign, the signares not only had exclusive access to imported goods in Saint-Louis, but also organized upriver trade for European company officials. They owned the majority of valuable property in the town, in the form of houses and canoes, and organized their own trade expeditions to acquire gold and slaves from markets on the upper Senegal. Martin Klein has pointed out elsewhere in this volume that, as slave owners, signares proved more effective than company officials at maintaining a reliable labor force for public works in the town and for upriver expeditions during the trading season.[26] Consequently, by the middle of the eighteenth century, company officials hired slaves from signares rather than purchasing them on the export market.

Slaves played key roles within signare households. Signares relied on household slaves to satisfy the need for productive and reproductive labor in the towns and in the homes that they shared with European men. Male and female slaves also lived and worked in signare homes in ways that replicated the Wolof institution of *jamm judu* or slaves attached to the lineage.[27] Women and girls made up a larger segment of the town's slave population because they fulfilled key functions as millet pounders, laundresses, wet nurses, and domestic servants. Antoine Edme Pruneau de Pommegorge, an eighteenth-century travel writer, used the term *raparille* to refer to the "dames de companies," or female slaves who accompanied signares as part of their public retinue. In this regard, slave women symbolized the honor and prestige of a signare household.[28]

The signare of the late eighteenth and early nineteenth centuries was a powerful social and economic figure in coastal Senegambia, essential to the success of French enterprise there. There are some clear resonances with elements that are common to depictions of mixed-race women in the West Atlantic. Pruneau de Pommegorge's 1789 description of Senegambia uses color terms that originated in the West Atlantic, including *mulâtresse, quarteronne,* and *négresse.* More notably, he ascribes to these women a love of extravagant sartorial display, observing that signares used the gold they obtained on trade expeditions to make jewelry and buy clothes. The "artistically arranged white handkerchief" that signares wore on their heads, the "French style blouse topped with a corset of taffeta or chiffon and a skirt of the same material, gold earrings and long chains of gold or silver," represent an ensemble that bears a striking resemblance to that worn by Thomas Ashe's 1808 New Orleans quadroon. Both the African signare and American quadroon wear a costume that mirrors the richness and style that Lady Montagu encountered among the women of the seraglio.

The resemblance of the signare of this era to the quadroon ends here, however. Pruneau de Pommegorge's signares are not dependent on the economic support of white men, but are rich on their own terms. They are monogamous, some "married in church and others à la mode du pays," and all conduct themselves impeccably.[29] The woman depicted in René Claude Geoffroy de Villeneuve's 1814 *Signar ou Femme de couleur du Sénégal* is unmistakably a woman in command of her own fate. She stands tall, her right hand outstretched toward an African settlement in the background, a gesture that suggests her authority over her native domain. The printed design of the fabric of her robe is exotic, but her ensemble signals restraint and dignity rather than opulent excess.[30] Pruneau de Pommegorge, Villeneuve, and their contemporaries neither ascribed essential racial characteristics to signares nor sought to convey them as erotic figures bent on the seduction of white men. Villeneuve's signare is not sequestered in a decadent seraglio, but stands free in the African landscape.

This powerful African woman disappeared both literally and figuratively in the 1840s and 1850s and was replaced by an image of the signare that more closely resembled the subordinate, Orientalized West Atlantic quadroon. As mid-nineteenth-century France pursued aggressive imperialist strategies that looked beyond Gorée, Saint-Louis, and the few riverine posts long under its control, signare authority began to decline.[31] France prohibited the transatlantic slave trade as a condition of the settlement that ended the Napoleonic Wars in 1815, which robbed signares of the income they earned by leasing out slaves to labor on the annual slaving convoy described in Martin Klein's essay in this volume. In 1816, the Bourbon monarchy regained possession of the Senegal colony, and French merchant interests shifted from mercantile companies to an export trade dominated by private firms. In Senegal, Bordeaux trade houses specialized in exporting gum arabic and other trade goods from the Senegal River valley. In the 1840s, British and French merchants adopted industrial vegetable oil processing factories in their metropolitan centers and began to introduce peanut culture to Senegalese farmers. By the 1860s, groundnuts became the dominant cash crop demanded by French industrialists, and Saint-Louis officials began to impose hegemony over the lower Senegal and the peanut basin north of the Gambia in order to secure the flow of cash crops and to suppress resistance from Muslim clerics who sought sovereignty over the Wolof kingdoms.[32]

As abolition gave way to British and French interest in "legitimate trade," commercial firms and households headed by French men replaced signares as the dominant economic, social, and cultural force in town life in Senegal. Catholic religious orders established and institutionalized their presence in Gorée and Saint-Louis after 1820, and promoted Christian marriage and the nuclear patriarchal family as the only acceptable family formation.[33] David Boilat, a mixed-race member of Senegal's first indigenous Catholic clergy and author of his own narrative about the peoples and societies of mid-nineteenth-century Senegal, lamented the immorality of signares' marriages outside of the Catholic Church and admonished the once-powerful women. In the 1820s, the Sisters of Saint Joseph de Cluny brought their mission to educate young girls to the Senegal colony and established specific classes for signares and young "demoiselles" to teach them the proper habits of middle-class women and to insist that they conform to Church teachings regarding companionate marriage, modesty, and propriety. Boilat's sketch *Signare* illustrates the ideal qualities that he promoted. The watercolor illustration shows a signare of medium brown hue, sitting upright in a high-back chair, dressed in a European gown of European design, draped with cloth in Senegalese style. She wears a conical head wrap and holds something, perhaps a Bible, in her hand. The sketch conveys the qualities of virtue and a mix of refined African and French bourgeois taste that Boilat considered the ideal to which signares should aspire.[34]

The métis priest Boilat and other religious personnel in nineteenth-century Senegal attempted to steer the signare toward a way of life that would be judged "respectable" and "civilized" by the colonizing French.

Many métisse women, whether they were signares or not, embraced this aim. Their efforts were doomed, however, by French colonial resistance to recognizing Africans, including the métis, as cultural, social, and political equals. As a consequence, the French gaze passed over the Catholic métisses who sought to emulate French feminine respectability and fixed instead on a newly constructed Orientalized version of the signare that better suited colonial ambitions.

In 1841, the French artist Stanislas Darondeau traveled to Senegal at the request of King Louis Philippe I and produced a series of drawings of signares.[35] These sketches show the women "in grand costume," dressed sumptuously in European dress and African fabrics in the style of the opulently attired signare established earlier by Pruneau de Pommegorge. But Darondeau rejects the regal outdoor signare of Villeneuve in favor of depictions of the interior life of the signare's household. One of his sketches shows a signare lounging on a settee, attended by a black woman who sits on a floor mat. Two children of light complexion wearing European dress, obviously the illicit progeny of the signare and a French man, stand in the corner observing the scene. Similarly, the sketch *Negresses Playing Kouri* shows a signare seated watching a black woman nurse an infant with four other black women seated on the floor playing the game and another standing over the scene.[36]

Although not outwardly sexual in nature, Darondeau's domestic interiors suggest that the signare and her companions (women of the towns and female servants) were idle and existed for the pleasure of men. The women are opulently and sensuously dressed, but their sartorial display is not for the eyes of all. Their time is spent not in directing the labor of their enslaved laptots, but in watching their maidservants play a board game to pass the time. They and their attendants show a preference for divans, platforms, and the floor over stiff-backed European chairs. Such non-Western furniture is as well suited to purposes of the sequestered all-female interior spaces of the signares' domain as to the seraglio. These images appear precisely at the moment that French officials ratcheted up military maneuvers in the interior while simultaneously warning their soldiers to avoid relationships with the métisses who sought marriages that conformed to the expectations of the Church and middle-class society. Instead, French men were steered toward temporary unions with exoticized signares whose ambition was not to join

French society but simply to live in sequestered luxury to satisfy the sexual requirements of male colonizers.

Although Darondeau died shortly after his travels to Senegal, Lt.-Col. Henri Frey reproduced these watercolor sketches to illustrate his own account of his travels to West Africa.[37] In 1885–1886, Frey headed a military campaign in the region that became French Guinea. Published in 1890, Frey's account likely reached a wider audience than Darondeau's original sketches. It circulated among interested naval officers and soldiers, colonial propagandists, geographers, civilian administrators, and a public interested in the Third Republic's colonial wars in West Africa, disseminating and popularizing Darondeau's exoticized version of the signare.

Frey's account appeared nine years after the naval officer and novelist Pierre Loti authored *Le Roman d'un Spahi.* Set in Saint-Louis, the story enters the world of a French cavalryman named Jean. Jean pines for the love of Jeanne, an unobtainable woman in Paris, but finds himself seduced by two women in Saint-Louis—Cora, a métisse, and Fatou Gaye, a captive living in Cora's house. In the novel, Jean seeks to marry Jeanne. He takes Fatou as his lover, describing her as a "dusky girl of the Khassonke race" who was captured in a raid of her homeland and sold as a slave by the Moors before being "bought back" and placed in Cora's house.[38] The soldier finds himself inexplicably attracted to Cora. Loti evokes familiar elements of exoticism in his description of Takusaan Ndar, the traditional promenade that signares and notable women of Saint-Louis (Ndar) took at dusk. One woman, writes Loti, "threw glances at Jean" with eyes that were dark and dreamy, half closed, and full of a Creole languor," a depiction that might have been lifted directly from Joseph Ingraham's description of the eyes of the New Orleans quadroon, Emelie, who had a "large orbed, jet-black eye, that seemed to float in lakes of liquid languor."[39]

Cora was the wife of a rich river merchant, but "the people of Saint Louis addressed her disdainfully by her Christian name, as a woman of color . . . reared in all the idleness and luxury of a rich Creole; white women kept her at a distance—a *fille de couleur*—she was repulsive to them."[40] In Senegal a mixed-race woman might not be denied Christian marriage to a white man, but she was tragic nonetheless, doomed never to enjoy the full respectability and status accorded to Christian French women. For Loti, the idea of the tragic mulatta provided a useful and convenient framework both to explain and condemn the existence of mixed-race society and a long history of sexual relations between African women and European men in Senegal. It is not surprising that the figure of the tragic mulatta appears at exactly the moment in Senegal's history when signares were losing their importance in the economic and social life of the towns to European officials and merchants, as well as Muslim clerics and traders and métis men.

Le Roman d'un Spahi and other works by Loti were translated into English beginning in the late nineteenth century. They reached an American audience primed by literary production featuring the tragic mulatta and quadroon to consume and apprehend Loti's transatlantic trope of the signare. Americans may not have understood what was at stake in Africa when the Orientalized signare emerged after the middle of the nineteenth century, but they recognized her type and may well have wondered if she was inspired by the tragic mixed-race protagonists of American literature.[41]

In the twentieth century, Senegalese writers appropriated the trope of the tragic mixed-race woman as a means of denouncing the cultural legacy of imperialism. Two postcolonial novels by Senegalese authors, Abdoulaye Sadji's *Nini: Mulâtresse du Sénégal* and Ousmane Socé Diop's *Karim: Roman sénégalais,* both depict life in Senegal's colonial capital for young Western-educated Senegalese men seeking to move into adulthood at the height of French rule.[42] In *Nini,* the title character lives with two unmarried mixed-race aunts in Saint-Louis. Rejected by a young Frenchman living in the capital, Nini also rejects the overtures of a young Senegalese man. She is at home in neither French nor African society. Like her aunts, who would have been the signares or mulâtresses of an earlier era, she is doomed to an unmarried life, one that does not reproduce future generations who will become citizens of either Senegal or France.

CONCLUSION

The connections between the New Orleans quadroon and the signare of Saint-Louis are neither direct nor perfectly sequential, but they are undeniable. The figures are linked at the most basic level by the connective tissue of the French Atlantic world. The administrative personnel of the Company of the Indies usually served at multiple sites in the course of their careers, crossing the Atlantic in the process and carrying with them practices and ideologies shaped by both policy and experience. Marie Baude, the subject of Jessica Johnson's essay in this volume, illustrates the challenge that mixed-race African women began to pose to the increasingly racialized early eighteenth-century French Atlantic world. In the late eighteenth century, when the mulâtresse of Saint-Domingue was cast as a principal culprit in the demise of French control of the colony, commentators like Moreau de Saint-Méry drew on the emergent discourse of Orientalism to establish Antillean mixed-race women as exemplars of a transgressive sexuality that vitiated the power and authority of white men. The Orientalized mulâtresse of Saint-Domingue became a quadroon in antebellum New Orleans, where the figure's association with the alien ways of the seraglio was expressed with both explicit and implicit allusions. Now, the mixed-race woman was not the villainess she was in Saint-Domingue, but instead the tragic sexual servant of triumphant white masculinity, condemned, like the concubines of the harem, to a life that would never grant her the respectability of Christian marriage. For proslavery advocates, the trope comfortingly confirmed white supremacy; for abolitionists, it exposed its evil immorality. The Oriental character of the quadroon was essential to both interpretations. By the time French colonial designs demanded a new version of the signare as subordinate and alien in her native land, Orientalism had been successfully deployed at other sites in the French Atlantic to recast the mixed-race woman in ways that allayed European anxieties and advanced their domination.

The trope of the Orientalized mixed-race woman was a product of the Atlantic World, spawned by its contested construction of race and citizenship. Circulated by those who participated in France's imperial projects over the course of more than three centuries, its contours shifted somewhat as it traversed time and space, but its essential character persisted. The figure became indispensable to the ideology of white supremacy that animated slavery and colonialism, and it remains unavoidable today for those who must contend with the legacies of these pernicious institutions.

NOTES

1. M. L. E. (Médéric Louis Élie) Moreau de Saint-Méry, *Description topographique, physique, civile, politique et historique de la partie française de l'Isle Saint-Domingue* (Philadelphia: By the author, 1797); François Alexandre Stanislas, Baron de Wimpffen, *Voyage to Saint Domingo, in the years 1788, 1789, and 1790,* trans J. Wright (London: T. Cadell Jr. and W. Davies, 1797), 111–13, published in French slightly later the same year as *A Saint-Domingue, pendant les années 1788, 1789 et 1790 par le Baron de Wimpffen* (Paris: Chez Cocheris, 1797).

2. Mary Wortley Montagu, "Extract from Lady M__y W__y M__e's Letters, written during her Travels in Europe, Asia, and Africa. Letter XXXIII. To the Countess of ______, her Sister. Relation of her Visit to the Grand Vizier's and Kahya's Ladies," *London Magazine or Gentlemen's Monthly Intelligence,* May 1763, 231–33.

3. Ibid., 232.

4. Ibid., 232–33.

5. Ibid., 232.

6. Ibid., 233.

7. Robert Battistini, "Glimpses of the Other before Orientalism: The Muslim World in Early American Periodicals, 1785–1800," *Early American Studies* 8:2 (Spring 2010): 446–74. Among the most representative accounts of Ottoman seraglios and harems published in the late 1790s and early 1800s in American periodicals are [James Dalloway] "Selections: Condition of the Female Sex at Constantinople," *Monthly Magazine and American Review (1799–1800),* August 1799, 1, 5, American Periodicals 381; [Harry Card], "On the Condition and Character of Women in different countries and ages," *American Review of History and Politics, and General Repository of Literature and State Paper* . . . October 1812, 4:2, American Periodicals 62; and [Edward Daniel Clarke], "Spirit of Magazines. Description of the Seraglio of the Grand Signior. From Clarke's Travels, Part 2," *Analetic Magazine* 1 (Jan. 1813), American Periodicals 48. All are excerpts of travel accounts by English authors.

8. Justin Girod de Chantrans, *Voyage d'un Suisse dans différentes colonies d'Amérique pendant la dernière guerre* (Paris: Neuchatel, 1785), 180, is representative of the versions of this critique that preceded Moreau de Saint-Méry and Wimpffen. John D. Garrigus, *Before Haiti: Race and Citizenship in French Saint-Domingue* (New York: Palgrave Macmillan, 2006), 109–70, explores this discourse fully.

9. Moreau de Saint-Méry, *Description,* 93.

10. Ibid., 92–93; Wimpffen, *Voyage to Saint Domingo,* 1:147–48.

11. Gabriel Debien and René J. Le Gardeur, "The Saint-Domingue Refugees in Louisiana, 1792–1804," in Carl A. Brasseaux and Glenn R. Conrad, eds., *The Road to Louisiana: The Saint-Domingue Refugees, 1792–1809,* trans. David Cheramie (Lafayette: Center for Louisiana Studies, 1992), 113–243; Paul F. Lachance, "The 1809 Immigration of Saint-Domingue Refugees to New Orleans: Reception, Integration, and Impact," in Brasseaux and Conrad, *The Road to Louisiana,* 245–84; Nathalie Dessens, *From Saint-Domingue to New Orleans: Migration and Influences* (Gainesville: University Press of Florida, 2007), 23–25.

12. Emily Clark, *The Strange History of the American Quadroon: Free Women of Color in the Revolutionary Atlantic World* (Chapel Hill: University of North Carolina Press, 2013), esp. 38–70.

13. Thomas Ashe, *Travels in America Performed in 1806 for the Purpose of Exploring the Rivers Alleghany, Monongahela, Ohio, and Mississippi, and Ascertaining the Produce and Condition of their Banks and Vicinity* (London: Richard Phillips, 1808), 3:269–70.

14. Ashe claimed to have seen the women of New Orleans with his own eyes, but others who traveled in his purported footsteps accused him of fabricating much of his account. Francis H. Herrick, "Thomas Ashe and the Authenticity of His Travels in America," *Mississippi Valley Historical Review* 13:1 (1926): 50–57.

15. Joseph Holt Ingraham, "The Quadroon of Orleans," in *The American Lounger; or, Tales, Sketches and Legends Gathered in Sundry Journeyings* (Philadelphia: Lea and Blanchard, Successors to Carey & Co., 1839): 255–71.

16. Nerina Rustomji, "American Visions of the *Houri,*" *Muslim World* 97:1 (2007): 79–92.

17. Ingraham, "The Quadroon of Orleans," 257–59.

18. James S. Peacocke, *Creole Orphans; or, Lights and Shadows of Southern Life. A Tale of Louisiana* (New York: Derby & Jackson, 1856), 10.

19. The literary criticism on the figure of the "Tragic Mulatto" originated with Sterling A. Brown, "Negro Character as seen by White Authors," *Journal of Negro Education* 2 (1933): 179–203. It has recently been most fully examined by Werner Sollors, *Neither Black nor White yet Both: Thematic Explorations of Interracial Literature* (New York: Oxford University Press, 1997).

20. See, e.g., Herbert Asbury, *The French Quarter; an Informal History of the New Orleans Underworld* (New York: A. A. Knopf, 1936); Sybil Kein, ed., *Creole: The History and Legacy of Louisiana's Free People of Color* (Baton Rouge: Louisiana State University Press, 2000); Judith Kelleher Schafer, *Brothels, Depravity, and Abandoned Women: Illegal Sex in Antebellum New Orleans* (Baton Rouge: Louisiana State University Press, 2011).

21. Clark, *Strange History of the American Quadroon.*

22. Emily Clark, "Atlantic Alliances: Marriage among People of African Descent in New Orleans," in Cécile Vidal, ed., *Louisiana: Crossroads of the Atlantic World* (Philadelphia: University of Pennsylvania Press, 2014), 165–83, and Clark, *Strange History of the American Quadroon.*

23. Deborah Gray White, *Ar'n't I a Woman? Female Slaves in the Plantation South* (New York: Norton, 1985), 27–61.

24. Three works of contemporary Senegalese fiction focus on the signare. Works of historical fiction, they provide a chronology of the signare in Senegalese society in the eighteenth, nineteenth, and twentieth centuries. See Abdoulaye Sadji, *Nini: Mulâtresse du Sénégal* (Paris: Présence africaine, 1954); Tita Mandeleau, *Signare Anna, ou le voyage aux escales* (Dakar: NEAS, 1991); and Fadel Dia, *La Raparille* (Paris: Présence Africaine, 2009).

25. For analysis of signare marriage, see George Brooks, *Eurafricans in Western Africa: Commerce, Social Status, Gender, and Religious Observance from the Sixteenth to the Eighteenth Century* (Athens: Ohio University Press, 2003), 122–60.

26. Notarized documents and population records attest to the fact that signares owned the majority of slaves in the towns until the 1848 decree that abolished slavery in areas under French control. On signares as slave owners, see Saliou Mbaye, "L'esclavage domestique à Saint Louis à travers les archives notariées (1817–1848)," in Djibril Samb, ed., *Saint Louis et l'esclavage* (Dakar: IFAN, Université Cheikh Anta Diop, 2000), 141–57, and Martin A. Klein, "The Role of Slavery in the Economic and Social History of Saint-Louis, Senegal," in this volume.

27. The term *raparille* seems to be a locally used term to refer to a captive who accompanied a signare that originated with the Portuguese *rapace* (m)/rapasse (fem). Pommegorge describes the "raparille" as the female domestic servant who lived with and depended upon signares. Sylvia Ba describes the word as used in Leopold Senghor's poetry as "a word of Portuguese origin that designates a young servant who accompanies a signare." See Antoine Edme Pruneau de Pommegorge, *Description de la Nigritie* (Paris: Chez Maradan, 1789), accessed December 16, 2015, http://gallica.bnf.fr/ark:/12148/bpt6k103355j/; and Sylvia Washington Ba, *The Concept of Negritude in the Poetry of Leopold Sedar Senghor* (Princeton, NJ: Princeton University Press, 1973), glossary.

28. Pruneau de Pommegorge, *Nigritie.*

29. Ibid., 6–7.

30. René Claude Geoffroy de Villeneuve, "Signare ou femme de couleur du Sénégal," *L'Afrique ou l'histoire, moeurs, usages et coutumes des Africains: Le Sénégal* (Paris: Nepveu, Libraire, 1814), vol. 1, facing 69.

31. Hilary Jones, *The Métis of Senegal: Urban Life and Politics in French West Africa* (Bloomington: Indiana University Press, 2013), chaps. 2 and 3.

32. On these nineteenth-century transformations, see Boubacar Barry and Leonhard Harding, eds., *Commerce et commerçants en Afrique de l'Ouest: Le Sénégal* (Paris: L'Harmattan, 1992), esp. 35–58; Yves Pehaut, "A l'époque de la 'traite' de l'arachide: Les 'bordelais' au Sénégal," *Revue historique de Bordeaux et du Département de la Gironde* (1883): 48–69; and George Brooks, "Peanuts and Colonialism: Consequences of the Commercialization of Peanuts in West Africa, 1830–1870," *Journal of African History* 16:1 (1975): 29–54.

33. Although signares, métis, and black Catholics professed Christianity long before 1820, the religious orders established a church, schools, and medical services for the Saint-Louis and Gorée population in the 1820s. See Joseph Roger de Benoist, *Histoire de l'Eglise catholique au Sénégal: Du milieu du XVe siècle à l'aube du troisième millénaire* (Paris: Editions Karthala, 2008), 61–82, 87–115.

34. The founder of the Sisters of Saint Joseph de Cluny took a group of Senegalese men to the headquarters of the Holy Ghost Fathers where three young boys succeeded in becoming ordained priests. Moussa, Fridol, and Boilat returned to Senegal in the 1830s to open their own schools and to serve as clergy under the authority of the priests appointed by the Spiritains to minister to the population of Saint-Louis and Gorée. Boilat wrote his account as a counterweight to European travel narratives. Boilat's analysis of signares was influenced by his mission to convert them. As a result, the account and the portrait of the signare that illustrates it reflect his ideal. David Boilat, *Esquisses sénégalaises* (Paris: P. Bertrand, 1853; Paris: Karthala, 1984). The portrait is the first illustration in the book. On the Sisters of Saint Joseph de Cluny,

see Geneviève Lecuir-Nemo, *Anne-Marie Javouhey: Fondatrice de la congrégation des soeurs de Saint-Joseph de Cluny (1779–1851)* (Paris: Editions Karthala, 2007), 67–92.

35. Stanislas Henri Benoit Darondeau (1807–1841) was a painter and engineer who exhibited at the Salon de Paris. He also traveled throughout the French overseas territories. He became known for his illustrations of Hawaii and Polynesia. In 1841, Darondeau accompanied an expedition to Senegal under Captain Bouet-Willaumez. Darondeau died upon his return to France. In 1843, the navy appointed Bouet-Willaumez governor of Senegal, where he imposed French control over territories for Bordeaux merchants to expand their trade relations. See a reproduction of these images in Colonel Henri-Nicolas Frey, *Illustrations de Côte occidentale d'Afrique: Vues, scènes, croquis* (Paris: C. Marpon et E. Flammarion, 1890), accessed July 29, 2015, http://gallica.bnf.fr/ark:/12148/btv1b23005610.r=Colonel+Frey.langEN.swf.

36. Darondeau, "Intérieur de Signare," fig. 9, and "Négresses jouant au Kouri," facing page 8, in Frey, *Illustrations de Côte occidentale d'Afrique,* accessed July 29, 2015, http://gallica.bnf.fr/ark:/12148/btv1b23005610.r=Colonel+Frey.langEN.swf.

37. Henri-Nicolas Frey wrote *Côte occidentale d'Afrique* as an account of his observations of the peoples of the West African coast from Morocco to Gabon. The work contains numerous lithograph illustrations from a variety of artists. For depictions of Senegal's signares, Frey relies on Darondeau's illustrations as well as illustrations by unknown artists. For an analysis of these depictions, see George Brooks, "Artists' Depictions of Senegalese Signares: Insights Concerning French Racist and Sexist Attitudes," *Genève-Afrique* 18:1 (1980): 77–89.

38. The French judiciary in Senegal enacted a policy called *rachat* or buying back, which allowed town residents to purchase slaves on upriver markets for the purpose of liberating them. Most, however, remained as servants in the households of their liberators. On *rachat,* see Martin A. Klein, *Slavery and Colonial Rule in French West Africa* (Cambridge: Cambridge University Press, 1998), 25–36; Trevor Getz, *Slavery and Reform in West Africa* (Athens: Ohio University Press, 2004), 44–53; and Bernard Moitt, "Slavery, Flight and Redemption in Senegal, 1819–1905," *Slavery and Abolition* 14:2 (1993): 70–86.

39. Pierre Loti, *Le Roman d'un Spahi* (Paris: Calman-Lévy, 1881; 37th edition, 1893). The quotes are taken from the English translation, *The Romance of a Spahi,* trans. M. L. Watkins (Chicago: Rand McNally, 1890), 39. Ingraham, "The Quadroon of Orleans," 258.

40. Loti, *The Romance,* 43.

41. The English translation of *Le Roman d'un Spahi* appeared as *The Romance of a Spahi* in 1890. The post–Civil War period saw a resurgence in the publication of American novels about New Orleans quadroons and the tragic mulatta, such as George Washington Cable's *Madame Delphine* (New York: C. Scribner's Sons, 1881), and Lydia Maria Child's *A Romance of the Republic* (Boston: Ticknor and Fields, 1867). US Library of Congress records show that *The Romance of a Spahi* circulated as part of a popular subscription series by Rand McNally for an $8.00 monthly fee. This may have been one of the first novels that introduced Senegal to US audiences.

42. Abdoulaye Sadji, *Nini: Mulâtresse du Sénégal* (Paris: Présence africaine, 1988); Ousmane Socé Diop, *Karim: Roman sénégalais* (Paris: Nouvelles éditions latines, 1948), originally published in 1935.

REFLECTIONS OF SENEGAMBIA IN NEW ORLEANS JAZZ

BRUCE BOYD RAEBURN

Is Senegambia reflected in New Orleans jazz and, if so, how should such connections be interpreted? The emergence of jazz in New Orleans from the postslavery African American vernacular and its apotheosis as a "great American art" by writers in New York and Paris in the 1930s would seemingly justify such questions. When increasing economic dependence on cultural tourism after World War II convinced civic leaders and jazz aficionados to capitalize on New Orleans's claim as the locus of jazz origins, the city's image turned Afrocentric, reifying the exoticism inherent in Storyville bordellos, jazz funerals, and "second line" parades.[1] As J. Mark Souther observes, "What had started out as a reinvigoration of a black music genre by jazz enthusiasts gradually became a cash cow for tourism promoters."[2] Matt Sakakeeny includes brass band, blues, rhythm & blues, soul, and funk in the tourism equation, arguing that "New Orleans Music" today is simply defined as black music, but promoted as exoticism. Regarding brass bands, he sees the tourist economy as affecting not only the market but also the reflexive nature of black performance: "The career of a contemporary brass band musician is a balancing act between *tradition* (community-based parades and performances) and *heritage* (staged exhibitions of tradition). Musicians circulate through various contexts as they fortify their association with New Orleans Music."[3] Does *heritage* erode *tradition?* For many New Orleans jazz musicians, Afrocentric tradition is an ontological issue, inextricably tied to identity and meaning, compared to which historical and economic considerations are secondary, yet specific African ethnic connections usually remain ambiguous, regardless of context.

While most histories explain jazz origins as a convergence of African and

European antecedents, details related to the musical practices of the dominant West African ethnic groups inhabiting New Orleans in the colonial period are usually lacking. George Lipsitz believes "the complex culture of New Orleans offers us an opportunity to rethink the concept of diaspora, to discern the ways in which New Orleans is always African—but never only African."[4] Lipsitz sees the city as "a significant center of the African diaspora," a bastion of African retentions, yet after acknowledging a Senegambian-Kongolese threshold in the eighteenth century, he employs Robert Farris Thompson's Yoruba model to describe core musical practices in New Orleans because "the brutal racial oppression mandated by the slave system compelled diverse African peoples to coalesce into a unified, if not always uniform, Afro-American culture."[5]

Yet the stated desire of some New Orleans jazz musicians to establish an explicit affiliation with Senegambia is reason enough to question this hypothesis. In this essay, I explore the strategies used by New Orleans jazz musicians to identify with Senegambia, emphasizing several key questions. How has the connection been sustained, transformed, imagined, and replenished?[6] Moreover, considering the preponderant influence of Islam in Senegambia for the past millennium, has Orientalism shaped perceptions of New Orleans jazz? In addressing these questions, I move beyond continuity narratives to examine alternative perspectives deriving from the actions of jazz musicians and related practitioners (such as Black Indians) who have sought out or created opportunities for enhancing their craft (or discovering new meanings within it) through association with Senegambia.

CONTINUITY NARRATIVES

As the research of Gwendolyn Midlo Hall and its application to New Orleans cultural development in the eighteenth century by Ned Sublette suggest, the characteristic heterophony and rhythms associated with New Orleans jazz stem from the French importation of Senegambian slaves with discrete musical practices from 1719 to 1731.[7] After the colony was ceded to Spain in 1763, Kongolese slaves with divergent musical practices predominated. Consequently, one can theorize a musical syncretism in New Orleans that had never existed in Africa and was also distinct from other French and Spanish colonial cultures. As a number of scholars have argued, New Orleans exhibited parallels to synergies animating Saint-Domingue (Haiti), the French Antilles, and Cuba.[8] Yet by comparison, New Orleans's role as a regional nineteenth-century Afrocentric entrepôt where the creolized culture of the Gulf of Mexico and Caribbean fused with the vernacularism of the Mississippi River valley (and thus the North American heartland) is both singular and significant, evident in a vast musical cornucopia including work songs, minstrelsy, spirituals, Creole songs, ragtime, blues, and jazz.

In *The World That Made New Orleans,* Sublette offers a concise accounting of Senegambian reflections in New Orleans music:

> It is worth noting the numerous correspondences between essential characteristics of African American music and those of [Senegambia] that relatively arid, Islamisized region of Africa. Very different from the communal, syllabic, highly polyrhythmic, drum-dominated music of the forested Kongo, this was a bardic, melismatic, swinging music, influenced by Koranic chanting, with a less polyrhythmic texture, favoring portable stringed instruments . . . the Senegambians had a bowed-instrument tradition, and had possibly had it as long as, or longer, than France. In the New World, the Senegambians' musical knowledge could be expressed on the European violin, as well as on the banjo, an instrument that derives from a Senegambian family of plucked instruments.[9]

Sublette correlates this influence with the rhythmic concept (or feeling) most emblematic of jazz, "swing":

> In *Cuba and Its Music* I speculated that the swing feel of jazz derives from a typical feel still easily audible in traditional music in the Senegambia and Mali today, and that New Orleans was a key point in its dissemination. To that I would like to add that there was a point of reinforcement between French New Orleans and Senegambian New Orleans: both sides played unequal eighth notes . . . I would also note the sometimes extreme fondness for melisma in New Orleans (e.g. the ornamentation of Aaron Neville's singing or James Booker's piano playing), which is an attribute of both the French Baroque and the music of the Islamized Senegalese.[10]

Michael Coolen provides further support in noting correspondences between Senegambian song forms (*fodet*) and chord changes in the blues—both cyclical in structure with alternating use of tonic and secondary dominant tones.[11] Taken in tandem, Sublette and Coolen offer compelling examples of reflections of Senegambia in jazz and blues (the most common raw material for jazz improvisation), although these comparisons are theoretical, based on contemporary parallels, rather than evidence of eighteenth-century diffusion. Interestingly, Aaron Neville cites "cowboy singers . . . with the yodeling and stuff" as the inspiration for his melismatic use of falsetto.[12]

The instruments and practices described by Sublette and Coolen were themselves the products of transculturation, deriving from what Peter van der Merwe refers to as "Near Eastern style," historically rooted in Mesopotamian and Arabic precedents (e.g. lutes and hourglass drums, vocal nasality incorporating expressive microtonal inflections, harmonic drones, polyrhythms) that were disseminated beyond the Mediterranean with the spread of Islam from the eleventh to the fifteenth centuries, penetrating both Europe and sub-Saharan Africa. As van der Merwe cautions, "it is often difficult to distinguish the 'Afro' from the 'Arab' in the Afro-Arab style," adding, "We must not attempt to provide our Africanisms with precise family trees. Their ancestry is far too mixed, confused, and obscure for that."[13] Afrocentrism pertaining to New Orleans music therefore encompasses an innate potential for Orientalism, although not necessarily in the pejorative sense applied by scholars who study the projection of Western desire through Orientalist stereotypes.[14]

Orientalism figures in discussions of jazz origins related to "Spanish tinge," meaning clave-based rhythms utilizing dotted-eighth-note syncopation such as *tresillo, cinquillo,* and *habanera* present in early jazz. In essays for the *Jazz Review* in 1959 titled "Creole Echoes," the jazz critic Ernest Borneman argued that a "mature and developed form of Afro-Latin music similar to that of Martinique, Guadeloupe, Trinidad, and Santo Domingo" in mid-nineteenth-century New Orleans was the threshold for the development of jazz. For Borneman, the proper dichotomy for interpreting jazz antecedents was not European-African syncretism but rather European/African versus Asian/Arabic, with a "reunion of the African and European strains of Mediterranean music during the Moorish conquest of Spain—a reunion which changed the structure of Spanish, Portuguese and Southern French music" prior to the colonization of the New World.

> When slavery brought Africans once more into contact with Europeans, the Africans recognized many familiar traits in the music of the Spanish, Portuguese and French settlers—but only a few familiar ones in the music of the other Europeans. Contrary to almost everything jazz critics have said, this familiarity was precisely in the field of harmony. While Anglo-Saxon music showed only harmonic similarities to African music, the French, Spanish and Portuguese settlers also showed similarities in the handling of rhythm and timbre. The slaves thus found it easier to assimilate the latter than the former, and this meant that Creole music had a head-start over the development of spirituals, blues, and other forms of Anglo-African music.[15]

In his conclusion Borneman undermined the viability of what was generally considered to be the Golden Age of jazz development, including the recorded masterworks of King Oliver and Louis Armstrong. Improvisation had long been looked upon as the essence of jazz performance, but Borneman was more interested in syncopation, a Creole rhythmic imperative:

> Jazz went tangent during the very years which, in recording history, appear to be the most fruitful ones—the years when the New Orleans jazzmen migrated to Chicago and were recorded there. . . . It must have been during these very years that jazz lost its 'Spanish tinge' and reduced itself to a series of improvisations in straight 2/4 and 4/4 time on Tin Pan Alley tunes. What got lost at that time was the essence of jazz: the African and Creole themes of the formative years, and the Creole manner of rhythmic accentuation.[16]

Borneman's "Spanish tinge" connotes a viable Orientalism, intrinsic to the creolized environment from which jazz emerged. Yet his analysis rests upon a myopic view of New Orleans culture, missing the complexity, contradictions, and ethnic variegation that existed within black, Afro-Creole, and white communities and the power of the blues (and Tin Pan Alley!) to inspire young musicians. In citing recordings of Creole songs by jazz artists, he neglects to mention their predilection for diversifying repertoire, interspersing Creole material with blues and popular songs.[17] It would appear that "Spanish tinge" was not so much forsaken by New Orleans jazz musicians as placed in perspective. Yet scholars such as John Szwed have argued that the tendency of American scholars to dismiss "Spanish tinge" as intermittent exoticism has also been harmful, diverting attention from transnational forces in the interpretation of jazz history.[18]

Borneman's Orientalism mingles with Afrocentrism: both are embedded in the concept of creolization, the transformative process underlying New Orleans's *couture de métissage.* Freddi Evans's *Congo Square: African Roots in New Orleans* provides an Afrocentric account of continuous syncretism at Place Congo through the 1850s and beyond. In discussing Senegambian contributions, she focuses on Benjamin Latrobe's 1819 sketches of the banza, a precursor of the banjo, noting Robert Farris Thompson's identification of carvings on the fingerboard as Kongolese. Evans also cites Theodore Pavie's observations from 1829–1830, where he describes banjos as integral to "the Dance of the Congos."[19] For Evans, Congo Square was an incubator of Afrocentric cultural continuity and reconfiguration, "fueled by the will to remember":

> The African cultural practices—rhythmic cells, songs, dances, musical instruments, orchestration, styles of drumming, and marketing practices—perpetuated at Congo Square on Sunday afternoons during the eighteenth and nineteenth centuries clearly influenced the local New Orleans culture. The Mardi Gras Indian tradition of integrating drumming/rhythm, song and dance, the waving of handkerchiefs while dancing, and giving money to impressive dancers are among these. African-derived habanera rhythm and its derivatives, found in the most popular Creole slave songs and the correlating dances at Congo Square, are also found at the core of early New Orleans jazz compositions, second line or parade beat, jazz funeral music, and Mardi Gras Indian chants and rhythms. . . . The cultural practices and performances that persisted around Congo Square bore fruit that continues to manifest itself and make New Orleans a distinct North American city.[20]

In her epilogue, Evans emphasizes the significance of Congo Square as a site of African memory and survival, noting an ordinance, enacted shortly after the book's publication, that returned its designation to Congo Square after more than a century as Beauregard Square, named after P. G. T. Beauregard, a Confederate general.[21]

Documentation and interpretation of African retentions in New Orleans remains challenging, yet historical verification is not always required to render a connection meaningful. The clarinetist and soprano saxophonist Sidney Bechet's apocryphal story of an enslaved grandfather Omar in *Treat It Gentle* has attracted considerable scholarly attention as myth. Much of the memoir is devoted to African cultural memory—how it informs a jazz musician's actions and imagination and the responsibilities that it entails:

> My grandfather was a slave. But he was a man that could do anything. He could sing; he danced, he was a leader. It was natural to him; and everyone followed him. . . . he beat out rhythms on drums at the Square—Congo Square they called it—and they'd all be gathered around him. . . . He had a power. He was a strong man. His name was Omar. What I'm saying is that he was a musician. No one had to explain notes or rhythm or feeling to him. It was all there inside him, something he was always sure of. All the things that was happening to him outside, they had to get there to be measured—there inside him where the music was.[22]

The narrative concerns Omar's love for a slave girl, her sadistic master, and the tragedy that ensues. References to *vodun,* African drumming, plantation balls, maroon colonies, pirate raids, allegations of black-on-white rape, and murder provide an exotic microcosm of antebellum Louisiana, infused with constant allusions to music. In the concluding chapter, Bechet reprises the Omar story to justify a manifesto:

> What I have to say, it's what the music has been saying to me and what I've been saying to it as far back as I can remember. The music makes a voice, and, no matter what happens, the man that cares to hear that voice, he *can* hear it. I don't mean there's any end to the things that make it hard for the people to hear the real voice the music has got in it. All I mean

> is the music is still there for any who want it. . . . Omar's voice, that's there . . . the blues, and the spirituals, and the remembering, and the suffering . . . that's all inside the music. And somehow when the music is played right it does an explaining of all those things.[23]

John Chilton has traced the family genealogy to Françoise Cocote, the mother of Sidney's grandfather, Jean Becher, a carpenter born circa 1802 and listed in the 1850 census as a mulatto married to a black woman. He was a successful *homme de couleur libre,* with assets amounting to $3,300 in 1860. His son Omar was Sidney's father, a shoemaker domiciled in the 7th Ward. Thus, Bechet most certainly did not have a slave grandfather who performed in Place Congo and lost his arm in a struggle for the affections of a slave girl. Given the details in question, Bechet's Omar story is probably a reworking of the Bras-Coupé folk tale included in George Washington Cable's *The Grandissimes.*[24]

Yet when a white scholar, Rod Jellema, argued during a conference in 1997 that the story was invented, the anger his comments elicited from Bechet relatives and audience members (notably Kalamu ya Salaam, who used the opportunity to read a poem he had written about Bechet) dramatically illustrated not only the symbolic power of myth but also the desire of those with a stake in the story to treat it as fact in order to strengthen its heuristic potency.[25]

In *Kinds of Blue: The Jazz Aesthetic in African American Narrative,* Jürgen Grandt extols Bechet's literary and musical talents as a griot conflating history and memory, imagining him as subverting slave heritage by deploying the discursive arsenal of jazz improvisation and African tradition to deconstruct not only history, but time itself:

> In interrogating the juncture between slavery and freedom, black and white, the individual and the collective, property and ownership by translating the literal into the figurative, the [Omar] passage is indicative of another narrative strategy that propels Bechet's entire autobiography. The narrative's jazz aesthetic probes and challenges the received binary pairs of the dominant culture, collapsing the absolute homogeneity of all concepts, categories, and frameworks . . . linear, historical time transforms

> into cyclical, cultural time and collapses historical as well as geographical distances.

Grandt sees the Omar story as "complete fabrication" and notes that "jazz scholars have long chastised Bechet for this and other discrepancies . . . Bechet claimed in a 1939 interview to be a native of Senegal."[26] Yet African retentions do not have to be historically demonstrable in order to factor effectively into jazz history—artistic inspiration and its products can derive from imagined realities. If one accepts Grandt's interpretation of Bechet's deconstructive intent, the interpolation of Senegalese heritage in an interview qualifies as a viable creative act, consonant with the prerogatives of a jazz artist whose work involves reconfiguring musical narratives and implying time.

Bechet's recounting of Africanisms manifested in the blues, spirituals, and jazz conforms to what David Scott calls "a narrative of continuities," a trope developed by the anthropologist Melville Herskovits to test the survival of African retentions in black American culture and to validate a useable, verifiable African past.[27] Herskovits's work reified a broader movement between the wars in which "across a range of Afro-American ideological positions—from the working-class disciples of Marcus Garvey to the intellectual organizers of Pan-Africanism and the artists and literati of the Harlem Renaissance—peoples of African descent were themselves reclaiming, in various inflections, a past called Africa, and placing it in the foreground of their assertions of cultural identity and community."[28] Scott's critique of continuity narratives resituates the African heritage discourse away from "corroboration or verification of authentic pasts" toward an emphasis on "tradition," in which participants "seek rather to describe the tradition of discourse in which they participate, the local network of power and knowledge in which they are employed, and the kinds of identities they serve to fashion."[29]

CRISIS NARRATIVES AND SANKOFA

Although continuity narratives related to slavery provide useful visions of cultural survival, they cannot explain all aspects of tradition building. The clarinetist George Lewis's great-grandmother was the daughter of a Senegambian slave, spoke Wolof, and taught bits of that language to his mother,

Alice Williams Zeno, along with some African recipes. Yet Tom Bethell, the clarinetist's biographer, describes Lewis's African past as "extremely distant" and rejects "the mysterious action of 'race memory' or . . . genetics (blacks having a better 'sense of rhythm' and so on)" as explanations for jazz origins in New Orleans. For Bethell, jazz was "an artistic response from blacks" to the repression of postslavery society.[30] It enabled the creation of new African American traditions, despite traumatic upheaval, regenerating what could be salvaged from a shattered past.

Radical discontinuities and even musical extinction within the African Diaspora are not uncommon, as Heidi Feldman has shown regarding the disappearance of Afro-Peruvian music and its resurrection from 1950 to 1970.[31] Borneman's interpretation of the dissolution of "Spanish tinge" would certainly qualify as discontinuity. Perennially, dire forebodings about the "death of jazz" have surfaced in New Orleans, especially with reference to brass bands (1930s, '40s, '70s).[32] In the 1940s the emergence of bebop was viewed as revolutionary in some circles and evolutionary in others but nevertheless promoted a culture of innovation that encouraged breaks with the past. It occurred simultaneously with a traditionalist New Orleans revival, splitting the jazz world into warring factions.[33] Thus, there were times when traditionalism was rejected by newcomers who embraced modernist idioms that were not only extraneous to the local tradition but also thought to be threatening to it.

A 2010 interview with jazz drummer Anthony Bazley presents a Senegambian connection to New Orleans jazz without invoking slavery-based continuity narratives. Bazley was born in the Carrollton section in 1934, and, like a number of local jazz musicians, claimed to be self-taught.[34] He started with a neighborhood band led by Curtis Mitchell. While a junior at Booker T. Washington High School, he worked professionally with the Johnson Brothers (including Plas and Raymond Johnson and Harold Battiste), thanks to the departing drummer, Edward Blackwell. Then he joined William Houston's big band, comprised of Orleans Parish School teachers and union officials, a prestige assignment.[35] Bazley left New Orleans as a show drummer with the United States Air Force, 1956–1957, traveling to Iceland, Greenland, Newfoundland, and Japan.

After military service, Bazley moved to California, where he attended the Los Angeles Music Conservatory and became an active studio musician, mentored by another transplanted New Orleans drummer, Earl Palmer.[36] From 1958 to 1963 he recorded extensively in Los Angeles with pianist Leroy Vinnegar, guitarist Wes Montgomery, alto saxophonist Herb Geller, tenor saxophonist Curtis Amy, flautist William Green, and vibraphonist Roy Ayers. He worked with notable beboppers, such as Eric Dolphy, Buddy Collette, Charles Lloyd, Teddy Edwards, Dexter Gordan, Hampton Hawes, and Harold Land, and played regularly with a band co-led by Amy and Ayers in 1964–1966.[37] By the 1970s, Bazley's modern jazz credentials were impeccable, and many of the younger musicians in New Orleans revered him.[38]

In discussing family background, Bazley revealed that his maternal grandfather, Toby Ritter, had been a Jew married to a "half-breed" Houma Indian. Then he described his father, Clarence Bazley, a cooper by trade, as "from Senegal."[39] As the interview progressed, however, it became clear that the details of his father's emigration from Senegal were rather hazy. The information had come from his paternal great-aunt, who told him "his [father's] people had migrated from Senegal to St. Thomas in the Virgin Islands first, then came to New Orleans." The use of the term "migrate" was particularly interesting, since it suggested that Bazley's ancestors had not been slaves and came to the United States voluntarily, albeit through a "back door." Bazley shared what he understood to be Senegalese terms used within the family: his father's nickname, "poo-pah" (which he thought meant "sunshine"), and "macoute" and "gunni" for his father's siblings.

The 1938 *Polk's New Orleans City Directory* places Clarence Bazley at 8716 Hickory Street, confirming the address given in the interview.[40] The 1930 United States Census provides more detail, but contradicts claims of African parentage—Clarence was a native Orleanian.[41] The 1920 US Census had Clarence Bazley (age fifteen) living in Holly Grove with his father Henderson Bazley (age forty), a longshoreman, his mother Anna (aged thirty-nine), a sister, Hazel (age sixteen), and a brother, Willie (age eleven). Both of Clarence's parents were identified as born in Louisiana, but Henderson's original entry of "unknown" for his father's place of birth was scratched out with "U.S." superimposed over it.[42] A Draft Registration Card identifies Henderson as "native born," giving his birth date as August 26, 1878.[43] Henderson was also included in the 1910 US Census with his wife Annie, Hazel, Clarence, and

William, but an alternative spelling of the surname as "Bazler" distinguishes this representation from later documents.[44]

Based on public records, Clarence Bazley was the son of an African American longshoreman born in Louisiana in 1878. By the time Tony was born, Henderson had been dead for more than a decade. Curiously, the 1880 census did not list any New Orleans Bazleys or Bazlers identified as black, so Henderson's parents are mysteriously absent. The most likely scenario for a Senegal to St. Thomas to New Orleans migration (if it happened at all) would therefore have been during Reconstruction, while the state constitution of 1868 was in effect—a time of hopeful possibility. Was Tony Bazley's great-grandfather one of the African seamen that figure so prominently in accounts of late eighteenth- and nineteenth-century transatlantic African to American cultural exchange?[45]

The significance of a free Senegambian ancestor for Tony Bazley is worth contemplating. One might construe the connection as validating his status within the New Orleans jazz community, or as an indication of his desire to be seen as a man connected to various worlds (African, Islamic, American), or both. A comparison of Bazley with Bechet provides additional insight. Bechet's is a slavery-based continuity narrative; Bazley's is a migration saga. Bechet came from a family of musicians; Bazley claimed to be the first member of his family to play music.[46] Bechet was a notorious traditionalist; Bazley preferred bebop, a jazz style that was not indigenous to New Orleans but that flourished there among young black (and white) musicians after 1945, despite efforts by traditionalists to suppress it.[47] Bechet's description of bebop as "lacking the memory of it . . . these new musicianers . . . they don't know where the music comes from and they don't know where it's going" depicts it as alien to his idea of a continuum of African spiritual tradition.[48] Bazley would obviously disagree. Yet despite their differences, Bazley and Bechet had at least one thing in common: whether imagined or real, when asked to specify their ethnic African heritage, they both claimed Senegal.

The terms mentioned by Bazley, "macoute" for Hazel and "gunni" for Willie, the father's younger brother, are susceptible to verification. In fact, *goné* is the Wolof word for "child." "Macoute" is not Wolof: it appears in Haitian Kreyol (famously in *tonton macoute* or in the name of Young Makout, a hip hop artist). "Poo-pah" and "Poo-pye" are also not found in Wolof, although *pappa* is the word for "father."[49] Conflation of Creole dialects with Africanisms in the Bazley household does not necessarily negate the Senegambian connection but instead contextualizes it within a dynamic cultural environment, a familial *couture de métissage* that also included Native American and Jewish heritage. Yet by the time Henderson Bazley was born, African heritage was being targeted for eradication—the result of post-Emancipation processes related more to ethnocentrism and apartheid than to syncretism.

A Bazley forbearer arriving in New Orleans between 1868 and 1878 would have been dismayed by how the term *Senegambian* was being expropriated and strategically deployed by whites in newspaper accounts of black political, cultural, and social activity. Gwen Hall's research illustrates how French slave traders and planters in the eighteenth century made a fetish of differentiating among Wolof, Mandinga, and Bambara according to their respective cultural traits.[50] By the 1870s, precision of language and function had given way to an ambiguous and undifferentiated use of "Senegambian" as a sarcastic signifier of anything "black." The ways in which the term was utilized in the white New Orleans press from the 1870s to the 1910s illustrate how a once specific and nuanced marker of African ethnic identity could be transformed into a racial epithet used to ridicule African heritage and promote apartheid.

Because the State Constitution of 1868 (backed by the presence of federal troops) was viewed as a realization of the civil and political rights provided for freedmen under the Fourteenth Amendment, the Reconstruction Era (1866–1877) was a time of rising political, social, and economic expectations for blacks in Louisiana, but it was marred by continuous conflict, evident in the Race Riot of 1866, the Colfax Massacre in 1873, and the Battle of Liberty Place in 1874. Contemporaneous newspaper accounts lampooning black governance were rife in the *Daily Picayune,* the organ for the Democratic Party. "Senegambian Gambols" (February 5, 1873) lamented the "more than usually strong picture of a colored Bedlam" in Republican Governor William Pitt Kellogg's "Bayonet Legislature"; "How Our Senegambian Legislators Are Manipulated" (July 23, 1874) blamed the "clannish and exclusive spirit of the colored people" for summoning up "the White League specter" and decried "the exclusive domination of the most ignorant class . . . for the aggrandizement of colored ignoramuses utterly unfit for the position to which they aspire."[51] Thirty-five years later, on April 14, 1908, the *Picayune* joyously reported that "there was no more Negro question in politics, that the kibosh had been put on the Senegambian all over the South," and that the Republican Party was willing to "endorse the sentiment."[52] The failure of Reconstruction and the disenfranchisement and subordination of blacks under Jim Crow laws bolstered by the *Plessy* decision in 1896 retired the issue of "Senegambian" political power from public attention, but the term continued to be applied to blackface minstrelsy and to describe violent crimes against blacks in New Orleans, including stabbings and assaults by police dogs.[53]

Of particular note was an incident occurring on Cypress Street in the "back o' town" section, reported in the *Daily Picayune* on August 22, 1898. "Senegambian Serenaders Indulge in a Row in Which the Peacemaker Is Cut" described an open-air Sunday evening performance by a black string band which was invaded by a group of "young white men" claiming to act as peacemakers breaking up a fight within the black audience: "During the melee one of the parties, said to be a negro, fired a pistol, and a white man named John Duffy, residing in the above neighborhood . . . received a cut about 6 inches in length on the right side of the head and another about an inch in length on the right side of the neck. . . . In the meantime Captain Boyle, Corporal Boyard and several officers hastened to the scene, but little information could be learned from the residents or those present."[54]

Whether descended from African slaves or migrants, blacks in New Orleans under segregation had reason to be concerned for their safety due to the predilection of whites to intervene in their affairs. Within two years of the Cypress Street event, the Robert Charles riot in nearby Central City illustrated what else could happen when a black man with a gun was confronted by law enforcement. The murderous white rampage that ensued after Charles killed a policeman lasted for days.[55] Yet African Americans found ways to use cultural tradition for defense and survival. During the onset of Jim Crow, music and related folk arts became one of the few means available for resisting oppression and coping with the erosion of civil liberties and economic opportunity that segregation entailed. Public displays of authentic African musical tradition, however, were no longer an option. As Jason Berry observes, "African drumming in New Orleans submerged long before the birth of jazz."[56] During segregation, whites attempted to expropriate the term "Creole," whiten genealogies, and erase African culture from the city's official history. In photographs of jazz bands from 1905 to 1930 one finds a preponderance of European instruments—no African drums, to be sure, although banjos became prevalent, especially after 1919.[57]

References to Senegambia in ragtime compositions such as George Rosey's "Senegambian March and Two-Step" (1899) and in Jazz Age tunes such as Clarence Todd's "Senegalese Stomp" (1926)—both of which were performed in New Orleans by the Creole violinist John Robichaux's orchestra—indicate that the term still retained some currency for black artists and audiences in the 1920s, but such fare also pandered to white bourgeois demands for exoticism.[58] The popularity of songs such as "The Sheik of Araby" and depictions of jazz bands in turbans revealed an Orientalist undercurrent that furthered the trend.[59] French and American intellectuals were initially more interested in equating jazz with African primitivism—calling it "jungle music"—than they were in trying to understand its connection to African American tradition. Before jazz achieved recognition as an American art, which afforded new opportunities for development and experimentation that could draw directly and unabashedly on African models, manifestations of African cultural memory such as Bechet revealed in *Treat It Gentle* remained hidden.

The emergence of new forms of modern jazz coinciding with the Civil Rights movement in the 1950s and '60s catalyzed a desire to render African connections to jazz more obvious and explicit, evident in the actions of New Orleans jazz musicians such as the drummer Edward Blackwell and saxophonists Harold Battiste and Earl Turbinton Jr. These were Tony Bazley's contemporaries, and in fashioning personal and musical identities for themselves, they drew heavily on traditional African techniques for performance, composition, and teaching, as did Bazley, whose nickname was "Oulabula."[60] Under their aegis, African tradition was rehabilitated as a means of ensuring the music's perpetuation and as a community resource. Blackwell became so thoroughly identified with this tendency, given his work with Ornette Coleman and trips to North Africa with Randy Weston, that some interviewers mistakenly assumed he had absorbed "Afro-Cuban" influences in New Orleans, which he denied, characterizing the New Orleans music scene he experienced in the 1940s and '50s as consisting only of "Dixieland and rhythm and blues." Yet in discussing the persistence of African sensibility in New Orleans drumming with Robert Palmer in October 1975, he stated: "the influence went on and on and was passed down . . . each drummer would take the history and use it and broaden it in some kind of way. And I think that led to the fact that you can always tell if a drummer's been in New Orleans."[61] When an opportunity to study African drumming with a Ghanaian master arose in the 1970s, he took advantage of it, just as he had in New Orleans when the traditional jazz drummer Paul Barbarin mentored him in the 1950s.[62] For Blackwell, boundaries between "African" and "American" or "traditional" and "modern" jazz were inconsequential, because the cultural memory he inherited in New Orleans and the desire to build upon it through transnational collaborations were his primary imperatives. As he told *Jazz Magazine*'s Aldo Romano in 1989: "Ce rythme s'est inscrit en moi."[63] The rhythm "inscribed itself" onto him.

Alto saxophonist Earl Turbinton Jr. considered the city's Afrocentric environment to be a powerful influence on all New Orleans musicians, regardless of genre: "It's the only place I've ever encountered musicians who play authentically and fluently, funk, Dixieland, gospel music, classical, bebop—all idioms, innately and fluently without having to study at Berklee or conservatories or copy off records. They're just born with it in New Orleans. This is where the music first got off the boats. I've tried to disprove it, but the only other place where I've seen such an overwhelming wealth in music and musicians is Africa."[64] The saxophonist, producer, and arranger Harold Battiste, whose talents graced the recordings of artists ranging from Sam Cooke to Sonny and Cher, sought inspiration in New Orleans's African roots. His *African Genesis Suite* was conceived in collaboration with Sonny Bono in November 1971, inspired by Robert Ardrey's book, *African Genesis: A Personal Investigation into the Animal Origins and Nature of Man.*[65]

Because Bazley, Blackwell, Battiste, and Turbinton consistently stressed the African nature of their native environment and aggressively sought opportunities to advance that connection through collaboration with African musicians, a threshold for the reclaiming of African tradition was established in New Orleans. Turbinton's Jazz Workshop in the late 1960s was a performance venue designed to attract young talent to serious jazz study, which included learning about tonal (or "melodic") approaches to the drums, as well as their spiritual dimension, according to African practices.[66] These musicians dressed daily in African garments, representing Afrocentrism as a natural part of New Orleans music, and because they all traveled extensively, they shaped perceptions abroad as well as at home. Since the devastation attending Hurricane Katrina, this sense of commitment to replenishing African tradition in New Orleans has only grown stronger.

In *New Orleans Suite: Music and Culture in Transition,* Eric Porter relates how Cherise Harrison-Nelson, a powerful female presence in the Black Indian masking tradition, incorporated Sankofa designs acquired during a Fulbright fellowship in Senegal and Ghana in the 1990s into beaded patchwork for Carnival suits in 2007 and 2008. Sankofa is an Akan symbol meaning "go back and get it," signifying the reclaiming of the past as a means of addressing the future, and Porter advises that "rather than simply (and anachronistically) reading these practices as a part of a centuries-old story of Akan influences in the new world . . . we need to understand them as imaginative acts of seizing the past to re-define life in the present and future."[67] Porter characterizes New Orleans as a "diaspora city," but with qualifications: "future writing about culture (and music in particular) in New Orleans may do well to foreground diaspora as an ongoing and evolving process. While recognizing the importance of narratives of creolization that link New Orleans to a colonial and postcolonial Caribbean, we can also see that creolization in the post-Katrina era is a multilayered process, constituted by many kinds of displacements and rebuilt human networks of both long and short duration. . . . the site of new creolizations, the meeting point of multiple diasporas and the crossing and intersections of diasporas."[68]

Today New Orleans musicians are implementing this vision of mixing and renewal by reintroducing Senegambian music into the city's eclectic art and music scenes. Jeff Klein's AfricaNOLA defines its mission as "bringing African musicians to New Orleans to live, perform, teach and share cultures that are uniquely intertwined with our own." Current projects include Kora Konnection, described as "an exotic blend of West African Mandinka music and Jazz Improvisation . . . led by two griots: Morikeba Kouyate, a kora master from Senegal, and Thiemo Djoubate, a balafon and djembe master from Guinea," and Africa Brass, a fusion of African drumming and New Orleans brass band heterophony. New Orleans saxophonist Tim Green, Jeff Klein on

African drums, and bass players James Singleton and Vince Mitchell complete the Kora Konnection lineup.[69] Such initiatives reinforce perceptions of New Orleans music as Afrocentric among locals and tourists alike, but they also increase the expressive choices available to all New Orleans musicians, regardless of racial or ethnic background. In this case, *heritage* does not erode *tradition*—it expands it.

Sankofa obliterates both distance and time and confirms David Scott's perspective on tradition as aligning past, present, and future in a meaningful way through a process of ongoing negotiation. For centuries, reflections of Senegambia in New Orleans culture have persisted, waxing and waning through slavery and apartheid, economic and social dislocation, the convolutions of the popular music industry and cultural tourism, and disasters both natural and man-made. New Orleans music remains a contested environment (as does its historiography), but in retrospect, a trend is apparent: repression and "coon song" caricatures of African ethnicity have been supplanted by serious multiethnic interest in nurturing and reclaiming African connections as intrinsic to jazz, a vaunted international treasure. The Afrocentric stamp on New Orleans music has become indelible, and access has been expanded to encompass the world—after all, those dollars are still needed to keep the music alive. Although identification of specific Senegambian musical traits dating back to the eighteenth century remains elusive, if not impossible to demonstrate, the *idea* of abiding Senegambian roots—and the act of reflecting upon them—conditions how New Orleans jazz musicians reconfigure tradition by referencing Senegambia as symbolic of a spiritual African homeland. As the stories of Sidney Bechet and Tony Bazley make clear, reflections of Senegambia can be imagined or real, but they continue to inspire musical regeneration through jazz, compelling New Orleans musicians to honor Afrocentric tradition, even as they transform it.

NOTES

1. Bruce Raeburn, *New Orleans Style and the Writing of American Jazz History* (Ann Arbor: University of Michigan Press, 2009), 217–58; Matt Sakakeeny, "New Orleans Music as a Circulatory System," *Black Music Research Journal* 31:2 (Fall 2011): 291–325. For a critique of

Eurocentric representations of New Orleans, see Rosanne Adderley, "Rebuilding an 'Historic' (Black) City: African-American History and the Public Profile of New Orleans around Hurricane Katrina," paper for "Katrina 2005," University of Lyon II, Lyon, France, March 31, 2011.

2. J. Mark Souther, *New Orleans on Parade: Tourism and the Transformation of the Crescent City* (Baton Rouge: Louisiana State University Press, 2006), 108.

3. Sakakeeny, "New Orleans Music," 321.

4. George Lipsitz, "New Orleans in the World and the World in New Orleans," *Black Music Research Journal* 31:2 (Fall 2011): 261–90; quotation on 261.

5. Ibid., 264–66.

6. See J. Lorand Matory, "Afro-Atlantic Culture: On the Live Dialogue between Africa and the Americas," in Kwame Anthony Appiah and Henry Louis Gates Jr., eds., *Africana: The Encyclopedia of the African and African American Experience,* 2nd ed. (New York: Oxford University Press, 2005), 1:93–103.

7. Gwendolyn Midlo Hall, *Africans in Colonial Louisiana: The Development of Afro-Creole Culture in the Eighteenth Century* (Baton Rouge: Louisiana State University Press, 1992), and Ned Sublette, *The World That Made New Orleans: From Spanish Silver to Congo Square* (Chicago: Lawrence Hill Books, 2008).

8. Roger Abraham, Robert Farris Thompson, John Szwed, and Nick Spitzer, *Blues for New Orleans: Mardi Gras and America's Creole Soul* (Philadelphia: University of Pennsylvania Press, 2006).

9. Sublette, *The World That Made New Orleans,* 60.

10. Ibid., 72–73.

11. Michael T. Coolen, "Senegambian Influences on Afro-American Musical Culture," *Black Music Research Journal* 11:1 (1991): 1–18; see 16.

12. Macon Fry, "Aaron Neville," *Wavelength* no. 65 (May 1985): 20–24; David Ritz with Art, Aaron, Charles, and Cyril Neville, *The Brothers* (New York: Little, Brown, 2000), 51–52. Lynn Abbott and Doug Seroff, "America's Blue Yodel," *Musical Traditions* no. 11 (1993): 2–11, shows yodeling as rooted in both Africa and Europe and subject to reciprocal transatlantic exchange.

13. Peter van der Merwe, *Origins of the Popular Style: The Antecedents of Twentieth-Century Popular Music* (New York: Oxford University Press, 2002; originally published 1989), 11–15, 29, 31.

14. Edward W. Said, *Orientalism* (New York: Random House, 1978), and critiques of Said in Robert Irwin, *Dangerous Knowledge: Orientalism and Its Discontents* (New York: Overlook Press, 2006), and Naomi Rosenblatt, "Orientalism in American Popular Culture," *Penn History Review* 16:2 (Spring 2009): 51–63.

15. Ernest Borneman, "Creole Echoes," *Jazz Review* 2:8 (September 1959): 13–15, quotation on 14; "Creole Echoes, Part II," *Jazz Review* 2:10 (November 1959): 26–27.

16. Borneman, "Creole Echoes," 14.

17. Borneman, "Creole Echoes, Part II," 27.

18. John Szwed, "Doctor Jazz: Appendix I—the Spanish Tinge," liner notes, *Jelly Roll Morton: The Complete Library of Congress Recordings by Alan Lomax,* Rounder 11661-1888-2 CD-al. (2005), pp. 33–36. Szwed does not cite Borneman but is clearly indebted to him, as is Thomas

Fiehrer in "From Quadrille to Stomp: The Creole Origins of Jazz," *Popular Music* 10:1 (1991): 21–38.

19. Freddi Williams Evans, *Congo Square: African Roots in New Orleans* (Lafayette: University of Louisiana at Lafayette Press, 2011), 70–71.

20. Ibid., 116, 117.

21. For Congo Square as "a spiritual place and a place to remember ancestors," see Katy Reckdahl, "No Bones about It," *New Orleans Times-Picayune,* April 7, 2012, B-1–2, in which Wynton Marsalis states that "the bloodlines of all important modern American music" can be traced to Congo Square.

22. Sidney Bechet with Joan Reid, Desmond Flower, and John Ciardi, *Treat It Gentle* (New York: Hill and Wang, 1960), 6.

23. Ibid., 217–18.

24. John Chilton, *Sidney Bechet: The Wizard of Jazz* (New York: Oxford University Press, 1987), 1, 3, 10, and George Washington Cable, *The Grandissimes, a Story of Creole Life* (New York: C. Scribner's Sons, 1880).

25. The author chaired the panel, "*Treat It Gentle* and the Jazz Narrative Tradition," with John Chilton, Rod Jellema, and Joseph Logsdon, Sidney Bechet Centennial Conference, New Orleans, Louisiana, May 6, 1997.

26. Jürgen E. Grandt, *Kinds of Blue: The Jazz Aesthetic in African American Narrative* (Columbus: Ohio State University Press, 2004), quotations on 5–6, 7; Bechet as *griot,* 112n6. However, Grandt misinterprets Bechet's statement on Senegalese nativity. In James P. Holloway, "He Played the Blues in London in 1919: A Study of Pops Bechet," *The Melody Maker* (December 23, 1939), Bechet claimed "his father was a Senegalese, his grandparents on his mother's side French" (p. 2).

27. David Scott, "That Event, This Memory: Notes on the Anthropology of African Diasporas in the New World," *Diaspora* 1:3 (1991): 261–84.

28. Ibid., 273.

29. Ibid., 279–80.

30. Tom Bethell, *George Lewis: A Jazzman from New Orleans* (Berkeley: University of California Press, 1977), 5–6, 9–12.

31. Heidi Feldman, *Black Rhythms of Peru: Reviving African Musical Heritage in the Black Pacific* (Middletown: Wesleyan University Press, 2006).

32. See Ellis Marsalis's remarks in Leo Touchet, *Rejoice When You Die: The New Orleans Jazz Funerals* (Baton Rouge: Louisiana State University Press, 1998), 1–3, and William Russell, liner notes, *New Orleans Parade: An Album of Six Marches by Bunk Johnson's Brass Band,* American Music 101–3 (1945).

33. Raeburn, *New Orleans Style,* 142–81.

34. Tony Bazley interview by Bruce Raeburn, October 9, 2010, DVD in author's possession. Bazley may have taken instruction from Yvonne Busch. See Al Kennedy, "Distant Music: Katrina Blasts through a Teacher's Golden Years," *New Orleans Times-Picayune,* March 22, 2006, Metro Section, 7.

35. Bazley interview; Vincent Fumar, "Popbeat: Drummer Decides to Try N.O. Again," *New Orleans Times-Picayune,* June 28, 1987, 16.

36. On Earl Palmer, see Tony Scherman, *Backbeat: Earl Palmer's Story* (Washington, DC: Smithsonian Institution Press, 1999).

37. See Walter Bruyninckx, *60 Years of Recorded Jazz, 1917–1977* (Mechelen, Belgium: Walter Bruyninckx, 1978), A169–70, A403, B270, G105, G544, M614, V119.

38. See Lolis Eric Elie, "Opportunity of a Lifetime," *New Orleans Times-Picayune,* June 13, 1997, B-1.

39. Bazley interview.

40. *Polk's New Orleans City Directory, 1938* (New Orleans: R. L. Polk, 1938), 167.

41. *Fifteenth Census of the United States: 1930,* Population Schedule, New Orleans, Louisiana, Orleans Parish, 17th Ward, Block 306, Enumeration District 36-274, Sheet No. 1A.

42. *Fourteenth Census of the United States: 1920,* Population Schedule, New Orleans, Louisiana, Orleans Parish, 17th Ward, Precinct 3, Sheet No. 20B.

43. Draft Registration Card for Henderson Bazley, New Orleans, Louisiana, witnessed on September 12, 1918; Draft Board: 13, Roll: 168492.

44. *Thirteenth Census of the United States: 1910,* Population Schedule, New Orleans, Louisiana, Orleans Parish, 17th Ward, Precinct 3, Sheet No. 26B.

45. See Matory, "Afro-Atlantic Culture," 93.

46. Bazley's mother sang in the choir at Morning Star Baptist Church. See her obituary, *New Orleans Times-Picayune,* January 10, 1995, B-4. On Bechet, see Chilton, 2–5.

47. Raeburn, *New Orleans Style,* 241–43.

48. Bechet, *Treat It Gentle,* 211–12.

49. I thank Dr. Omar Ka, associate Ppofessor of Wolof & French, Department of Modern Languages, University of Maryland, Baltimore County, and Dr. Fehintola Mosadomi, coordinator of Yoruba studies at the University of Texas–Austin, for this information.

50. Hall, *Africans in Colonial Louisiana,* 29, 40–55.

51. "Senegambian Gambols," *Daily Picayune,* February 5, 1873, 1, and "How Our Senegambian Legislators Are Manipulated," *Daily Picayune,* July 23, 1874, 4.

52. "Pharr Faction for White Man's Party," *Daily Picayune,* April 14, 1908.

53. "Amusements: Faranta's Pavilion Summer Theatre—New Faces! All Stars! Latest Novelties! Faranta's Senegambian Minstrels," *Daily Picayune,* May 3, 1883; "A Midnight Stabbing, in which a Sicilian Smites a Senegambian," *New Orleans Times-Picayune,* November 22, 1900, 8; and Clem G. Hearsey, "Curious Pets in New Orleans," *Daily Picayune,* October 20, 1912, in which the author recounts the tale of a "burly Senegambian" being "apprehended" by a police dog in a game of "catch the nigger."

54. "Senegambian Serenaders Indulge in a Row in Which the Peacemaker Is Cut," *Daily Picayune,* August 22, 1898, 3.

55. See William Ivy Hair, *Carnival of Fury: Robert Charles and the New Orleans Race Riot of 1900* (Baton Rouge: Louisiana State University Press, 1976).

56. Jason Berry, "African Cultural Memory in New Orleans Music," *Black Music Research Journal* 8:1 (1988): 3–12; see 7.

57. Al Rose and Edmond Souchon, *New Orleans Jazz: A Family Album,* 3rd ed (Baton Rouge: Louisiana State University Press, 1984).

58. See the John Robichaux sheet music collection at the Hogan Jazz Archive, Tulane University (HJA). *Senegalese Stomp* was recorded by New Orleans pianist Clarence Williams's Blue Seven in 1926.

59. See photograph of Bechet with Benny Peyton's Band (London, 1919) in Rose and Souchon, *New Orleans Jazz,* 273.

60. Bestowed by Babatunde Olatunji; Bazley interview. For context, see Robin D. G. Kelley, *Africa Speaks, America Answers: Modern Jazz in Revolutionary Times* (Cambridge, MA: Harvard University Press, 2012).

61. Edward Blackwell, transcribed interview by Robert Palmer, October 1975, p. 16, HJA.

62. Kalamu ya Salaam, "Edward Blackwell—The Rhythm King," *Coda Magazine,* no. 218 (February 1988), 4–6, and Blackwell interview, 14.

63. Aldo Romano, "Drums Conversation: Ed Blackwell par Aldo Romano," *Jazz Magazine,* no. 388 (December 1989), 38–41; quotation on 40.

64. John Alan Simon, "Earl Turbinton Jr.," *Down Beat* 26:46 (September 7, 1978): 26, 46; see 26.

65. Harold R. Battiste Jr. with Karen Celestan, *Unfinished Blues: Memories of a New Orleans Music Man* (New Orleans: Historic New Orleans Collection, 2010), 114–15.

66. Earl Turbinton Jr., interview by Lorraine Farr, September 1, 1990, audio CD, HJA.

67. Lewis Watts and Eric Porter, *New Orleans Suite: Music and Culture in Transition* (Berkeley: University of California Press, 2013), 87.

68. Ibid., 84.

69. For further detail, see www.africanola.org. Since 2010, there has also been a third project, the AfricanZydeco Revue, involving Kouyate, Dioubate, and zydeco accordionist Cedric Watson.

ACKNOWLEDGMENTS

A collected volume invariably accrues more debts of thanks than any other form of publication. A project that begins its life as an idea spawned by three scholars—one Senegalese, one French, and one American—adds the debts of each of them to the list. The roll of debts becomes even longer when the idea takes shape in two sequential conferences held a year apart on opposite sides of the Atlantic in the cities that give their names to the volume: Saint-Louis, Senegal, and New Orleans, Louisiana. A well-known African proverb observes that it takes a village to raise a child. It literally took a world to make this book. The editors take great pleasure now in acknowledging the many people and institutions that contributed to making this book a reality.

The essays in this volume began as papers presented at colloquiums on the connected and comparative histories of Saint-Louis, Senegal, and New Orleans, Louisiana, held in Saint-Louis June 4–7, 2012, and April 23–25, 2013. Such international gatherings require substantial public and private support, and we were given both in abundance, beginning with the national governments of Senegal, France, and the United States. We are grateful to the Service de Coopération et d'Action culturelle (SCAC) of the French Embassy in Dakar, the US Embassy in Dakar, and the French Ministère chargé de l'outre-mer.

In Senegal, coeditor Ibrahima Thioub's home institution, the University Cheikh Anta Diop in Dakar, took on the enormous task of organizing logistics and securing essential financial support from agencies and institutions in Senegal. Thioub also elicited time, talent, and treasure from his own institution to make the 2012 conference happen, including resources from the Centre africain de recherches sur les traites et les esclavages (CARTE). In Saint-Louis, the University Gaston Berger welcomed us to their campus, gave us a beautiful meeting space, and made sure that we were never without good food to sustain us. The City of Saint-Louis and the Regional Council of Saint-Louis received us with the legendary Senegalese hospitality known as *teranga.*

From France came major support secured through the efforts of coeditor Cécile Vidal, including funds from the École des hautes études en sciences sociales, the Centre d'études nord-américaines, Mondes Américains-UMR 8168 (CNRS/EHESS), the Centre de recherches sur le Brésil colonial et contemporain, and the Institut des Amériques.

Tulane alumnus Alan Lawrence made two very generous gifts in memory of fellow alumnus James E. Hailer to support each of the two meetings. Tulane University and the New Orleans Center for the Gulf South at Tulane's School of Liberal Arts and the Clement Chambers Benenson Professorship in American Colonial History provided support for the Saint-Louis meeting.

For the second meeting in New Orleans in 2013, support was provided once again by the University Cheikh Anta Diop, the CARTE, and the University Gaston Berger, the City of Saint-Louis and the Regional Council of Saint-Louis, the Service d'action culturelle of the French Embassy in Dakar, the US Embassy in Dakar, the Ministère chargé de l'outre-mer, the École des hautes études en sciences sociales, the Centre d'études nord-américaines, Mondes Américains-UMR 8168 (CNRS/EHESS), the Centre de recherches sur le Brésil colonial et contemporain, the Institut des Amériques, Tulane University and the New Orleans Center for the Gulf South at Tulane's School of Liberal Arts, and the Clement Chambers Benenson Professorship in American Colonial History.

New sponsors for the 2013 meeting in New Orleans included the Historic New Orleans Collection, WWNO Radio, the Consul Général of France in New Orleans, the New Orleans Jazz and Heritage Foundation, the University of New Orleans Midlo Center for New Orleans Studies, Le Musée de FPC, Tulane University Law School's Payson Center for International Development, the Organisation internationale de la francophonie, and the Comité pour la mémoire et l'histoire de l'esclavage.

Radio France Internationale undertook an exclusive partnership with the colloquium series. Valérie Nivelon, host of "La Marche du Monde," produced two special programs on the conferences, recording live in both Saint-Louis and New Orleans.

Music was an integral part of both meetings, and we were extraordinarily fortunate to have at both the Saint-Louis and New Orleans meetings the Dia brothers' Band of Njum Waalo, a traditional Senegalese musical ensemble led by master xalam/hodu player Demma Dia. Asali DeVan Ecclesiastes, coordinator of the Congo Square African Marketplace at the New Orleans Jazz & Heritage Festival, generously created a performance space for the Njum Waalo Band that allowed them to share their art with thousands on the festival grounds. In Saint-Louis the Senegalese musician Vieux Mac Faye and Louisiana blues musician Larry Garner participated. New Orleans banjo virtuoso Don Vappie joined the Njum Waalo Band in an exploration of the ties between the stringed instrument traditions of New Orleans and Senegal in 2013. Cherice Harrison Nelson and the Guardians of the Flame Maroon Society made a surprise appearance at the conclusion of one of the conference sessions, creating, together with the members of the Njum Waalo Band, an electrifying demonstration of the living connection between the mirror cities of New Orleans and Saint-Louis.

Two individuals deserve special thanks for the daunting organizational planning that ambitious international conferences of this kind entail. Ibrahima Seck, then of the University Cheikh Anta Diop and now of Whitney Plantation, managed a thousand details with confidence, grace, and aplomb. He made sure that some two dozen international participants were conveyed safely from the airport to their rooms at the Maison de l'Université at Cheikh Anta Diop, thence to Saint-Louis, and finally back to the airport again on a bus generously provided by the university. He arranged lodging and meals in Dakar and Saint-Louis, and helped everyone find whatever they needed, or thought they needed, from ATM machines to bookshops. In New Orleans, Liz Skilton, then a graduate student at Tulane and now assistant professor of history at the University of Louisiana–Lafayette, was equally adept at making things happen, keeping us all on track and coping with unanticipated crises from monumental traffic delays to a flash flood.

Presses that take on publication of a collected volume are a special breed, and we are very grateful to the editors and staff of Louisiana State University Press not only for acceptance of this project, but for their enthusiasm at every stage. From the time we first began to discuss publication, we agreed that LSU Press was our top choice and approached its acquisitions editor for Atlantic history, Alisa Plant. Alisa was immediately receptive and encouraging, and we experienced the same level of care and interest from everyone at LSU Press who touched the project from that initial conversation to publication. Director MaryKatherine Callaway embraced the project and made us feel at home with the business side of book publishing. Rand Dotson, editor-in-chief, has been enthusiastic, patient, and forbearing as we worked to marshal our contributors and wrestle with the myriad of linguistic and cultural translations that arise when contributors hail from three different continents and a variety of academic traditions. Gary Von Euer's copyediting was a paragon of thoroughness and acute sensitivity to the substance as well as the form of what the authors were attempting to say. The entire volume is better because he put his practiced hand to it.

Finally, we wish to thank not only each of the contributors to this volume, but all of the scholars who took up the challenge of writing original papers for the two linked conferences. This volume could only include a portion of the pathbreaking work presented at those meetings, but each of the essays published here bears the imprint of the research and analysis introduced in the body of scholarship produced for the meetings and was improved by the animated, thought-provoking discussions that flowed around the meeting table in French and English, Wolof and Pulaar.

SELECTED BIBLIOGRAPHY

SAINT-LOUIS, SENEGAL

Aïdara, Abdoul Hadir. *L'esclavage à Saint-Louis du Sénégal début XVIIIe siècle à 1848.* Saint-Louis: CRDS, 1996.

Alquier, P. "St-Louis du Sénégal, pendant la Révolution et l'Empire." *Bulletin du Comité d'études historiques et scientifiques de l'Afrique occidentale française* 5 (1929): 277–320 and 411–63.

Aubert, Guillaume. "'Nègres ou mulâtres nous sommes tous Français': Race, genre et nation à Gorée et à Saint-Louis du Sénégal, fin XVIIe—fin XVIIIe siècle." In *Français? La nation en débat entre colonies et métropole, XVIe–XIXe siècle,* edited by Cécile Vidal, 125–47. Paris: Éditions de l'École des hautes études en sciences sociales, 2014.

Badji, Mamadou. "L'abolition de l'esclavage au Sénégal: Entre plasticité du droit colonial et respect de l'État de droit," *Droit et cultures* 52:2 (2006), http://droitcultures.revues.org/729.

Barry, Boubacar. *Le royaume du Waalo: Le Sénégal avant la conquête.* Paris: Karthala, 1985.

———. *Senegambia and the Atlantic Slave Trade.* Cambridge: Cambridge University Press, 1998 (1st edition, 1988).

———. *La Sénégambie du XVe au XIXe siècle: Traite négrière, Islam, et conquête coloniale.* Paris: L'Harmattan, 1988.

Bathily, A. *Les portes de l'or: Le royaume de Galam (Sénégal) de l'ère musulmane au temps des négriers (XVIIIe–XIXe siècles).* Paris: L'Harmattan, 1989.

Becker, Charles, Victor Martin, Jean Schmitz, and Monique Chastanet, with Jean-François Maurel and Saliou Mbaye. *Les premiers recensements au Sénégal et l'évolution démographique: Présentation de documents.* Dakar: ORSTOM, 1983.

Benoist, Joseph Roger de. *Histoire de l'Église catholique au Sénégal.* Paris: Karthala, 2008.

Bonnardel, Régine. "1789: Le Cahier de doléances des Saint-Louisiens (Sénégal). Mythe et réalité." In *Esclavage, colonisation, libérations nationales de 1789 à nos jours,* 51–59. Paris: L'Harmattan, 1990.

Botte, Roger. "L'esclavage africain après l'abolition de 1848: Servitude et droit du sol." *Annales HSS* 55:5 (2000): 1009–37.

Bouche, Denise. *Les villages de liberté en Afrique noire française (1887–1950).* Paris: Mouton et Cie, 1968.

Boulègue, Jean. *Les Luso-Africains de Sénégambie XVIe–XIXe siècle.* Dakar: Université de Dakar, 1972.

Brasseur, Paule. "Le Sénégal et sa lente intégration au mouvement abolitionniste (1815–1830)." In *Rétablissement de l'esclavage dans les colonies françaises, 1802: Ruptures et continuités de la politique coloniale française (1800–1830). Aux origines d'Haïti,* edited by Yves Bénot and Marcel Dorigny, 375–86. Paris: Maisonneuve et Larose, 2003.

Brooks, George. "Artists' Depictions of Senegalese Signares: Insights Concerning French Racist and Sexist Attitudes in the Nineteenth Century," *Genève-Afrique* 18:1 (1980): 75–90.

———. *Eurafricans in Western Africa: Commerce, Social Status, Gender, and Religious Observance from the Sixteenth to the Eighteenth Century.* Athens: Ohio University Press, 2003.

———. "The *Signares* of Saint-Louis and Gorée: Women Entrepreneurs in Eighteenth-Century Senegal." In *Women in Africa: Studies in Social and Economic Change,* edited by Nancy J. Hafkin and Edna G. Bay, 19–44. Stanford, CA: Stanford University Press, 1976.

Camara, Camille. *Saint-Louis-du-Sénégal: Évolution d'une ville en milieu africain.* Dakar: Institut Fondamental d'Afrique Noire, 1968.

Coquery-Vidrovitch, Catherine. "Nationalité et citoyenneté en Afrique occidentale française: Originaires et citoyens dans le Sénégal colonial." *Journal of African History* 42:2 (2001): 285–305.

Crowder, Michael. *Senegal: A Study of French Assimilation Policy.* London: Methuen, 1967.

Curtin, Philip. *Economic Change in Pre-colonial Africa: Senegambia in the Era of the Slave Trade.* Madison: University of Wisconsin Press, 1975.

Delcourt, André. *La France et les établissements français au Sénégal entre 1713 et 1763.* Dakar: Institut Fondamental d'Afrique Noire, 1952.

Deroure, François. "La vie quotidienne à Saint-Louis par ses archives (1779–1809)." *Bulletin de l'Institut Fondamental d'Afrique Noire* 26 (1964): 397–437.

Diagne, Babacar. "Saint-Louis du Sénégal et sa population au XIXe siècle: Les mutations politiques, économiques et sociales d'une ville coloniale." Thèse de troisième cycle, Université Cheikh Anta Diop, 2004.

Diop, Abdoulaye Sokhna. "La fondation de Saint-Louis du Sénégal." *Bulletin de l'Institut Fondamental d'Afrique Noire* 38:2 (1975): 318–39.

Diouf, Mamadou. "Assimilation coloniale et identités religieuses de la civilité des originaires des quatre communes (Sénégal)." *Canadian Journal of African Studies / Revue canadienne des études africaines* 34:3 (2000): 565–87.

———. "L'idée municipale: Une idée neuve en Afrique." *Politique africaine* 74:2 (1992): 13–23.

———. "Islam, the 'Originaires,' and the Making of Public Space in a Colonial City." In *Tolerance, Democracy, and Sufis in Senegal,* edited by Mamadou Diouf, 180–204. New York: Columbia University Press, 2013.

Dozon, Jean-Pierre. *Saint-Louis du Sénégal—Palimpseste d'une ville.* Paris: Karthala, 2012.

Getz, Trevor R. *Slavery and Reform in West Africa: Toward Emancipation in Nineteenth-Century Senegal and the Gold Coast.* Athens: Ohio University Press, 2004.

Guèye, Mbaye. "La fin de l'esclavage à Saint-Louis et à Gorée en 1848." *Bulletin de l'Institut Fondamental d'Afrique Noire, Série B* 28:3–4 (1966): 637–56.

Hardy, Georges. *La mise en valeur du Sénégal de 1817 à 1854.* Paris: E. Larose, 1921.

Johnson, G. Wesley. *The Emergence of Black Politics in Senegal: The Struggle for Power in the Four Communes, 1900–1920.* Stanford, CA: Stanford University Press, 1971.

Jones, Hilary. *The Métis of Senegal: Urban Life and Politics in French West Africa.* Bloomington: Indiana University Press, 2013.

Jore, Léonce. *Les établissements français sur la côte occidentale d'Afrique de 1758 à 1809.* Paris: Maisonneuve et Larose, 1965.

Ka, Ibrahima. "L'évolution sociale à Saint-Louis du Sénégal du XIXe siècle au début du XXe siècle." Thèse du 3e cycle, Université de Dakar, 1981.

Kane, Oumar. *La première hégémonie peule: Le Fuuta Tooro de Koli Teŋella à Almaami Abdul.* Paris and Dakar: Karthala and Presses universitaires de Dakar, 2004.

Klein, Martin A. *Slavery and Colonial Rule in French West Africa.* Cambridge: Cambridge University Press, 1998.

———. "Slaves, Gum, and Peanuts: Adaptation to the End of the Slave Trade in Senegal, 1817–48." *William and Mary Quarterly* 66:4 (2009): 895–914.

Lacroix, Jean-Bernard. *Les Français au Sénégal au temps de la Compagnie des Indes de 1719 à 1758.* Vincennes: Service historique de la Marine, 1986.

Lecuir-Nemo, Geneviève. *Anne-Marie Javouhey: Fondatrice de la congrégation des soeurs de Saint-Joseph de Cluny (1779–1851).* Paris: Karthala, 2007.

Ly, Abdoulaye. *La Compagnie du Sénégal.* Paris et Dakar: Karthala et IFAN, 1993 (1st éd. 1958).

Marcson, Michael. "European-African Interaction in the Pre-Colonial Period: Saint Louis, Senegal, 1758–1854." PhD diss., Princeton University, 1976.

Mbodj, Mohamed. "The Abolition of Slavery in Senegal, 1820–1890: Crisis or the Rise of a New Entrepreneurial Class?" In *Breaking the Chains: Slavery, Bon-*

dage, and Emancipation in Modern Africa and Asia, edited by Martin A. Klein, 197–214. Madison: University of Wisconsin Press, 1993.

Moitt, Bernard. "Slavery, Flight and Redemption in Senegal, 1819–1905." *Slavery and Abolition* 14:2 (1993): 70–86.

Morénas, Joseph Elzéar. *Précis historique de la traite des noirs et de l'esclavage colonial.* Geneva: Slatkine Reprints, 1978.

Ngalamulume, Kalala J. "Leisure in Colonial Saint-Louis (Senegal), 1850–1920." In *Leisure in Urban Africa,* edited by Paul Tiyambe Zeleza and Cassandra Rachel Veney, 71–83. Trenton, NJ: Africa World Press, 2003.

Pasquier, Roger. "À propos de l'émancipation des esclaves au Sénégal en 1848." *Revue française d'histoire d'outre-mer* 54:194–97 (1967): 188–208.

———. "Villes du Sénégal au XIXe siècle." *Revue française d'histoire d'outre-mer* 47:168–69 (1960): 387–426.

Renault, François. *L'abolition de l'esclavage au Sénégal: L'attitude de l'administration française, 1848–1905.* Paris: Société française d'histoire d'outre-mer, 1972.

———. *Libération d'esclaves et nouvelle servitude: Les rachats de captifs pour le compte de l'administration française après l'abolition de l'esclavage.* Abidjan: NEA, 1976.

Reyss, Natalie. "Saint-Louis du Sénégal à l'époque précoloniale: L'émergence d'une société métisse originale, 1650–1854." Thèse de 3eme Cycle, Université Paris I, 1983.

Robinson, David. *Paths of Accommodation: Muslim Societies and French Colonial Authorities in Senegal and Mauritania, 1880–1920.* Athens: Ohio University Press, 2000.

Sackur, Amanda. "The Development of Creole Society and Culture in Saint-Louis and Gorée 1719–1817." PhD diss., University of London, 1999.

———. "The French Revolution and Race Relations in Senegal, 1780–1810." In *People and Empires in African History: Essays in Memory of Michael Crowder,* edited by J. F. Ade Ajayi and J. D. Y. Peel, 69–87. London: Longman, 1992.

Samb, Djibril, ed. *Saint-Louis et l'esclavage: Actes du Symposium international sur "La traite négrière à Saint-Louis du Sénégal et dans son arrière-pays"* (Saint-Louis, 18, 19, et 20 décembre 1998). Dakar: IFAN and Université Cheikh Anta Diop de Dakar, 2000.

Sankalé, Sylvain. *À la mode du pays: Chroniques saint-louisiennes. Saint-Louis du Sénégal, 1788–1835.* Paris: Riveneuve, 2008.

Searing, James. *West African Slavery and Atlantic Commerce: The Senegal River Valley, 1700–1860.* Cambridge: Cambridge University Press, 1993.

Sinou, Alain. *Comptoirs et villes coloniales du Sénégal: Saint-Louis, Gorée, Dakar.* Paris: Karthala and ORSTOM, 1993.

———. "Saint-Louis du Sénégal au début du XIXe siècle: Du comptoir à la ville." *Cahiers d'études africaines* 29:115 (1989): 377–95.

Thioub, Ibrahima. "L'esclavage à Saint-Louis du Sénégal au XVIIIe–XIXe siècle." *Jahrbuch 2008/2009, Wissenschaftskolleg zu Berlin* (2010): 334–356.

Webb, James L. A., Jr. "The Trade in Gum Arabic: Prelude to French Conquest in Senegal." *Journal of African American History* 26:2 (1985): 149–68.

White, Owen. *Children of the French Empire: Miscegenation and Colonial Society in French West Africa, 1895–1960.* Oxford: Oxford University Press, 1999.

Zuccarelli, François. "Le régime des engagés à temps au Sénégal." *Cahiers d'études africaines* 7:2 (1962): 420–61.

———. *La vie politique sénégalaise, 1798–1940.* Paris: CHEAM, 1987.

NEW ORLEANS

Bell, Caryn Cossé. *Revolution, Romanticism, and the Afro-Creole Protest Tradition in Louisiana, 1718–1868.* Baton Rouge: Louisiana State University Press, 2004.

Berry, Jason, Jonathan Foose, and Tad Jones. *Up from the Cradle: New Orleans Music since World War II.* Athens: University of Georgia Press, 1986.

Boelhower, William. ed. *New Orleans in the Atlantic World: Between Land and Sea.* New York: Routledge, 2009.

Bourdelais, Marjorie. *La Nouvelle-Orléans: Croissance démographique, intégrations urbaine et sociale (1803–1860).* Bern: Peter Lang, 2012.

Campanella, Richard. *Bienville's Dilemma: A Historical Geography of New Orleans.* Lafayette: Center for Louisiana Studies, University of Louisiana at Lafayette, 2008.

Clark, Emily. *Masterless Mistresses: The New Orleans Ursulines and the Development of a New World Society, 1727–1834.* Chapel Hill: University of North Carolina Press, 2007.

———. *The Strange History of the American Quadroon.* Chapel Hill: University of North Carolina Press, 2013.

Clark, John G. *New Orleans, 1718–1812: An Economic History.* Baton Rouge: Louisiana State University Press, 1970.

Dawdy, Shannon Lee. *Building the Devil's Empire: French Colonial New Orleans.* Chicago: University of Chicago Press, 2008.

Dessens, Nathalie. *Creole City: A Chronicle of Early American New Orleans.* Gainesville: University Press of Florida, 2015.

———. *From Saint-Domingue to New Orleans: Migration and Influences.* Gainesville: University Press of Florida, 2007.

Din, Gilbert C. *Spaniards, Planters, and Slaves: The Spanish Regulation of Slavery in Louisiana, 1763–1803.* College Station: Texas A&M University Press, 1999.

Din, Gilbert C., and John E. Harkins. *The New Orleans Cabildo: Colonial Louisiana's First City Government, 1769–1803.* Baton Rouge: Louisiana State University Press, 1996.

Dubé, Alexandre. "Les biens publics: Culture politique de la Louisiane française, 1730–1770." PhD diss., McGill University, 2009.

Evans, Freddi Williams. *Congo Square: African Roots in New Orleans.* Lafayette: University of Louisiana at Lafayette, 2011.

Faber, Eberhard L. *Building the Land of Dreams: New Orleans and the Transformation of Early America.* Princeton, NJ: Princeton University Press, 2016.

Fairclough, Adam. *Race and Democracy: The Civil Rights Struggle in Louisiana, 1915–1972.* 2nd ed. Athens: University of Georgia Press, 2008.

Giraud, Marcel *Histoire de la Louisiane française,* 4 vols. Paris: puf, 1953–1974.

———. *A History of French Louisiana, vol. 5.* Baton Rouge: Louisiana State University Press, 1991.

Gould, Virginia Meacham. "In Full Enjoyment of Their Liberty: The Free Women of Color of the Gulf Ports of New Orleans, Mobile, and Pensacola, 1760–1860." PhD diss., Emory University, 1991.

Greenwald, Erin M. *Marc-Antoine Caillot and the Company of the Indies in Louisiana.* Baton Rouge: Louisiana State University Press, 2016.

Guenin-Lelle, Dianne. *The Story of French New Orleans: History of a Creole City.* Jackson: University Press of Mississippi, 2016.

Hall, Gwendolyn M. *Africans in Colonial Louisiana: The Development of Afro-Creole Culture in the Eighteenth Century.* Baton Rouge: Louisiana State University Press, 1992.

Hanger, Kimberly S. *Bounded Lives, Bounded Places: Free Black Society in Colonial New Orleans, 1769–1803.* Durham, NC: Duke University Press, 1997.

Hirsch, Arnold R., and Joseph Logsdon, eds. *Creole New Orleans: Race and Americanization.* Baton Rouge: Louisiana State University Press, 1992.

Ingersoll, Thomas N. *Mammon and Manon in Early New Orleans: The First Slave Society in the Deep South, 1718–1819.* Knoxville: University of Tennessee Press, 1999.

Johnson, Rashauna. *Slavery's Metropolis: Unfree Labor in New Orleans during the Age of Revolutions.* Cambridge: Cambridge University Press, 2016.

Johnson, Walter. *Soul by Soul: Life inside the Antebellum Slave Market.* Cambridge, MA: Harvard University Press, 1999.

Langlois, Gilles-Antoine. *Des villes pour la Louisiane française: Théorie et pratique de l'urbanistique coloniale au 18e siècle.* Paris: L'Harmattan, 2003.

Marler, Scott P. *The Merchants' Capital: New Orleans and the Political Economy of the Nineteenth-Century South.* Cambridge: Cambridge University Press, 2013.

Nystrom, Justin A. *New Orleans after the Civil War: Race, Politics, and a New Birth of Freedom.* Baltimore: Johns Hopkins University Press, 2010.

Polfliet, Marieke. "Émigration et politisation: Les Français de New York et La Nouvelle-Orléans dans la première moitié du XIXe siècle (1803–1860)." PhD diss., Université de Nice, 2013.

Powell, Lawrence N. *The Accidental City: Improvising New Orleans.* Cambridge, MA: Harvard University Press, 2012.

Raeburn, Bruce Boyd. *New Orleans Style and the Writing of American Jazz History.* Ann Arbor: University of Michigan Press, 2009.

Sacher, John M. *A Perfect War of Politics: Parties, Politicians, and Democracy in Louisiana, 1824–1861.* Baton Rouge: Louisiana State University Press, 2007.

Schafer, Judith Kelleher. *Becoming Free, Remaining Free: Manumission and Enslavement in New Orleans, 1846–1862.* Baton Rouge: Louisiana State University Press, 2003.

———. *Brothels, Depravity, and Abandoned Women: Illegal Sex in Antebellum New Orleans.* Baton Rouge: Louisiana State University Press, 2009.

Scott, Rebecca. *Degrees of Freedom: Louisiana and Cuba after Slavery.* Cambridge, MA: Belknap Press of Harvard University Press, 2005.

Spear, Jennifer M. *Race, Sex, and Social Order in Early New Orleans.* Baltimore: Johns Hopkins University Press, 2009.

Sublette, Ned. *The World That Made New Orleans: From Spanish Silver to Congo Square.* Chicago: Lawrence Hill Books, 2008.

Thompson, Shirley Elizabeth. *Exiles at Home: The Struggle to Become American in Creole New Orleans.* Cambridge, MA: Harvard University Press, 2009.

Vidal, Cécile. *Caribbean New Orleans: Empire, Race, and the Making of a Slave Society.* Chapel Hill: University of North Carolina Press, 2019.

———, ed. *Louisiana: Crossroads of the Atlantic World.* Philadelphia: University of Pennsylvania Press, 2013.

Walker, Daniel E. *No More, No More: Slavery and Cultural Resistance in Havana and New Orleans.* Minneapolis: University of Minnesota Press, 2004.

SAINT-LOUIS AND NEW ORLEANS

Johnson, Jessica Marie. "Freedom, Kinship, and Property: Free Women of African Descent in the French Atlantic, 1685–1810." PhD diss., University of Maryland, 2012.

Scott, Rebecca, and Jean Hébrard. *Freedom Papers: An Atlantic Odyssey in the Age of Emancipation.* Cambridge: Cambridge University Press, 2012.

Seck, Ibrahima. "The Relationships between St. Louis, Senegal, Its Hinterlands, and Colonial Louisiana." In *French Colonial Louisiana and the Atlantic World,* edited by Bradley G. Bond, 265–90. Baton Rouge: Louisiana State University Press, 2005.

———. "La traite négrière entre Saint-Louis du Sénégal, les Antilles et la vallée du Mississippi au XIXe siècle." In *Saint-Louis et l'esclavage: Actes du Symposium international sur "La traite négrière à Saint-Louis du Sénégal et dans son arrière-pays,"* edited by Djibril Samb, 217–35. Saint-Louis, 18, 19, et 20 décembre 1998. Dakar: IFAN and Université Cheikh Anta Diop, 2000.

CONTRIBUTORS

EMILY CLARK is Clement Chambers Benenson Professor of American Colonial History at Tulane University in New Orleans. She is the author or editor of four books about New Orleans, including the prizewinning *Masterless Mistresses: The New Orleans Ursulines and the Development of a New World Society, 1727–1834* (2007).

JESSICA MARIE JOHNSON is assistant professor of history at Johns Hopkins University. She is at work on a monograph about free women of color in the French Atlantic world and is the founder and curator of *African Diaspora, Ph.D.*

HILARY JONES is associate professor of history at Florida International University in Miami. She is a historian of West Africa and the author of *The Métis of Senegal: Urban Life and Politics in French West Africa* (2013).

MARTIN A. KLEIN is professor emeritus of history at the University of Toronto. He is the author or editor of numerous works on West Africa, including *African Voices on Slavery and the Slave Trade* (edited with Alice Bellagamba and Sandra E. Greene, 2013), *The Bitter Legacy: African Slavery Past and Present* (edited with Alice Bellagamba and Sandra E. Greene, 2013), *Slavery and Colonial Rule in French West Africa* (1998), and *Breaking the Chains: Slavery, Bondage and Emancipation in Modern Africa and Asia* (1993).

LARISSA KOPYTOFF is a visiting instructor of history at the University of South Florida, St. Petersburg.

MARIEKE POLFLIET received her PhD from the University of Nice Sophia Antipolis, Nice, in 2013. She is a historian of the French Atlantic world.

BRUCE BOYD RAEBURN, now retired, is the former curator of the Hogan Jazz Archive at Tulane University in New Orleans. He is a historian of New Orleans jazz and the author of numerous articles, including "Expanding Parameters on Brass Bands in Early New Orleans Jazz" (2008) and "Music Flows like Water: Alligator Horses, Minstrels, Roustabouts, Bluesmen, and Jazz on the Mississippi River" (2009).

REBECCA J. SCOTT is Charles Gibson Distinguished University Professor of History and Professor of Law at the University of Michigan. A historian of Latin America and the Atlantic world, she is the author or editor of several volumes, including the prizewinning *Freedom Papers: An Atlantic Odyssey in the Age of Emancipation* (with Jean Hébrard, 2012).

IBRA SENE is assistant professor of history at the College of Wooster, Wooster, Ohio. A historian of Senegal, he is the author of numerous articles and book chapters, including "Slavery, History, and Memory: A Report on the African Burial Ground in New York City" (2008) and "Race and Imprisonment in Colonial Senegal: Evidence from the Prison of Saint-Louis (1860–1940)."

IBRAHIMA THIOUB is rector and professor of history at the University Cheikh Anta Diop, Dakar. He is the author of many works on the history of Senegal, including "Stigmas and Memory of Slavery in West Africa: Skin Color and Blood as Social Fracture Lines," *New Global Studies*, 6:3 (2012) (French version, "Stigmates et mémoires de l'esclavage en Afrique de l'ouest: Le sang et la couleur de peau comme lignes de fracture," *Nouvelles Annales Africaines*, édition spéciale, 2012).

CÉCILE VIDAL is professor of history at the École des hautes études en sciences sociales, Paris. Among her many works on French Atlantic history are the prizewinning *Histoire de l'Amérique française* (with Gilles Havard, 2003), the edited volume *Louisiana: Crossroads of the Atlantic World* (2013), and the monograph *Caribbean New Orleans: Empire, Race, and the Making of a Slave Society* (2019).

INDEX

Acadians, 5
Adrianople, 192, 194
Africa, 2, 12, 15
African American, 17, 210, 212, 217, 219, 221, 223, 224
Africans, 17
Agui, Samba, 45, 48
Aix-en-Provence, 108
Akan symbol, 226
Alleghenies, 4
Alsace, 136
America, 2, 36, 127, 130, 138, 197
Americas, 2, 12, 15, 56, 76, 106, 159, 160
Amy, Curtis, 220
Anderson, David M., 106
André, 59, 60, 63
Angoulvant, Gabriel, 181
Anne St., New Orleans, 66
Antilles, 10, 125, 126, 127, 128, 129, 156
Applebaum, Anne, 105
Aquino, Philip, 151
Arago, François, 154, 155
Aram, Marie, 66
Ardrey, Robert, 225
Arkansas, 90
Armstrong, Louis, 214
Ashe, Thomas, 195, 200
Atlantic world, 2, 12, 13, 15, 18, 19, 55, 56, 57, 67, 68, 126, 128, 138, 146, 191, 198, 205
Aubin, François, 62
Augustin, Étienne, 151
Auvergne, 136
Ayers, Roy, 220
Balize, 58
Baltimore, MD, 161
Bamana, 65
Bambara, 37, 42, 51n6, 222
Barbarin, Paul, 225
Basil, 63
Basses-Pyrénées, 153
Basse-Terre, 155
Bates, Edward, 160, 161
Battiste, Harold, 219, 224, 225
Baude, Marie, 19, 55, 56, 57, 59, 60, 61, 62, 63, 67, 68, 205
Baude, Sieur, 61
Baudin, Auguste, 46
Bawol, 3, 14, 61, 110
Bayot, Marie Françoise, 153
Bayou Road, 66
Bazley, Anthony, 219, 221, 224, 227
Bazley, Clarence, 220, 221
Bazley, Hazel, 220
Bazley, Henderson, 220, 221, 222
Bazley, William/Willie, 221
Beauregard Square, 216
Becher, Jean, 217
Bechet, Sidney, 216, 217, 218, 221, 224, 227
Benton, Lauren, 105
Berlin, Ira, 11
Bernault, Florence, 105
Berry, Jason, 223
Bethell, Tom, 219
Bienville, Jean-Baptiste LeMoyne de, 79
Black Indians, 211
Blackwell, Edward, 219, 224, 225

Blanc, Louis, 161
Boilat, David, 201
Bonaparte, Louis-Napoléon, 132
Bonaparte, Napoléon, 171
Bono, Sonny, 225
Booker, James, 212
Bordeaux, 157, 201
Borneman, Ernest, 213, 214, 215, 219
Boston, MA, 157
Bou el-Mogdad, 49
Bourbon monarchy, 200
Bourbon St., New Orleans, 66
Bras-Coupé, 217
Brazil, 12
British North America, 76
Brittany, 82
Bundu, 11

Cable, George Washington, 217
Caledonia, 154
California, 219
Camara, Marie-Caroline, 11
Cape Verde, 36
Caribbean, 6, 64, 153, 160, 226
Carrère, Frédéric, 174
Carrollton, 219
Casamance, 110
Cavillier, Charles, 62
Cavillier, Paula, 62
Championet, Baron, 196
Chaperon, Joseph, 80
Charles, Robert, 223
Charlotte, 9
Charron, Marie, 62
Charron, Pierre, 62
Chase, Salmon, 160
Chicago, IL, 214
Chickasaw, 15, 65, 80
Chilton, John, 217
Choctaw, 3, 65
Civil War, 7, 17, 139, 148, 149, 159, 160
Claiborne, William C. C., 151, 152
Clozel, François, 181
Cocote, Françoise, 217
Coleman, Ornette, 224
Colfax Massacre, 222
Collette, Buddy, 220
Congo, 23
Congo, Louis, 65, 66
Congo Square, 215, 216, 235
Cooke, Sam, 225
Coolen, Michael, 213
Cooper, Frederick, 182
Cora, 203
Côte d'Ivoire, 181
Creole, 10, 11, 126, 135, 215
Cuba, 10, 12, 212
Curtin, Philip, 1
Cypress Street, 223

d'Erneville, Charles Jean Baptiste, 9
d'Erneville, Pierre Henri, 9
d'Erneville family, 9
Dabouc, 85
Dahomey, 181
Daily Picayune, 223
Dakar, 4, 8, 107, 112, 113, 115, 168, 169, 175, 181
damels, 61, 62
Darby, Jonathan, 65
Darondeau, Stanislas, 202, 203
Deep South, 7, 17
Desdunes, Rodolphe, 161
Diagne, Blaise, 22, 175, 176
Diop, Ousmane Socé, 204
Diouf, Mamadou, 6, 49, 117
Djolof, 3
Djoubate, Thiemo, 226
Dolphy, Eric, 220
Dominique, 63
Douglass, Frederick, 152, 161
Dred Scott v. Sandford, 148, 160

Duffy, John, 223
Dumaine St., New Orleans, 66
Duoy, 66
Durkheim, Emile, 104

East Africa, 106
Economy Hall, 160
Edwards, Teddy, 220
Elkins, Caroline, 105
England, 193
Espent (colonial inspector), 115
Europe, 2, 7, 12, 14, 15, 16, 17, 22, 134, 137, 153, 154, 155, 176, 192, 213
Evans, Freddi, 215, 216

Fabre (Swiss sergeant), 85
Faidherbe, Louis Léon César, 4, 46, 47, 110, 173, 174
Feldman, Heidi, 219
Ferro, Marc, 105
Feuiltaine, Antoine, 39
Feuiltaine, Marie, 39
Fleuriau, Pélagie, 9
Fort Saint-Joseph, 14, 37
Foucault, Michel, 104, 106, 116
Foulhouze, James, 136
France, 5, 7, 61, 64, 67, 82, 108, 114, 127, 128, 131, 132, 138, 147, 150, 152, 153, 154, 158, 159, 161, 173, 175, 176, 181, 182, 198, 200
François alias Cariton, 86
French Antilles, 2, 23, 212
French Canada, 106
French Empire, 2, 5, 13, 14, 125, 126, 127, 155
French Guinea, 203
French Guyana, 106
French-Native alliance, 15
French Regime, 9, 14
French Soudan, 178
French West Africa, 4, 17, 107, 169, 180, 198
Frey, Henri, 203
Fuladu, 110
Fulbe, 49
Fuuta Tooro, 1, 3, 14
Fyson, Donald, 106

Gajaaga, 3, 14, 37
Galam, 14, 36, 109
Gambia, 37, 63, 201
Gambia River, 3, 4, 110
Gamian (gunsmith), 64
Gandiole, 38, 41
Garvey, Marcus, 218
Geller, Herb, 220
Germany, 7, 193
Goodrich, 154
Gordan, Dexter, 220
Gorée, 4, 6, 9, 36, 40, 42, 43, 55, 56, 57, 58, 59, 60, 61, 62, 65, 66, 67, 107, 112, 113, 134, 168, 169, 171, 172, 175, 198, 200, 201
Gorée, Joseph de, 62
Gorée, Michel de, 62, 63
Grandt, Jürgen, 217, 218
Gravier Street, 138
Great Britain, 17
Great Lakes, 4
Green, Tim, 226
Green, William, 220
Greenland, 219
Grenoble, 9
Guadeloupe, 126, 129, 155, 173, 213
Guèye, M'Baye, 41, 44
Guinea, 226
Gulf Coast, 55, 56, 57, 58, 64, 65
Gulf of Mexico, 2, 3, 4, 212
Guyana, 173

Haalpulaar, 3
Haiti, 5, 146, 151, 156, 212
Hall, Gwendolyn Midlo, 211, 222
Harrison-Nelson, Cherise, 226
Havana, 79
Hawes, Hampton, 220

Hébrard, Jean, 9
Hémard, Charles, 139
Henriette (prison warden), 115
Herskovits, Melville, 218
Hickory Street, 220
Holly Grove, 220
Hôtel de Mars, 88
Houma, 65, 220
Houston, William, 219
Houzeau, Jean-Charles, 134, 159
Hugo, Victor, 161
Hurricane Katrina, 226
Hyacinthe (Capuchin missionary), 1

Iceland, 219
Illinois Country, 2, 80
India, 173
Indian country, 15
Indian Ocean, 153
Indies, 2, 8, 9, 62, 64
Ingraham, Joseph Holt, 196–98, 203
Ireland, 7

Jajolet, Michel, sieur De La Courbe, 40
Japan, 219
Jean-Baptiste (free black), 87, 89, 90
Jefferson, Thomas, 5
Jellema, Rod, 217
Jim Crow, 18, 223
Joal, 57, 60, 61
Johnson, Jessica, 205
Johnson, Plas, 219
Johnson, Raymond, 219
Jolly, Anne Françoise, 86
Jolly, Antoine, 86
Jones, Hilary, 170
Joupillon, 85
Jupiter alias Gamelle, 86, 87, 88

Kaabu, 110
Kaarta, 37
Kajoor, 1, 3, 14, 61, 110
Kamata, Mariam, 44
Kayes, 178
Kellogg, William Pitt, 222
Kenya, 106
Kerlérec, Louis Billouart de, 82
Kinds of Blue (Grandt), 217, 229
King Oliver, 214
Klein, Jeff, 226
Klein, Martin, 200
Kongo, 212
Kongolese, 211
Kopytoff, Larissa, 117
Kouyate, Morikeba, 226

L'Abeille de La Nouvelle-Orléans, 128
L'Esperance, 63
L'Orléanais, 128, 157
L'Union, 158, 159, 160
La Carpentras, 86
la femme Pinet, 19, 55, 56, 57, 59, 66, 67
La Galathée, 55, 57, 58, 59, 65
La Gautreau, 86
La Tribune, 159
Lake Pontchartrain, 3
Lallande, Charles, 148, 149
Lamartine, Alphonse de, 159, 161
Land, Harold, 220
Langue de Barbarie, 3
Larue, Étienne, 66, 90, 91
Larue, Sieur, 90
Latrobe, Benjamin, 215
Laussat, Pierre-Clément de, 150
Lavie, M., 157
Law, John, 64
Le Bilan, Antoine, 62
Le Courrier de la Louisiane, 128, 154, 155, 156
Le Page du Pratz, Antoine-Simon, 75, 89
Leclerc expedition, 5
LeGrain, Pierre, 59, 60, 63
Legrose, Marie, 43

Les Cayes, 58
Lewis, George, 218, 219
Liberty Place, 222
Lincoln, Abraham, 137, 160
Lipsitz, George, 211
Lloyd, Charles, 220
Lorraine, 136, 139
Los Angeles, CA, 219, 220
Loti, Pierre, 203, 204
Louis Philippe I, 202
Louisbourg, 87, 88
Louisiana Purchase, 5, 6
Louison, 90
Lydon, Ghislaine, 174

Malespine, Aimé, 137
Mali, 37, 212
Malietal, *nègre libre,* 62
Mandinga, 222
Mandingo, 65
Manuel, Gabriel, 61
Marcson, Michael David, 44
Marie, *négresse,* 66
Marie Anne, Senegalese "free negress," 1
Marly, Jean Baptiste, 66
Martinique, 126, 129, 155, 156, 173, 213
Mauritania, 4, 110
Maximilian, 161
Mexican War, 126, 155
Mexico, 147, 160
Mezelliers, 66
Miller, Catherine, 9
Mingo, Jean, 65, 66
"Mississippi Bubble," 64
Mississippi colony, 4, 8, 57, 67, 81
Mississippi River, 3, 5, 55, 58, 64, 86, 90
Mississippi River valley, 1, 2, 3, 8, 14, 15, 212
Mitchell, Curtis, 219
Mitchell, Vince, 227
Moitt, Bernard, 46
Môle St. Nicholas, 151
Monroe Doctrine, 147, 160
Montagu, Mary Wortley, 192, 193, 194, 195, 196, 200
Montgomery, Wes, 220
Moors, 38, 49, 203
Moreau de Saint-Méry, Médéric Louis Élie, 192, 194, 195, 198, 205
Mount Washington, 157
Murat, Lucien, 136

Nantes, 63
Napoleon III, 136, 146, 147, 160, 161
Natchez (Native Americans), 15, 65, 66, 73, 80
Natchez fort, 88
Natchez Wars, 8, 14
Native Americans, 3, 14, 17, 88
Ndar, 5, 108
Neville, Aaron, 212, 213
New Caledonia, 106
New Jersey, 136
New World, 214
New York, 157, 210
Newfoundland, 219
Niang, Amadou, 179
Niger Valley, 3
Nini (title character), 204
North Africa, 224
North America, 2, 3, 4

Omar (in *Treat It Gentle*), 216–18
originaires, 103, 117, 168, 169, 170, 171, 172, 174, 175, 176, 177, 178, 179, 181, 182
Ottoman, 194

Palmer, Earl, 220
Palmer, Robert 225
Paris, 82, 114, 147, 154, 155, 157, 158, 159, 173, 210
Pateloux, Hélène, 9

Pau, France, 153, 157
Pavie, Theodore, 215
Peacocke, James, 197
Pelletan, Eugène, 159
Périer, Étienne, 58
Perrot, 86
Peul, 3
Pierre alias Jassemin, 88
Pinet, Jean, 55, 59, 60, 61, 63, 64, 65, 67
Place Congo, 215, 217
Place d'Armes, 87
Plessy, Homer, 161, 162
Plessy v. Ferguson, 162, 223
Pochenet, Pierre Antoine, 89, 90
Portendick, 4
Porter, Eric, 226
Portudal, 61
Poulard, 9
Pradel, Jean de, 86
Pruneau de Pommegorge, Antoine, 199, 200, 202

Quinet, Edgar, 161

Rassac, Redon de, 80
Reclus, Élisée, 137
Reid, Mayne, 196
Renault, François, 134
Réunion, 173
Revels, Hiram, 148, 149
Revue des Deux Mondes, 157
Ritter, Toby, 220
Roberts, Richard, 172, 174
Robichaux, John, 224
Rochefort, 61
Rochemore, Vincent-Gaspard, 78, 81
Rocky Mountains, 4
Roger, Aimé, 128, 131, 132, 137
Roger, Jacques-Françoise (baron Roger), 108, 109
Romano, Aldo, 225
Rosalie, black woman of the Poulard nation, 9
Rosey, George, 224
Rothman, David, 104
Roudanez, Louis Charles, 159
Rouen, 8
Rue Royale, 66
Rufisque, 61, 62, 168, 175
Ryan, Mary, 138

Saalum, 3, 110
Sackur, Karen Amanda, 39, 40
Sadji, Abdoulaye, 204
Saint-Domingue, 5, 10, 15, 58, 90, 126, 127, 128, 129, 146, 191, 194, 195, 205, 212
Saint Pierre, 129
Sakakeeny, Matt, 210
Salaam, Kalamu ya, 217
Sankalé, Sylvain, 39
Sankofa, 226, 227
Santo Domingo, 213
Schoelcher, Victor, 126, 133, 155, 161
Scipion, free man of color, 66
Scott, David, 218, 227
Scott, Rebecca, 9
Segou, 37
Semaine, Marie Thereze Yacam, 62
Senegal River, 3, 10, 36, 37, 38, 42, 47, 61, 106, 107, 109, 110, 169, 171, 173, 178
Senegal River valley, 49, 201
Senegambia, 1, 3, 4, 8, 9, 14, 15, 16, 36, 37, 55, 56, 57, 199, 210, 211, 212, 213, 224, 227
Seven Years War, 4, 6, 15, 78, 79, 87
Sierra Leone, 36
Siin, 3, 61, 110
Simon, free man of color, 66
Singleton, James, 227
Soninke, 3, 49
Sonny and Cher, 225

Souther, J. Mark, 210
Sozie, enslaved man, 88
Spain, 5, 211
Spanish, 2, 4, 5, 7, 9, 14, 15, 78, 126, 212, 213, 214, 215, 219
St. Louis Cathedral, 196
St. Thomas, 220, 221
Sublette, Ned, 211, 213
sub-Saharan Africa, 213
Swan, Samuel, 41, 44
Szwed, John, 215

Taney, Roger B. (chief justice), 148, 160
Testut, Charles, 137
Thérèse, wife of Jean Mingo, 65, 66
Thioub, Ibrahima, 116
Thompson, Robert Farris, 211, 215
Tinchant, Edouard, 160, 161
Tinchant, Louis, 153, 157, 158
Tinchant, Jacques, 153
Tinchant, Joseph, 157, 158, 160
Tioucou, François, 66
Todd, Clarence, 224
Toth, Stephen, 106
Treat It Gentle (Bechet), 216, 224, 229
Treaty of Cession, 146
Treaty of Fontainebleau, 5
Treaty of Paris, 5, 16
Treaty of San Ildefonso, 5
Trévigne, Paul, 159
Tribune, 158, 160
Trinidad, 213
Turbinton, Earl, Jr., 224, 225

United Kingdom, 10
United States, 5, 7, 10, 17, 126, 130, 131, 134, 137, 138, 146, 147, 149, 151, 152, 154, 159, 161, 220
Upper South, 7
Ursulines, 90

Valentin, Durand, 173
van der Merwe, Peter, 213
Vanon, Simon, 1
Vaudreuil, Pierre de Rigaud de, 83
Venus, wife of Jean Baptiste Marly, 66
Villebois de La Rouvillière, Honoré Michel de, 79, 83, 89
Villeneuve, René Claude Geoffroy de, 200, 202
Vincent, Elisabeth, 153
Vinnegar, Leroy, 220

Waalo, 1, 3, 61, 110
Walsh v. Lallande, 148–49
Washington, Booker T., 219
Washington, DC, 160
Weil, François, 128
Weil, Patrick, 182
West Africa, 2, 3, 37, 56, 57, 103, 106, 117, 168, 170, 174, 175, 177, 181, 182, 198, 203
Western Europe, 104
Western Sahara, 3
Weston, Randy, 224
Willaumez, Bouët, 109
Wimpffen, François Alexandre Stanislas, 192, 194, 195, 198
Wolof, 1, 4, 5, 44, 49, 61, 65, 199, 201, 218, 221, 222
World War II, 182, 210

Xavier, person of color, 66

Yoruba, 211

Zeno, Alice Williams, 219
Zinoman, Peter, 105